IN THE LAST RESORT

IN THE
LAST
RESORT

*A Critical Study of
The Supreme Court
of Canada*

Paul Weiler

*Chairman
Labour Relations Board
British Columbia*

*Professor of Law
Osgoode Hall Law School
(on leave)*

Carswell/Methuen, Toronto

Library of Congress Catalog Card Number 74-76831.
ISBN 0 459 31330 4

Printed and bound in Canada
by The Carswell Company Limited

1 2 3 4 5   78 77 76 75 74

To my wife Barbara

PREFACE

In this book, I have not attempted a comprehensive treatment of the Supreme Court of Canada. In the presently underdeveloped stage of investigation of that body, such a study may be impractical for anyone; it is certainly beyond my reach. Such a work would have to draw on a number of disciplines and perspectives of the judicial process. As anyone familiar with the literature will realize, an ecumenical spirit does not prevail in the scholarly world concerning the validity of all of these alternatives. Accordingly, anyone who is going to paint only a partial picture of a court must be careful to define the scope and limitations of his effort from the outset.

First let me say what this book does not do. I have not engaged in quantitative analysis of the judges' voting behaviour; I have not attempted sociological analysis of the judges' backgrounds, the inner workings of the Supreme Court, or the impact of its decisions on Canadian society; I have not written a history of the Court; I have not even described in any systematic way the legal doctrines the Court has introduced into Canadian law. None of these omissions implies any disrespect for these techniques of analysis. I have tried to read every study published on the Supreme Court of Canada, from whatever discipline, and have made use of all these perspectives in this and other writings of mine about the Court. However, my objective here is much more restricted in compass. This is an essay in legal philosophy, an attempt to develop a theory of the role of law in courts, which can be used to appraise the legal reasoning and decisions of the Supreme Court.

In order more adequately to convey my intentions, some further details about the background of this book may be helpful. In 1969, along with two of my colleagues at the Osgoode Hall Law School, I received a grant from the Canada Council to study the Supreme Court of Canada. Since then I have written and published several articles on the contribution of the Court to the evolution of selected fields of Canadian law since 1949 (when it succeeded the Privy Council as our final court of appeal). Each piece involved a detailed examination of every decision of the Court in the area in question, in order to discern the extent of the influence of its judges on the growth of Canadian law and to evaluate the quality of this product.

For each of these studies, I had to develop a thesis about the proper scope of the judicial function which would serve as a vantage point for my selection and analysis of the decisions. Because of the lengthy detail in which the various articles described what the Supreme Court was actually doing, these views of what it should have been doing tended to recede into the background. In this book I have tried to draw them together into a more or less systematic theory of how the judicial function should be carried on in Canada. Since the Supreme

Court, from its position at the top of our judicial hierarchy, sets the tone for our judicial process as a whole, it was natural to focus my illustrations on the structure and work of that Court alone. The theory is used to appraise some examples of the Supreme Court's performance while these same illustrations put flesh on the abstract propositions of the overall scheme.

The first part of the book sets out my general views of the proper conception of law in appellate courts. Chapter 1 analyses the nature of a "court", as embodied in the changing structure of the Supreme Court of Canada. Chapter 2 formulates my proposal for the kind of legal reasoning which we should expect from such a judicial institution.

In the second part, I undertake the examination of the actual performance of the Supreme Court as seen through the lenses of my ideal picture of the judicial function. The Supreme Court of Canada is an especially helpful vehicle with which to develop such a picture because it has an unusually broad jurisdiction as a final court of appeal. Too many jurisprudential analyses of legal reasoning have focused on just a few cases drawn from a selected area of judicial work. Perhaps the need to test my own position across a somewhat broader perspective may have helped me avoid some of these pitfalls. In any event, I have looked at recent cases in the law of torts, criminal law, labour law, constitutional federalism, and civil liberties respectively. In the final chapter, I summarize my hopes and expectations about the future evolution of the Supreme Court in the 70's and beyond.

In order to develop clearly my message about how the Court should be performing, I have had to be selective in the use of examples in the middle section of this book. I could review only a few cases in each chapter and could then focus on only some facets of the legal problems presented by any one such decision. The reader has a right to suspect that my choice of examples is not representative of the thrust of the Supreme Court's activity and that my analysis of any one decision simplifies and distorts the legal issues. This may well be a danger because I have deliberately chosen those actual cases and issues which best help me communicate my view of how a final court of appeal should function. This, after all, is the theme of the book. The only response that I can make to the sceptical reader is that I have published comprehensive surveys of the recent decisions of the Supreme Court in all of the areas I will review, except that of civil liberties. He will find the references at the beginning of each chapter and this may give him some aid in checking whether I have rendered a fair picture of the Court's actual performance.

I should mention two omissions from the book. First of all, I did not include treatment of the Court's contribution to Quebec's civil law system or its involvement in commercial and business law. These are important gaps in any attempt at a systematic analysis of the judicial function in Canada but I do not have the background in these areas to undertake such studies. I look forward to someone else filling the gap. Secondly, I have deliberately decided to confine footnote references to an absolute minimum. No one realizes more than I do my indebtedness to the scholarly literature of both the philosophy of judging and the analysis of different areas of substantive law. The interested reader will find this fully documented in my earlier articles on which I have drawn for the various chapters in this book. However, I prefer to leave the argument formulated in this work to stand on its own without meticulously tracking down the sources in which I originally located its parts.

This brings us to the final matter with which I must deal in this preface. Canadian judges and lawyers are not used to systematic criticism of a court's performance. My earlier publications about the Supreme Court caused a certain fluttering in the legal dovecotes when they first appeared. One gained the impression that this was unseemly behaviour on the part of an academic. It smacked of American iconoclasm, not the true Canadian (or should I say British) tradition of reverence for our judicial institutions. Criticism of a judge's reasoning might properly appear in the course of analysis of an area of law, but it should be hesitant and obscure; certainly one should not administer a general rebuke for a court's style of work as a whole.

There is a germ of truth in the call for restraint in criticizing the judiciary. We have a deeply embedded convention that judges do not enter the public lists and fight back against their attackers. Accordingly, a critic must try to be fair and impersonal in the comments that he makes. I have tried to give a true picture of what I see as the overall trend in the Supreme Court's performance. My focus has been the visible content of the opinions of the Court, not the personal attitudes of any one of the individual judges.

Our legal establishment is not satisfied by that level of restraint. It appears to assume that judges in their work speak only as the impersonal voice of "the Law". If someone disagrees with the results in a case, he should blame the legal system, not the individual judge. The quality of our law is the legislature's responsibility, not the court's. With this view I heartily disagree. Judges do have an independent influence on the evolution of our law. If their craftsmanship deteriorates, we, the consumers of that law, will suffer. Academics would shirk their responsibility to the Canadian public if they did not present forthright and understandable criticism of inadequate judicial performance wherever it is found. The decisions of the Supreme Court of Canada can have a real impact on the quality of our law and our lives. If that quality deteriorates, the citizens of Canada have the right to know about it and to understand how it may be improved.

This judgment of the role of the Supreme Court is not self-evidently true. I know many lawyers and judges who heartily disagree with it. Indeed, it is the primary objective of this book to try to demonstrate its validity. Accordingly, the critical tone I have taken in my appraisal

of the Supreme Court's work must await its justification in the acceptance of the thesis I am trying to convey. I will leave the issue by
quoting this comment of Mr. Justice Frankfurter, one of history's
greatest English-speaking judges and legal scholars:

> Judges as persons, or courts as institutions, are entitled to no greater
> immunity from criticism than other persons or institutions. Just because
> the holders of judicial office are identified with the interests of justice
> they may forget their common human frailties and fallibilities . . .
> Therefore judges must be kept mindful of their limitations and of
> their ultimate public responsibility by a vigorous stream of criticism
> expressed with candor however blunt.
>
> *Bridges v. California* (1941), 314 U.S. 252 at 289.

*　　*　　*

I wish to acknowledge the contribution of several institutions and
individuals without whose assistance this book might not have seen
the light of day. The Canada Council provided funding for the research
into the work of the Supreme Court of Canada upon which this study
is based. For the last several summers, these funds furnished me with
the help and pleasant company of a series of student researchers —
Paul Cavalluzzo, Paul Lannon, George Adams, Joe Weiler, Geoff Kane,
Cliff Shannon and Art Haladner. Our efforts originally bore fruit in
articles published in the Canadian Bar Review, University of Toronto
Law Journal, Osgoode Hall Law Journal, and the book, *Law and Social
Change*. The editors of these publications kindly consented to my draw-
ing on these earlier writings in this work. The Osgoode Hall Law School
of York University allowed me a year's sabbatical leave free of all
teaching and administrative commitments and the Faculty of Law of
the University of British Columbia extended me its hospitality and its
facilities during that year while I wrote this book. To each of these,
I express my appreciation.

Several members of these two law faculties read earlier drafts of
different chapters and made many helpful suggestions for improvement;
in particular, Harry Arthurs, Tony Hooper, and Alan Grant of Osgoode
Hall Law School and Peter Burns and Jim Matkin of the University of
British Columbia, Faculty of Law. I do want to mention, especially,
my colleague Peter Hogg at Osgoode Hall, who read the whole manuscript of the book as well as several of the earlier articles, and whose
contribution has been invaluable to me. While I take full responsibility
for any legal fallacies and stylistic infelicities which remain, I am
grateful for their time and effort in making these much fewer than
they would otherwise have been. But my greatest debt is owed to
Mrs. Ruby Richardson, my secretary at Osgoode Hall, who has tran-
scribed more versions of my thoughts on the Supreme Court of Canada
than I care to remember, and who cheerfully and diligently typed this
manuscript at long distance during the last year. My thanks.

Paul Weiler

POSTSCRIPT

Just prior to publication of this book, the Supreme Court began to take a somewhat different shape. Two new members were appointed, following an earlier addition in March 1973. Even more important, Mr. Justice Bora Laskin was made Chief Justice of the Supreme Court of Canada.

This last appointment generated considerable controversy in the Canadian legal establishment. It departed from an informal seniority system which appeared to be the pattern in the last half-dozen selections for that post. I must say that I find incongruous the notion that the Chief Justice of our highest court should be chosen on the basis of seniority. Indeed, the very fact that it has been seriously entertained is an indictment of prevailing Canadian assumptions about law and the judicial process which I will criticize in this book. The selection of Bora Laskin, whose background, abilities, and actual performance stamped him as clearly the logical candidate in the entire legal community, is some evidence that the Prime Minister, at least, would prefer a more creative mood on our final court.

In the final chapter of the book, I struck a mildly optimistic note about the future of the Court and certainly that hope has a somewhat firmer foundation as I write this now. But there are no grounds for complacency. A Chief Justice has only one vote among nine. His influence and leadership rest largely on his powers of persuasion and example. And these are frail instruments with which to dislodge the Supreme Court of Canada from the style of legal craftsmanship into which it has settled in recent years.

January 1974   P. W.

CONTENTS

CHAPTER 4

CHAPTER 5

CHAPTER 6

PART I

On Law
in the
Supreme Court:

A preliminary view

CHAPTER 1

The Supreme Court of Canada: Its Structure and Capacities

INTRODUCTION

A strange malaise has overtaken the Supreme Court of Canada in recent years. The condition takes several forms: our lawyers encounter difficulty in finding legal guidance in Supreme Court authorities; the judges and scholars of other countries rarely cite Canadian judicial opinions as persuasive precedents; in the law schools we are often disappointed in comparing the Supreme Court's analysis of a legal problem with the contribution of other national courts. Each of these failings testifies to one pervasive concern. Our final court of appeal is not providing sufficient illumination and excitement in the evolution of Canadian law.

Disenchantment with the Supreme Court of Canada is by no means universal among the Canadian bench and bar. A large segment of our legal establishment positively prefers a court which is non-political, dispassionate, and above the battles in Canadian society. It recoils with horror at the suggestion that our judges might emulate the "activism" of American courts; undoubtedly such attitudes have been reinforced by the stormy controversies which envelop the United States Supreme Court. These Canadian lawyers believe that our Supreme Court can only remain a "quiet court in an unquiet country"[1] if it sticks rigidly to the task of administering the law as it *is*; our judges must resist the temptation to remake the law as some academic thinks it *ought to be*. The spirit of Canadian nationalism may be affronted because the work of our final court attracts so little attention in the outside legal world, but surely there are other avenues for raising our national self-esteem.

In my view these failures of the Supreme Court do matter. The Court is an important part of the governmental structure in Canada. It exercises substantial, independent power in laying down the general legal standards by which our lives are regulated. In some areas—the administration of the British North America Act and the Bill of Rights—the judges tell the elected legislators what they can and cannot do. Their judgments

---

[1] Cf. Cheffins, "The Quiet Court in an Unquiet Country" (1966), 2 O.H.L.J. 259.

about important issues of public policy are not readily reversible by the representative institutions of our government, especially in the constitutional area. The personal influence of Supreme Court judges on Canadian law is no secret to the insider and some members candidly recognize this in public addresses. For these reasons, criticism of the reasoning in Supreme Court is not merely of aesthetic concern; deficiencies in the Court's performance have an important impact on the quality of Canadian law and life. I am going to try to explain what has gone wrong in our highest court and to suggest in which direction improvement lies.

My diagnosis of the malady of the Supreme Court is quite simple and can be summed up in one short sentence: Our judges share an outmoded and unduly narrow conception of the role of law in courts. I will defend this thesis through a detailed examination of selected cases from various areas of the Court's jurisdiction. Because any such appraisal must be undertaken from a particular perspective, I will first set out my own views about a more adequate theory. In this chapter I will analyze the significance of the fact that the Supreme Court is a "court". In the next chapter I will focus on the nature and role of "law" in judicial decision-making.[2]

A court is an instrument of government. Like any social tool it has a complex internal structure. The structure of a court is designed for the performance of important specialized tasks in the over-all work of government. Once an observer understands the thrust of this design, he can trace its implications for the use of this judicial instrument in different areas of social life. From this perspective, two contrasting deficiencies in a court's work might be discerned. A court may ignore the necessary limits on its proper role and such over-reaching may cause a serious "self-inflicted wound". There are many who believe this to be true of the United States Supreme Court in recent years. Less visible but equally harmful is the failure of a court to fulfill all its responsibilities within its own distinctive sphere. This can lead to atrophy of its judicial capacities and the eventual irrelevance of that court. It is this second danger to which the Supreme Court of Canada may now be exposed.

Some readers may question this talk of tools, instruments, designs and structures. Does not such language tend to reify the court, to treat it as a separate "thing"? Surely the Supreme Court is just a group of nine men, doing their job in a building in Ottawa with the help of lawyers, law clerks, staff and the like. This picture leaves out one important dimension to the social reality of a court. The Supreme Court of Canada is an

---

2 The theoretical framework for this analysis of the policy of the courts is developed in detail in my article, "Two Models of Judicial Decision-making" (1968), 46 Can. Bar Rev. 406. The interested reader will find there extensive references to the scholarly literature as well as greater elaboration of many of the factors which I touch on in this chapter.

institution, something more than the immediate preferences and actions of its members at any one time.[3]

When a newly appointed judge arrives in Ottawa, he will find a firm and durable social arrangement facing him. He may have very definite ideas of what he wants to accomplish on the Court, but will discover that that body does not yield readily to his views about judging. There are a great many people who co-operate in the work of a court, and they have their own well established ways of doing things. Deeply ingrained standards of behaviour exist to channel and co-ordinate these many individual efforts. Our newcomer will be expected to assimilate the features of his judicial role from this same source.

It is this network of expectations and patterns of behaviour, one which endures while judges come and go, that entitles us to speak of the Supreme Court of Canada as something more than its individual members. Yet even as the judge adjusts to this structure and his judicial role becomes second nature to him, he remains a human being. He can appreciate the way the existing conventions of the judicial office are founded on a shared, though largely implicit, idea of how a society wants its judges to function. The social expectations defining the judicial institution have developed over centuries and are not frozen in their current shape. As we refine and enlarge our views of what courts are for, the individual parts can be rewritten and the structure redesigned. As long as its human members are reflective and critical about what they are doing, the judicial process will continue to evolve.

Accordingly, there is a range of possible choices about what a court might be like. At any one time the Supreme Court will occupy an identifiable position in this range. Constant gradual alteration will be taking place in this position, impelled by changing views of what we want our court to do. The best way to gain some distance from the details of our own existing institution, and to appreciate the potential alternatives, is to compare its structure with those in other societies. As in so many other works about Canadian institutions, the natural comparison is with the courts of Britain and the United States. Not until late 1949 was the Supreme Court of Canada freed of formal legal control by the Privy Council (essentially the House of Lords by another name), and we are a long way yet from shaking off the legal and judicial conventions by which we were formerly governed. Yet we cannot avoid the powerful influence of our neighbour to the south, and this is especially true in the case of the United States Supreme Court. Since our own Court has come to perform the same distinctive judicial function of supervising legislative action under a federal constitution and a Bill of Rights, we should expect to find interesting resemblances in the evolution of their respective designs.

---

[3] The implications of this fact are nicely developed in a lecture by a recently appointed Justice of our Supreme Court; see Laskin, "The Institutional Character of the Judge" (1972), 7 Israel Law Review 329.

When I first made these comparisons, I was immediately struck by the differences. The British House of Lords, the United States Supreme Court, and the Supreme Court of Canada are all described by the same English phrase—"a final court of appeal". One would certainly expect a basic similarity in reality to justify this linguistic usage. Yet not only are there many variations in surface appearance—the judges' titles, their dress, ceremonial court procedures—but there are also fundamental differences at the heart of their operations. On reflection, this should not be so surprising; we also find significant differences in the *legislative* institutions in these three countries. Yet the problem is posed for our understanding of a "court". What is the key that will allow us to identify the common core of the institution and still explain the crucial variations in real life?

My hypothesis is that the answer is to be found in the functions we want this social instrument to perform. Any appellate court can be located somewhere between the two extreme points on the one scale. The polar alternatives can be labelled: (i) the judge as adjudicator, and (ii) the judge as political actor. Under the first label, the judge's function is to resolve a concrete dispute between two adversaries. Under the second, the judge adopts general policies for the community and gives them the force of law. I must emphasize that these two labels denote *ideal* types; any real-life court inevitably performs a mixture of both functions and thus is positioned somewhere between these artificial models. However, differences in the mix and the position are critical.

What do these technical labels mean? The judicial process as a whole is largely oriented towards the role of adjudication. In any society, especially one as complex and interdependent as ours, there will be clashes of interest leading to private disputes. Two men get in a fight and one is injured. A house is rented and the roof leaks. A car is sold and the purchaser fails to continue his payments. Some of these disputes will be voluntarily and amicably resolved; for those that are not settled, some alternative to self-help is required. For this purpose society provides an adjudicator—an official to whom the parties may go with their dispute, present their respective sides, and then receive an authoritative and impartial decision as to their rights. This is the standard concept of a judge and is still a fair picture of the function of a trial court. When we add appellate courts to this scene, the focus of the judicial mission is subtly altered.

An appeal court may certainly be seen as an adjunct to the system of adjudication. It provides litigants with an opportunity to have the original decision reviewed, especially if one side thinks the trial judge has made a legal error. The same adversarial format prevails, each side trying to win its case through the force of the argument it provides. However, for reasons I will develop in the next chapter, the system of law to which they direct their arguments is constantly moving, even in its application to individual cases. This process is especially pronounced at the appellate level, where one lawyer vigorously disputes the legal rulings made by the trial judge. In deciding the appeal, judges move gradually but inevitably from *applying* the law to *interpreting* the law to *creating* the law. There is no formula which distinguishes these functions within the fluid reality of the legal process. Once the appeal court has made its decision and expressed it in a legal opinion, its conclusion will have an independent legal authority. Because judicial decisions are reported and followed as precedents in later cases, every such decision helps crystallize the law by which we are ruled. Because a final court of appeal has such authority over a large number of judges and courts, its opinions will eventually place a personal stamp on the character of the legal system it administers. When this court resolves an immediate lawsuit by adopting a novel legal doctrine, one which embodies a preferred policy, its judges function as important political actors in the system of government. This second function—policy-making—is performed by an institution which is designed to perform the first—adjudication.

Though I made the point not far back, it is important enough that I will repeat it here. Any final court of appeal, including the Supreme Court of Canada, performs *both* of these functions as an inevitable consequence of its place in the legal and political system. Through the same proceedings, it resolves litigation between identifiable individuals and contributes to the evolution of the general law. Because an appellate court performs both of these tasks, its internal arrangements must necessarily be more complicated than a body which need perform only one function. We can best appreciate the present character of the Supreme Court of Canada if we understand it as an uneasy compromise between the sometimes conflicting demands of adjudication and policy-making. Many variations in this compromise are possible and it is now time to look at the one we have in Canada.

Up until now I have spoken of the structure and design of the Court without trying to break this down into its constituent parts. There are three key elements in the make-up of any court. The first is its *jurisdiction*. By this I mean the kinds of lawsuits and litigants which are brought before the court and the path they must take in getting there. The second is its *personnel*. Who are the people who get appointed to the court, who makes the selection, and what is the status of a judge once he arrives? The third is its *decision-making procedure*. How is a decision of the court made, who participates in this process, and what is the contribution of each? These are the questions I will ask about the Supreme Court of Canada in order to sketch a picture of the institution sufficient for my thesis about its responsibilities to Canadian society.[4]

---

4 The principal source of material on the Supreme Court of Canada is Russell, *Bilingualism and Biculturalism in the Supreme Court of Canada* (1969). For the House of Lords I have relied primarily on the recent study of that body by Blom-Cooper and Drewry, *Final Appeal* (1972). The material on the United States Supreme Court is so voluminous that any attempted citation of sources is

THE JURISDICTION OF
THE SUPREME COURT

There are not many legal topics which are as dry and technical as the law defining the jurisdiction of an appellate court. Yet this element is absolutely vital in understanding the nature of that court. Henry Hart once said that "the hard fact must be faced that the Justices of the Supreme Court . . . can at best put their full minds to no more than a tiny handful of the trouble cases which year by year are tossed up to them out of the great sea of millions and even billions of concrete situations to which their opinions relate".[5] The jurisdictional rules reflect our society's decisions about how best to ration the scarce time of its Supreme Court judges. Analysis of these choices allows us to trace our basic understanding of the mission we have set for the Court in the governing of the Canadian nation. This judgment establishes the general tone for the structure of the Court. The other key elements—membership, appointment process and decision-making procedure—flow naturally from this fundamental conception. What are these implications of recent developments in the jurisdiction of the Supreme Court of Canada and the pattern of actual cases they have produced?

One striking feature in recent history is the dramatic increase in the number of cases the Court has actually heard and decided.[6] In 1949, the membership of the Court was increased to its current size of nine judges. In the year 1950, the Court delivered 62 judgments, of which 45 were considered of sufficient legal significance to be reported. In 1960, the Court decided 119 cases, of which 78 were reported. In 1970, the Court's caseload had increased to the extent of requiring 137 judgments, of which 102 were reported. To give some perspective to these figures, I might note that the House of Lords, the final court of appeal for Great Britain (which has a population much greater than that of Canada), hears only about 35 appeals per year, approximately one quarter of the number reaching the Supreme Court of Canada. When the work load of a body increases by well over 100% in a twenty year period, and the number of people available to do the work remains precisely the same, something must give. There were two possibilities in the Supreme Court. One was to increase the number of cases heard by the bare quorum of 5 of the 9 judges; this has occurred somewhat more frequently

---

pointless here. There is a good comparative study, Karlen, *Appellate Court in the United States and England* (1963), which did give me some valuable aid putting the Supreme Court of Canada in comparative perspective.

5 This remark of Professor Hart about the U.S. Supreme Court is equally appropriate for our own. It is quoted in Russell, "The Jurisdiction of the Supreme Court of Canada" (1968), 6 O.H.L.J. 1 at 31, the best analysis of features of the Supreme Court's jurisdiction.

6 These figures were computed by student researchers from the volumes of the Supreme Court Reports, including the listing of unreported decisions.

and the Court now does a little over three-quarters of its work through this minimum panel (compared to a little over 50% in 1950). The other was to reduce the number of opinions written by the judges giving a legal justification for their decisions; there has been a radical change in this direction, with almost half the decided cases in 1970 carrying only one opinion for the whole court (compared to a little over 20% in 1950). The consequences each of these trends has for the quality of Canadian law I will assess later.

While the total number of cases in the Court's work load has increased sharply, the proportion of cases in the several important categories has remained remarkably stable. More than one-half of the Court's work load has consistently been composed of private law cases, involving disputes between individuals in automobile accident cases, contract actions, property claims, etc. In fact, 57 of the 102 reported cases in 1970 fell into this category, and the vast majority of unreported decisions (many of which were appeals dismissed from the bench without any reasons at all) were of the same kind. Criminal law cases constitute a stable 20% of the Court's reported decisions, constitutional cases fluctuate in very small numbers (averaging less than three a year over the whole period), and administrative law cases (including expropriation and taxation appeals) have assumed greater importance in recent years and account for about the same proportion as criminal law in the Court's work load. A substantial majority of the private law cases, and a significant proportion of the public law cases are essentially disputes about concrete issues in the evidence, the trial, the quantum of damages awarded, etc. This is true, not only of unreported decisions which may have no opinions at all, but also of many of the judgments which are reported because they may be considered of some general legal interest. The characteristic tone of the Court's work is heavily oriented toward the merits of a concrete dispute involving an identifiable individual, whether he be opposed by the government or another private individual.

What are the legal rules which shape this pattern and what theory of the institutions do they express? The Supreme Court of Canada is a final court of appeal. As a "court" it does not write its legal opinions in the abstract, no matter how interested someone may be in the legal conclusion. There is one long-standing exception to this rule which is distinctive of the Supreme Court. Canadian governments can refer troublesome legal questions to the Court (directly or indirectly) for "advice" as to the correct legal answer. This device has been almost totally reserved for constitutional questions (though the *Truscott* case is a noted exception), and has fallen somewhat out of favour in recent years (and the cases in which it still is used are good examples of why it should be in disfavour).[7]

---

7 Many constitutional lawyers might strongly dispute this *ipse dixit* of mine. We shall look at an example of the use of the Reference device in the chapter on constitutional law where I shall elaborate a little further. My feelings about con-

Save for this example, the Supreme Court is moved to action by appeals from lawsuits, prosecutions, etc., which are immediately focused on some harm to an identifiable individual. The formulation of the general law is a by-product of this effort.

A good example of the restrictions imposed by this stance was the second *Saumur*[8] decision. Saumur was a member of the Jehovah's Witnesses who fought a running battle with Quebec's Duplessis government in the Supreme Court throughout the fifties. In his own case, Saumur succeeded in having a Quebec by-law declared invalid by the Court insofar as it allowed the Chief of Police to prohibit the distribution of religious pamphlets on the streets. It took a great deal of legal effort and imagination from the Supreme Court majority to reach this civil libertarian conclusion and the variety of opinions left a possible loophole. The Duplessis government moved immediately to take advantage of it through an amendment[9] to the Quebec *Freedom of Worship Act*, R.S.Q. 1941, c. 307. This new provision was still constitutionally dubious, and Saumur quickly asked for a judicial declaration that the new provision was invalid. He had not himself been prosecuted and could show no specific threat to his own interests. On the other hand, it was obvious that the law was designed to have a harmful result on his own religious sect and to undo the legal immunity he had won in the Supreme Court. Yet the Court eventually held that his second suit was improper. The function of courts is not to give advisory legal opinions, no matter how real the interest of the applicant in having a legal issue definitely settled. Instead, courts are confined to resolving concrete questions of legal rights in specific circumstances, and they give their general views about the law only in passing.

The tradition that courts are put into motion only by an immediate lawsuit is an implication of the adjudicative function. Once it is seen that

---

stitutional references cannot be totally severed from my attitude to the Court's constitutional role generally. However, two further points can be made at this stage. First, it appears that the possibility of references was one of the historical factors which led to the original creation of the Supreme Court. Secondly, though, this function must be parasitic on the Court's adjudicative role. Why would the Canadian government go to the trouble and expense of referring a legal question to the Supreme Court rather than its own law officers in the justice department? Is it because the judges are so much more expert in the law? Surely that is not the reason. What the government is primarily interested in is knowing now what the Court would decide about a problem raised in litigation later. It is because courts *settle* the law in litigation that their "advice" is more valuable than that of ordinary lawyers. The reason why references are confined almost exclusively to constitutional cases is that in that area the legislature cannot settle and clarify the law itself by statute.

8 *Saumur v. A.G. Que.*, [1964] S.C.R. 252, 45 D.L.R. (2d) 627. This case is analyzed in Cavarzan, *Civil Liberties and the Supreme Court* (1965), LL.M. thesis for Osgoode Hall Law School, at 72-75 where a very different evaluation of the conclusion is arrived at.

9 An Act Respecting Freedom of Worship and the Maintenance of Good Order, 1953-54 (Que.), c. 15.

that same appellate court is responsible for basic questions of law, there will be a temptation to obtain the court's views as quickly and efficiently as possible. Observers will be impatient if a court respects this traditional restraint. Yet there are reasons of substance behind this self-denying ordinance. It preserves one of the main virtues of judicial law-making, that it emerges from a situation where a real, human conflict dramatizes the policy choice to be made. It protects the integrity of the adversary process. As we shall see, courts rely heavily on the research and arguments of the opposing counsel for the materials on which they will base their decision. To ensure their best efforts, it is desirable to see that each side has a real stake in the legal outcome as it applies to his situation.

Finally, a refusal to give legal "advice" will often keep a court out of a political struggle in which its position and authority can only suffer. This is exemplified by such recent constitutional references as those in the *Offshore Mineral Rights* and *Chicken and Egg War* cases which I will deal with in more detail in the chapter on federalism. The cumulative force of these three reasons justifies the *Saumur* holding through which the Supreme Court re-emphasized the principle that policy-making from a court should take place within the process of adjudication.

If a Supreme Court decision must be initiated by the trial of a concrete dispute, might we not then conclude that the criterion for allocating the scarce time of the Court should be the importance of the immediate dispute to the litigants involved in it? This does appear to be the rationale of the existing doctrines. Take the rules governing criminal law appeals as an example. In capital murder cases, there is an absolute right of appeal in matters of law or mixed questions of law and fact. In indictable offences, there is a right of appeal on questions of law where there is disagreement among the lower court judges as to the law applicable to the case. For summary offences, there is no right of appeal at all (though there is the possibility of securing an appeal through the discretionary leave of the court). These are, no doubt, rough and ready rules for defining the degree of pressing interest among the litigants and, if anything, are exceeded in this respect by the rule granting appeals as of right in civil cases.

For civil appeals there is a single criterion—does the monetary amount in dispute exceed $10,000?—a standard which was fixed in 1956 (when it was raised from $2,000). Such a criterion may well be considered a mark of the unfeeling crassness of the Canadian character and is certainly an unsophisticated measure of the individual importance of even a civil claim. Is a $9,500 tort judgment sought by a widow really less important than a $95,000 tax claim litigated by a large corporation? Even if we must accept the need to frame our rules in crude terms which cannot capture fine distinctions in reality, the differences between criminal and civil appeals are inexcusable. Any question which is not purely factual, including even the quantum of damages, can be appealed in a civil case (where over $10,000 is in dispute), while only pure questions of law (and

11

none involving the quantum of sentence) can generate an appeal as of right in a non-capital criminal case, and then only if there was some legal disagreement in the lower courts. Whatever be the justification for these limitations there surely can be no argument for imposing them on claims involving personal liberty, but not on claims for money or property.

These are issues which arise if we want to tinker with the rules generated by the orientation of the Court towards the adjudication of concrete disputes. There is a growing consensus among students of the Court that this whole perspective is fundamentally inadequate. It is argued that the Court's role should primarily be the shaping of Canadian law in the interests of the country as a whole. The interests of the litigants in a fair trial of their dispute may require one appeal to the provincial court of appeal, but does it require a second appeal to the Supreme Court? It is true that a further appeal might possibly discover and correct errors in the earlier proceedings. It is equally possible, though, that the second appeal can add errors as it gets farther away from the original events and trial. More important, it is certain that a second appeal imposes lengthy delays and great expense on the person who was successful below. There must be some finality to litigation and, on balance, it would seem that justice to the immediate litigants is most adequately served by confining them to one appeal as of right.[10]

What should the Supreme Court of Canada be for? I suggest that the criterion for rationing its time should not be based on the degree of need in the individual case. The Supreme Court has a substantial influence on the development of Canadian law, as I will show in later chapters. Like the House of Lords it has ultimate judicial control of the total expanse of the nation's law. Like the Supreme Court of the United States it exercises the special constitutional power of controlling the behaviour of the legislature. Judicial views in this latter area are, as a practical matter, almost irreversible by elected institutions. Legislative alterations of judicial interpretations of the Criminal Code, important regulatory statutes, or even the fine points of private law are achievable only with great difficulty and after long delay. If and when the Court errs, it harms the interests of a great many Canadians besides those involved in the immediate litigation. The jurisdiction of the Supreme Court must be designed to maximize the likelihood that when its judges settle the policy of our law, they do it well.

There is widespread agreement about one vehicle for approaching this objective. Appeals as of right must be abolished; a litigant should

---

10   Indeed, for this very reason, the original jurisdiction of the Supreme Court was not irrational, historically. In 1875, several of the provinces did not have intermediate courts of appeal, and the Supreme Court did perform this function, with a possibility of further appeal to the Privy Council. Since both of these factors have disappeared, the time for revision of the Supreme Court's jurisdiction is long overdue.

have access to the Supreme Court of Canada only when it is determined that his lawsuit raises a legal issue of importance to the nation. There is a strange quirk in the jurisdiction of our Court. It has authority over a wider sphere of legal issues than either the House of Lords or the United States Supreme Court. Unfortunately, it has much less control over the kinds of appeals which will present these legal issues. When appeals lie as a matter of right rather than with judicial permission, we give private litigants the power to allocate the scarce time of our Supreme Court judges. We should not be surprised that they exercise this power in their own private interests rather than the public interest in the quality of Canadian law. The jurisdiction of the Court has been slowly evolving towards a system of appeals with leave; we should adopt the principle that no case should be before the Supreme Court of Canada until it has been certified as *worthy* of being there. I would add that only the judges of the Supreme Court should have the power to grant such leave. At present, provincial appellate courts can also grant permission for an appeal to the Supreme Court from their own decisions, and no doubt this is of some added convenience. However, not only is a court of appeal not a totally disinterested bystander, but it also sees only a small slice of the Supreme Court's total work, and is not in any position to judge how the Supreme Court's efforts should be distributed. It is high time that we erased these two practices which have produced a situation in which only 20% of the cases that reach the Supreme Court of Canada are there by permission of that court.

What are the likely virtues in the alternative system? The most obvious benefit is that it will place some limits on the total number of appeals heard by the Court, with a corresponding increase in the time available to deal with those which are heard. Mr. Justice Frankfurter put it this way:

> the judgments of this Court are collective judgments. Such judgments presuppose ample time and freshness of mind for private study and reflection in preparation for discussion at Conference. Without adequate study there cannot be adequate reflection; without adequate reflection there cannot be adequate discussion; without adequate discussion there cannot be that fruitful interchange of minds which is indispensable to thoughtful unhurried decision and its formulation in learned and impressive opinions. It is therefore imperative that the docket of the Court be kept down so that its volume does not preclude wise adjudication. This can be avoided only if the Court rigorously excludes any case from coming here that does not rise to the significance of inescapability in meeting the responsibilities vested in this Court.[11]

We have a Gresham's law in effect here; bad appeals drive out the good ones. This is graphically displayed by the common practice of the

---

11 This oft-quoted comment of Mr. Justice Frankfurter is included in Kurland, *Mr. Justice Frankfurter and the Constitution* (1971), at 18.

Court dismissing appeals from the bench without reasons, and without even calling on counsel for the respondent to answer his opponent's unsuccessful argument.[12] At the same time the Supreme Court has been insensitive to requests for leave to appeal in cases of real constitutional or civil libertarian importance.[13] If we do nothing, the situation will worsen with the decline in the real value of the $10,000 monetary limit. Appeals as of right would become an overwhelming part of the Court's work. The best way to prevent private litigants taking up even more space on the Court's docket in their own monetary interest is to abolish appeals as of right altogether.

At the moment, though, we would be deceiving ourselves if we tried to explain deficiencies in the Court's performance by saying that the judges are overworked. By contrast, the Supreme Court of the United States faces many times the number of cases that our Court does, and resolves substantially more appeals on the merits; every one of these cases is disposed of by the full nine-man court.[14] The work load of individual judges in the U.S. Supreme Court is thus significantly greater than that of our judges.[15] If a reader should pick up a volume of the reports from the two courts for any one year and casually browse through it, the comparison will not be flattering, to say the least, to the Supreme Court of Canada. The range of materials considered, the depth of the analysis of the issues of legal policy, even the literary quality of the opinions, are all astonishingly different. Perhaps this is wistful Canadian nationalism, but I believe that some of this difference is the result of jurisdictional factors quite apart from the total number of appeals that are generated.

The present jurisdictional rules naturally generate a characteristic tone in the composition of our Court's appellate work. Most of a Supreme Court judge's efforts in any one year is directed at the assessment of the factual merits of a concrete dispute. As a consequence, he will develop habits of perception and analysis which he cannot easily shuck off when

---

12 Mr. Justice Laskin discloses that appeals disposed of immediately from the Bench numbered 32 in 1969, 44 in 1970, and 40 in 1971.

13 Examples which come immediately to mind include *R. v. Klassen* (1959), 31 C.R. 275, 29 W.W.R. 369, 20 D.L.R. (2d) 406 (Man. C.A.); *Koss v. Konn* (1961), 36 W.W.R. 100, 30 D.L.R. (2d) 242 (B.C. C.A.); *Cameron v. R.*, [1966] 2 O.R. 777, 49 C.R. 49, [1966] 4 C.C.C. 273, 58 D.L.R. (2d) 486; affirmed 1 C.R.N.S. 227, [1967] 2 C.C.C. 195n, 62 D.L.R. (2d) 328n (Can.); and *R. v. Harrold*, [1971] 3 W.W.R. 365, 3 C.C.C. (2d) 387, 19 D.L.R. (3d) 471. Leave to appeal to Supreme Court of Canada refused 3 C.C.C. (2d) 387n, 19 D.L.R. (3d) 471n (B.C. C.A.).

14 In the 1971 term, the U.S. Supreme Court's total case load was 3,645 cases. Of these, 3,196 were denials of applications for review and 449 were decisions on the merits of the case. The Court heard full argument in 192 cases and delivered full opinions in 168. The U.S. Supreme Court's work load shows the same dramatic rate of increase as our own. In the 1958 term it disposed of 1,738 motions and 126 appeals.

15 These figures are derived from the section on statistics in "The Supreme Court, 1971 Term" (1972), 86 Harv. L.R. at 279-306.

he meets a major issue of legal policy. The reader of a volume of Supreme Court of Canada Reports cannot help but be struck by the overwhelming proportion of the pages which are devoted to reiteration of the facts and the procedural history of the case, quotation of testimony from the transcript and analysis of passages from the trial judge's address to the jury. In many cases, these are the only materials relevant to the issues in dispute before the Court. The judge can honestly perform his job only by making a real effort to decide the just result for these immediate facts. Still, in any one year there is a significant number of cases in which the Court must resolve basic issues in the development of Canadian law. In these cases, the judges must turn their attention to the general implications of the doctrine they are adopting in the course of adjudicating the concrete disputes. The capacity to perform this policy-making job well is gained and maintained only by judges who concentrate their time and energies on it. Unlike either the House of Lords or the United States Supreme Court, our Supreme Court judges are prevented from focusing their attention on the task of judicial development of Canadian law. As a result, in the cases where they must still perform this task, they do not display the ability to do it very well.

In sum, the present jurisdiction of the Supreme Court of Canada is a strange mixture of adjudicative and policy-making emphases. Like the United States Supreme Court, our Court makes basic policy decisions controlling the division of legislative authority, enforcing the Bill of Rights, and limiting the jurisdiction of administrative agencies. Yet this work is only part of the Court's function as a general court of appeal (like the House of Lords) to which private litigants have access as a matter of right simply because of the monetary amount of their dispute, rather than the public interest in the legal issues reflected in the case. Ironically, though, while both the House of Lords and the United States Supreme Court are limited to developing legal doctrines in the course of resolving a concrete dispute, our Court can be asked to lay down legal doctrines in the abstract matters of public controversy where the law is in doubt. Both of these Canadian anomalies—the appeal as of right and the reference—are now in retreat, and hopefully we can anticipate a future framework which will permit our Court to focus on matters of general import raised by specific litigation.[16]

APPOINTMENTS TO THE
SUPREME COURT OF CANADA

The evolution of its jurisdiction is at the root of the changing character of the Supreme Court in Canadian society because it defines

---

[16] Whether the Supreme Court of Canada should emulate its American counterpart and become a specialized tribunal concentrating on matters of federal public law is also a matter of current debate. I shall deal with this jurisdictional problem in connection with my discussion of the specific areas of law in question.

the primary function we want the Court to perform. Intimately connected with this element is the question of the membership of the Court: what kind of person is appointed as a Supreme Court justice and how is he selected? The kind of person we want on the Court should be substantially influenced by the type of work he is to perform; contrariwise, the nature of the tasks we would give the Court must be kept within the capacities of the typical appointee. To return to our basic alternatives, it is clear that somewhat different qualities will be useful for the role of impartial adjudication of concrete disputes among individuals, in contrast with the wise and statesmanlike development of legal policies for the country as a whole. There is, however, a third complicating factor. Membership on the Court is one of the most prestigious positions to which a Canadian can aspire. It may be sought after and accorded by reason primarily of the status it confers, rather than the ability of the individual to excel in his performance of the dominant role of the Court at any one time. When we examine the actual patterns of recruitment of Supreme Court justices, no single explanation is sufficient to understand what has emerged.

A. D. MacLean, at one time secretary to Prime Minister R. B. Bennett, commented on the latter's view of selection of a Supreme Court judge:

> In choosing men for appointment he would like to make merit the chief consideration. Instead, he has found that party, race, religion, occupation, and geographical location of the nominee are more important than his qualifications.[17]

Of course the definition of merit is a personal thing and is heavily dependent on one's view of what the judge is supposed to do—what this "merit" is for. It is interesting that a Prime Minister should feel compelled to ignore his own view of a candidate's legitimate qualifications and make his selection on the basis of what he believes are irrelevant factors. This is a testimonial to the power of convention in Canadian political life. There are no constitutional and only minimal statutory qualifications required of a Supreme Court appointee. Yet such firm patterns have emerged in the characteristics of the typical judge that we can draw a very clear picture of a selection some time before it is made.

Let us take as an example the appointment of a successor to Mr. Justice Hall, who is the next justice slated to retire. What picture could we draw of his replacement simply by extrapolating from past experience? He will be a male lawyer of about 50 years of age. He will live in Western Canada, be English-speaking, of British ancestry, and quite likely Roman Catholic. He will come from a family which was comfort-

---

17 As quoted in Adams and Cavalluzzo, "The Supreme Court of Canada: A Biographical Study" (1969), 7 O.H.L.J. 60 at 63. This study, and the Russell book cited in fn. 4, *ante*, are my primary sources of information for this section.

ably well-off, with a father who was either a professional man or a businessman. In his family background there will likely be some prominent involvement in public and/or legal life. These favourable circumstances will provide him with a good education and entrance into a successful law practice. Assuming that the Liberals are still in power in Ottawa, the new appointee will likely be a member of the Liberal party.[18]

How can one have any confidence in these predictions? The Supreme Court Act places only the barest limitation on the qualifications for a Supreme Court judge. He must be a lawyer with ten years experience (or a judge). This is hardly surprising, though not, I would suppose, self-evidently valid. Not only must all of the judges be experienced in *law*, but some must be competent in the *civil law*. This is the source of the requirement that three judges must be appointed from the bar of Quebec. In turn, though, this statutory rule has generated an elaborate system of geographic and linguistic representation which is the most obvious conventional restraint on the appointment process. Because Quebec is legally entitled to three Supreme Court judges, Ontario must be politically entitled to the same number as the other dominant provincal partner in Canada. This distribution leaves only three seats for the rest of Canada and it appears clear from the experience of the last 25 years that two are to be allocated to the Western provinces and one to the Maritimes.

But geography in Canada is not only of regional significance, it reflects linguistic, cultural and religious divisions and these are also vital elements in the make-up of the Court. There are three judicial seats for Quebec; two of them go to French Canadians, but one is often filled from the English minority in that province. Consistent with our usual failure to give French Canada reciprocal privileges in the rest of the country, there is no French Canadian justice from outside Quebec and this national "partner" has been consistently under-represented on the Court. Yet equality between the two founding races appears to be established for the Chief Justiceship. In the last 40 years and 6 nominations, the post has rotated between English-Canadian and French-Canadian appointees (and only once in history was the Chief Justice not promoted from within the Court).

If the key attribute in selection of a judge should be legal skill and experience—as appears from the face of the Supreme Court Act—then

---

18 This passage was written in the summer of 1972. Just before the manuscript was ready to go to the publisher, Mr. Justice R. G. Dickson of the Manitoba Court of Appeal was appointed to replace Mr. Justice Hall, effective March 26, 1973. I decided to leave the text unchanged as a test of the validity of predictions we can make of the characteristics of future Supreme Court justices, relying simply on past trends. From the biographical data I have been able to locate on Mr. Justice Dickson, the only factor which proved incorrect is his religion. He is a member of the Church of England, not a Roman Catholic.

these regional and ethnic constraints would seem to be undesirable. It is not likely that the best legal talent is distributed in as systematic a geographic way as is implied by these patterns of selection. However, if a dominant feature of the work of the Court is its policy-making role in our system of government, the same conclusion is not so apparent. Just as for the cabinet, there is real virtue in giving different regions and groups significant representation on a body which will have an important impact on their lives. From this perspective, the problem is that these extra-legal factors are too narrowly defined, rather than too widely. If we want a group of individuals who have some experience of the needs and aspirations of a wide range of the Canadian populace, we will not find it on the Supreme Court. Instead, this body is a prime example of the "vertical mosaic" of Canadian society.

The most obvious limitation in the membership of the Court is that it is an all-male society. There have been 51 judges of the Court and not one has been a woman. This is not peculiarly Canadian male chauvinism since the same is true of the highest appellate courts in England and the United States. Nor do I expect a female appointee in the foreseeable future. In an age of women's liberation, I suppose nothing more need be said. The second basic limitation is in terms of age. It is not unusual for a Supreme Court judge to be appointed in his middle forties, although the average age at the time of appointment is in the middle fifties. The real problem is the length of a judge's stay on the Court. Only fairly recently was a retirement age established, and even then it was set at the age of 75. The significance of this is emphasized by the unusual longevity of our judges. In recent years they simply have not died in office.[19] This combination of factors has produced a court whose current membership has an average of 68 and whose members have sat on the Supreme Court (let alone on the bench as a whole) for an average of 12 years. One cannot over-estimate the importance of these figures. We are asking a small group of men to handle an ever-increasing work load, involving vital decisions of public policy, at a time when many of them are long past the age of normal retirement. We allow this task to be performed by men who have often sat in the insulated Supreme Court chambers in Ottawa for over twenty years (the longevity record is held by Chief Justice Duff: over 37 years). Someone once said that judges deal today with the problems of tomorrow by applying the solutions of yesterday. One need go no further than these chronological facts to understand the reason.

Other vital features of the national experience are basically lacking on the Court. It was not until the most recent appointment of Mr. Justice Laskin—the 51st member of the Court—that a person who was not a member of our dominant racial and religious groups, British and French,

---

[19] The only one in recent years was Mr. Justice Nolan, who died in 1957.

Protestant and Catholic, reached the Court.[20] Not only is there an ethnic bias in the Court's membership, but there is also a class bias. The somewhat incomplete surveys of fathers' occupations and of early education indicate a heavy emphasis on upper class, well-to-do, professional families with some history of involvement in public life, including the bench. The early life of most Supreme Court judges will be spent in the atmosphere of a family which enjoys real status in the community, for these several reasons of race, religion, money, father's profession, family background, and the like.

None of these facts should be surprising. They do not require an explanation in terms of some "power elite" conspiracy. Instead, they are traceable to the kind of image that a Prime Minister will have in mind in looking for a Supreme Court justice. The candidate must be a middle-aged lawyer of some distinction, and he must be part of the establishment so we can be sure of his "judicial" temperament. It is very natural that well-to-do families of the founding races and religions in Canada, especially those with a background of professional and/or public involvement, will produce the sons who will get the right kind of education, and thus the entrée into the kind of practice or position which produces a likely candidate for the Court. I return to the comment I made earlier. A position on the Court is a very prestigious end to a legal career and, as we shall see, it is awarded in a very quiet way by a small group of people. One can certainly anticipate that the dominant groups in our society will receive a disproportionate number of these prizes. Indeed, is it unfair to suggest that Mr. Justice Laskin's appointment was a long overdue recognition of the prominent place of Jewish lawyers in Canadian law (as well, as I have no doubt, of the fact that this appointment was highly deserved on its individual merits)?

It is not enough, of course, to have the right background to secure appointment to the Supreme Court. There are many lawyers who satisfy the above description but there are only a few judges. What have the successful candidates done to single themselves out from the field before they are appointed? In this connection Canada certainly reflects the pattern in the United States rather than in England. The customary route to the House of Lords is a successful career as a barrister, appointment to the High Court, and then promotion to the Court of Appeals and the House of Lords. This pattern reflects the traditional ideal of adjudication —the judge must have achieved professional expertise in the existing law and then worked his way up to the highest court via the judicial route, not political life. Such a sequence would be extremely unusual in the Supreme Courts of both Canada and the United States.

---

20 I might add that while Catholics are somewhat under-represented on the Court, there has developed a tradition that one of the seats from outside Quebec will be occupied by a Catholic. Mr. Justice Hall fitted this description and for this reason I predicted that his successor would also be a Roman Catholic. That pattern has been interrupted in the case of Mr. Justice Dickson.

For one thing, political affiliation and involvement is much more important in both of these countries. There is substantial evidence that membership in the political party in power in Ottawa enhances one's chances of being selected by its Prime Minister. The selection of a prominent member of an opposition party is not unheard of, but provokes comment when it occurs (and I should note that none of the minority parties in Canada have ever been represented on the Court). Despite these truths, I do not believe that simple partisan politics is a very significant factor in the selection. It may narrow the search to likely candidates in one political party, but the appointment is too important to be given as a reward for efforts on behalf of the party (something which may not be thought true of lower judicial office). Something else is required to bring our prospective candidate to the attention of those who must choose.

Ordinarily, this something else is previous involvement in public life, rather than a reputation as a successful lawyer. Occasionally, a counsel held in high professional esteem will be appointed directly to the Court —this seems to have been the reason for the choice of Mr. Justice Cartwright—but this is the exception, not the rule. For a long time, political life was the preferred route and a surprising number of Supreme Court judges came directly from the federal Cabinet. In recent years this avenue has receded in importance, though Mr. Justice Abbott did move directly over from the Ministry of Finance. Now the likely career in public life is more likely to be an important, appointed post in government (exemplified on the current court by Justices Spence, Pigeon and Fauteux). One would think that an obvious factor in appointments to the Supreme Court would be prior judicial experience in a lower court. For a long time this was a prime prerequisite, and about two-thirds of the justices had served some apprenticeship in a lower court. In the last 35 years or so, this route also has declined in importance and only one-third or so have satisfied this condition (although five are on the present court, Justices Fauteux, Hall, Laskin, Spence and Judson). I might also add that if a judge on a lower court is appointed to the Supreme Court, it is likely to be within six or seven years of his original elevation to the bench. A trend in recent years has been the selection of judges with close, continuing association with the law schools (including Justices Fauteux, Pigeon, Martland, Ritchie), culminating in the recent appointment of one of the most distinguished full-time Canadian law professors, Mr. Justice Laskin.

In sum, then, the somewhat stereotyped view of Canadian judges— that they are selected simply from the comfortable, insulated practice of corporation law—does not hold true of the members of the Supreme Court. Taken collectively, they have had a substantial range of experience in Canadian public life, whether in politics, government, education, royal commissions, law societies, etc. The breadth of such experience seems especially pronounced in the case of the appointees consistently selected from Quebec.

When we return, then, to the perspective from which we began—the capacity of the members of the Court to play an important policy-making role in Canadian society—the picture is very mixed. The judges are drawn from a very narrow stratum in Canadian society—ageing, male lawyers. In their early youth, they were unlikely to experience any of the important deprivations which it is a primary object of public policy to ameliorate. Yet male lawyers—I dare say from basically comfortable backgrounds—dominate Canadian political life generally. Moreover, the lawyers who reach the Supreme Court of Canada have had a fairly broad range of experience in public life which gives them some equipment to respond in a statesmanlike way to the problems which come before them. In this respect they are much closer to the United States Supreme Court than is commonly believed.

We are light years removed from the United States though in our method of appointment of Supreme Court justices. No doubt there are many Canadians who think it is a good thing that we have not experienced the kind of unseemly battles which occurred over the recent Fortas, Haynsworth, and Carswell nominations. They would say that the prestige of the Court can only be harmed if its "dirty linen is washed in public". In Canada, typically, the selection is made by the Prime Minister and his Minister of Justice after a quiet investigation, and then announced as a *fait accompli* to the public. Yet the fact that this decision, which is of vital importance to the future quality of Canadian law, is made at such low visibility and with only the most informal consultation, should be a cause for disquiet in a democracy. The decision to appoint a tenured Supreme Court justice has implications long past the time a Prime Minister leaves office and we should have some assurances that the process will produce the right selection.[21]

The direction in which the procedure should be revised is itself debatable, and this is one reason why the *status quo* remains unchanged. The lawyers—or at least their official organ, the Canadian Bar Association —strongly believe that the government should be required to seek (and perhaps even take) their professional advice. Again, if one conceives of the primary function of the Court as the application of the law to resolve concrete disputes, this is a reasonable proposal. Who is better equipped to assess the technical legal ability of a prospective judge than

---

21 As stated earlier, a judge is usually on the Court for some fifteen years or so until he dies or retires. There have been only nine appointments in the 22 years since 1950 (in 1949, the Court was expanded to nine members and two appointments had necessarily to be made then). In that time we have had four Prime Ministers and they have the opportunity of making a new appointment every 2½ years. At this rate, it takes a very considerable time to revise the composition of the Court to bring its views into line with popular aspirations. Accordingly, the original decision is crucial.

his professional peers? When the full realization of the Supreme Court's impact on the development of Canadian law strikes home, I think we must agree that this direction of reform would be disastrous. The system of appointments is already too insulated from participation by the people who are going to be governed by the decisions made at the Supreme Court level.

A much preferable course would be to require the Prime Minister to submit his nominee to a committee of Parliament for questioning about his qualifications and aspirations for the post. I know that it is a radical break with the Canadian legal tradition to suggest that a judge's personal views should be open to examination. The tradition is based on an out-moded assumption that the work of the Court is the completely imper-sonal product of "The Law", and both should by now be discarded. I also realize that it is very unlikely that a Prime Minister will see his appointment rejected by the Parliament he controls (unlike the experi-ence in the United States). It would nevertheless be a salutary exercise to require the person making the selection to anticipate some question-ing and debate about the quality of his choice. In fact, this is the most likely vehicle for beginning the public dialogue about the kind of Supreme Court we really want.

The over-all picture with regard to Supreme Court appointments is equally as disjointed as it is for jurisdiction. We are a long way from the adjudicative ideal of the House of Lords—the standard progression from a prominent barrister, to the trial court, and on up to the final court of appeal. The membership of the Supreme Court of Canada, by contrast, reflects a much more varied background and is deliberately made repre-sentative of several different segments in Canadian society. These pat-terns are even more pronounced than they are in the United States Supreme Court, where such "non-legal" factors are openly accepted as legitimate criteria for selection to a major policy-making organ of the government. Yet our actual procedure for selection follows the British model of an invisible and genteel review of possible candidates. There are straws in the wind which suggest that the suitability of a prospective appointee, especially for the performance of the constitutional function, may be subjected to debate and ratification in a public forum.

Recognition of these different avenues by which the judges find their way to the several highest courts should not obscure the essential simi-larity in their status when they arrive. Members of these appeal courts are all tenured judges, holding office until they die or resign. There is provision for impeachment for cause, for some form of unseemly or un-judicial conduct (an obvious though very unlikely example is the ac-ceptance of a bribe). But that is all. The essential trait of the judicial attitude is impartial and impersonal judgment. The critical convention which preserves this atmosphere is the principle that a judge cannot be removed from office on the ground that the public or the government does not agree with the decisions that judge has honestly reached. This principle is the natural implication of the judge's adjudicative role. We want to create an insulated setting in which our judges feel free to search for a disinterested conclusion about the legal merits of a concrete dispute, whatever be the popular emotions it has aroused. Suppose the focus of the appellate institution was turned squarely on policy-making. Could we still justify exemption of our judges alone of our public officials from normal accountability for performance to the voters or their elected representatives?

THE SUPREME COURT'S DECISION-MAKING PROCEDURE[22]

The third key element in the structure of the Supreme Court is the procedure it follows in reaching its decisions. How are judges allocated to the panel which hears a particular case? What are the kinds of materials and resources available to the judges in reaching their decision? Who has access to the Court to try to influence the result? What is the process by which the judges deliberate and arrive at their final judgment? Clearly, one who wants to understand how the structure of the Court shapes its product will have to analyze these immediate factors as well as the more remote patterns in the Court's jurisdiction and membership. It is also true that assessment of the existing arrangements will depend on the critic's conception of what the Court product should be like—the restrained adjudication of a concrete dispute or innovative policy-making for society as a whole.

The Supreme Court of Canada, unlike the Supreme Court of the United States, is not required to sit with its full membership of nine judges. Instead, its legal quorum is three judges for a motion for leave to appeal and five judges for the hearing of an appeal on the merits; and in four out of five cases only the bare quorum is empanelled. Occasionally, a larger panel of seven judges, or more often the full nine man court, will be constituted to hear more important and more contentious cases. It is still not unusual for major constitutional, civil liberties, or other legal issues to be resolved by much less than the full court. There can be no doubt that this practice is a more efficient and expeditious method of resolving a large number of appeals of concrete disputes. It is also apparent that the American practice gives much greater recognition to the general law-making character of these decisions by requiring that each be the product of the deliberations of the full collective body.

The Canadian procedure would appear to give significant influence to the Chief Justice, who decides the number of judges to be included

---

22 There is a good description of Supreme Court procedure in Russell, cited in fn. 4, *ante*, at 79-97, viewed naturally enough from the perspective of his bilingual concerns; an updated description is provided in Laskin, article cited in fn. 3, *ante*.

on the panel and which judges are to fill it. Analysis of the substantial influence attained by the Chief Justice of the United States Supreme Court locates its source in his very subtle powers of chairing the conferences of the judges after the hearing and then assigning the writing of the court's opinion (if he is in the majority on that case). The formal powers given to the Chief Justice in Canada would seem to afford him substantially more potential for pursuing his personal views, in the light of what he knows of the attitudes of his fellow judges. However, there has never been any suggestion that our Chief Justices have tried to exercise this power, and there is no evidence that they have done so. An occasional Chief Justice has placed his personal stamp on an aspect of law by virtue of his long seniority and accepted expertise, but not apparently by reason of his office. For example, we do not refer in Canada to the passing of the "Cartwright Court", as it is very common in the United States to speak of the passing of the "Warren Court".

How then are judges allocated to the panels? Statistical studies show that the primary basis is geography. Cases are listed on the docket by four areas—Maritimes, Quebec, Ontario, and the West. Judges from these areas will almost always be allocated to the cases from their own region (though this is less true of Ontario judges), and in recent years have tended to write the opinions of the Court. Regional specialization still leaves some room for a division of labour according to interest or expertise in a subject matter. For example, Chief Justices Cartwright and Fauteux sat on almost all of the criminal law cases, Justices Rand and Judson in administrative (and labour) law, Mr. Justice Abbott in tax cases, while Mr. Justice Martland writes the opinions in oil and gas cases (though this last is also explained by the geographic factor). However, the primary tone of the Court, especially in recent years, is against the emergence of such legal personalities. Each judge is a generalist, he is formally equal in his vote, and basically equal in shaping the course of decisions (even, as stated above, equal in influence to the Chief Justice).

A more vital difference between these several final courts is in the materials which are provided to them. All three courts share in varying degrees the essential constituent of adjudication—the adversary process. The parties to the immediate dispute provide the arguments on the basis of which the judges decide what are the appropriate legal standards for resolving the issues in the case. In the House of Lords, this is still strikingly the case. Prior to the hearing, the parties provide the Court and each other with only a very short outline of the line of argument they intend to adopt and the legal authorities they will rely on. The judges do not usually analyze this document in any detail beforehand, apparently on the assumption that this would detract from the right of counsel to make his case before judges who do not have any preconceptions. Oral argument is not limited in time, lasts an average of three days and occasionally up to twenty days, and is the primary external influence on the Court's conclusion. The process is very much an extension of the adversarial character of the trial process. The pervasive risk of such an adversarial process is that the result may turn on the quality—even more the equality—of opposing counsel. I think this is a risk worth running as far as the merits of the individual dispute are concerned; yet one cannot help but feel qualms about the kind of legal policies which this process may impose on the rest of us.

The procedure in the Supreme Court of Canada is substantially different and this has been accentuated by changes in recent years. In the first place, Supreme Court factums are much larger—often over 100 pages —and make a much more sustained argument in their own right. The judges are assisted by a clerk who can make some analysis of the issues in the case and critical points in contending positions, and provide this for the judge before the hearing. However, when one examines these factums the sources referred to are almost exclusively conventional legal materials. Moreover, the factums are not prepared one in response to the other, and so there is no explicit joinder of issue prior to the hearing. At the hearing, oral argument is again unlimited; lawyers on each side spend a great deal of time reading from the record of the case or from prior judicial authorities, and a typical hearing will last up to two full days. Finally, the immediate parties to the dispute are the only sources of education which the judges have. Although there is provision for intervention in a case by third parties who have an interest in the issue, this is rarely used outside constitutional matters.

The United States Supreme Court forms a fascinating contrast here, and one which illustrates the direction in which our Court's procedure may well move as its jurisdiction changes. In the first place, the written briefs are by far the most important vehicle for the parties' influence on that court. A good brief on an important point will often be a small monograph of real intellectual achievement. It will contain not only a canvass of the relevant legal materials, but also reference to law review articles, statistical data, social science studies, classic works in philosophy or history, etc. It is also very common for other individuals or groups to submit an *amicus curiae* brief without actually becoming a party to the case. This document will often illuminate the implications of a possible general decision of the court for other interests which may not be the primary concern of the individuals who are immediately involved.

The judges, by reason of their specialized jurisdiction, are already acquainted with much of this material, and their general views and attitudes may be well known from their previous opinions or even extra-judicial writing. They have a small research staff—several law clerks— who are charged with the responsibility of preparing a detailed analysis of the ramifications of the case. This kind of preparation by the judge is made possible by the fact that oral argument is rigidly limited, one hour to each side on the case. During this argument, reading from the brief or other materials is frowned upon, and counsel can assume the judges are already familiar with these sources. Instead, they are supposed to concentrate on the key lines of their argument and be prepared for stiff questioning about the "soft spots" which have been noted by the judges. Rather than the forensic atmosphere of the adversary process, the procedure is much more akin to a research seminar among highly experienced experts devoted to the solution of a major problem of public policy. To the extent that the work of our Court becomes concentrated on such issues, and consciously so, we can expect the recent trends in Supreme Court procedure towards this model to continue.

What happens when the hearing is over? In the Supreme Court of Canada it is not at all unusual for the panel to deliver its decisions at the end, without giving any reasons, and even without calling on counsel for the respondent. As stated earlier, this is due to our procedure for appeals as of right at the election of the litigant, who may not be personally convinced of the truth that his appeal has no merit. In the House of Lords and in the United States Supreme Court, where the case is there only because it has been certified as raising a difficult legal issue, the judges will almost always reserve their decision until after further reflection. There the resemblance ends. The Lords basically reach their conclusions independently, without formal consultation with each other, write their opinions and when the individual decisions are totalled up, render judgment one way or the other. In the United States Supreme Court, there is a firm practice of a preliminary conference and tentative assessment, assignment of the writing of an opinion of the court with extensive informal consultation, and then a final conference where the matter is fully thrashed out, and the judges reach their conclusion—whether to join in the opinion of the court or write a concurring or dissenting opinion. The procedure is designed to maximize the collective deliberation and exchange of views on the merits of the problem and then to secure an opinion of the court majority which clearly expresses the minimum common views which they share and are making into law.

Here also we can discern substantial changes in the procedure of our own Supreme Court. In the Fifties, the Court used an extreme version of the process in the House of Lords. Many cases generated a long string of opinions from the sitting judges, each of which reproduced the total history of the case, reviewed the same authorities, and ended with the conclusion of the individual judge. It was obvious that there was little or no prior consultation between them, no attempt by the others to rely on the work of one judge in setting out and analyzing the accepted framework for the contentious issues, and then no joinder of issue on the merits of the points on which they differed. Even where the Court was unanimous or almost so in its voting, the proliferation of opinions written completely independently of each other made it extremely difficult to extract from the case a legal rule which the majority had agreed to adopt as part of the law. We knew what the majority had agreed to as the judgment in the immediate dispute, but we did not know the legal reason for this judgment.

26

As a result of criticism of this practice, and after some changeover in the Supreme Court's membership, there have been clearly evident changes. Conferences of the sitting judges on any particular case are now an established practice, and the judges do endeavour to reach a common ground. Apparently there is also an effort to have one opinion written for the Court (sometimes, in fact, without even a named author) and the incidence of concurring and dissenting opinions has been sharply reduced. Indeed, the pendulum may have swung too far in the opposite direction. It may be that agreement on one common opinion has increased the clarity in the product of the Court, but this has been achieved at some expense to the quality of the product. The opinions on which the Court agrees are much shorter in length and much shallower in scope. In particular, there is very little real argument or analysis of the precise legal issues which were in doubt and are now being settled. In turn, this failing is aggravated by the usual absence of additional opinions which themselves grapple with the difficult problems and in so doing highlight the inadequacy of the majority's approach.

In summary, there is a very clear relationship between the procedures that develop in a court and the view taken of its primary function. What can we expect in a body oriented to the adjudication of concrete disputes within the established law? A random selection of a panel of judges from the court as a whole is acceptable; the judges will rely on traditional legal materials presented by the parties to the instant dispute; they will be heavily influenced by the abilities of opposing counsel in oral argument; the conclusion of the court will reflect individual decisions by each judge on the merits. To an outsider such as myself this seems a fair picture of the procedure of the House of Lords.

Suppose a court gradually begins to focus on the resolution of basic questions of legal policy, especially in the area of public law. Social conflicts would first generate extensive law review analysis and social scientific research into the dimensions of the problem. Eventually a law suit would be selected, in the discretion of the court, as the vehicle for bringing the general issue forward for judicial resolution. The immediate parties would prepare very extensive briefs analyzing all of the materials relevant to the issue, both legal and non-legal, and these would be supplemented by *amicus curiae* briefs for other groups who were vitally affected by the resolution of the general legal problem, though not by the instant litigation. These briefs would be thoroughly analyzed by the judges and their staffs and then counsel would be invited for a short period of searching questioning. Finally, the judges would retire for collective deliberation for a lengthy period, which would eventually result in a collective opinion of the Court majority, but one which was subjected to exacting scrutiny by other judges who might not fully agree. It is hard to reject the American view that this second procedure is a much more adequate way of achieving important legal innovations.

27

Though slowly and somewhat fitfully, this is the direction in which the Supreme Court of Canada is moving.

Yet all three courts exhibit a fundamental similarity in their procedures, one which is typically judicial rather than legislative. Once the representations from the parties are complete, the judges deliberate in complete privacy before reaching their conclusion. They do not debate the issues in a public forum; they do not receive delegations or take opinion polls; they do not take part in television interviews about the course of the debate; they do not submit "White Papers" or draft proposals and ask for public reaction with a view to reconsideration of the new policy. There is nothing improper about any of these tactics; indeed we expect legislators in a democracy to take them. However, we do believe they are totally inappropriate for a court charged with adjudicating a concrete dispute, e.g., a man's criminal guilt. A court may change a great deal to accommodate its new policy-making function, but it will still remain a very different entity from a legislature, as long as the residues of its adjudicative mission linger on.

CONCLUSION

We are now in a position to view in the concrete the abstract hypothesis with which I began my analysis of the structure of the Supreme Court. The important elements of any court are influenced by the nature of the tasks it has to perform; any appellate court is engaged in two basic functions, the adjudication of concrete disputes and the elaboration of general legal policy; the shape of a particular court depends on the emphasis which is placed in that society on one or other of these functions. One can identify the central core of the notion of a "court", and see that it is satisfied by the three examples I have been reviewing. A court is a body of *lawyers*, hearing lawsuits about *concrete disputes*, on the basis of representations from the immediate *adversarial* parties, which it resolves after internal judicial *deliberation* about the appropriate *legal doctrines*. This framework derives its meaning from the distinctive governmental task of adjudication. As I shall show in the next chapter, and then throughout the book, a final appellate court also has a major influence on the development of the law as it administers the system in individual cases. When the implications of this second function are perceived, the structure of the institution will be altered gradually to improve the performance of this vital task.

If the notion of a "court" is to retain any intrinsic meaning, the restrictions imposed by some such minimal definition must be observed. Comparative analysis does disclose how flexible these limits are. Any one of the key elements in my definition admits of wide variation in the way in which it is realized. Exactly what kinds of lawyers will hear what kinds of disputes? How much reliance will be placed on adversarial arguments and how many interested parties will be admitted to the debate? What procedures will be adopted for judicial deliberation? And how bound by legal doctrine will a court feel itself to be? The cumulative product of several sets of answers can be final courts of appeal which differ almost as much as they resemble one another.

Logically one could imagine many possible combinations of social decisions about each of these critical elements (*i.e.*, what kinds of disputes, lawyers or procedures?). Realistically we should expect the several components of any one court to cluster around a basic orientation. At least to a Canadian observer, the House of Lords seems primarily oriented towards the adjudicative model. Many of the characteristics of the Supreme Court of Canada reflect this British influence on our legal traditions. By contrast, the Supreme Court of the United States has moved as far as any court I know of towards specialization in the shaping of public policy. The growing politicization of its structure is pressing at the outer boundaries of our conception of a court. Formally at least, our Supreme Court enjoys much the same constitutional authority over legislative behaviour as its American counterpart. Because the actual exercise of these critical powers has such an enduring impact on Canadian society, the need for wise judicial policy-making is acute. If changes in the judicial structure are believed necessary for this purpose, the Canadian public and politicians will demand them. We can already sense the drift in jurisdiction, appointments, and procedure towards the American model, for better or for worse.

This comparative experience should not be absorbed uncritically. We can learn from the British and the Americans, but neither foreign pattern can be wholly transplanted into Canada. An appellate court in any society is part of a law-making partnership. The terms of any such partnership will depend on the nature and capacities of all its members. The relationship of executive to legislature differs markedly in these three countries and for good reasons; it would be surprising if the same were not true of the judiciary. Analogies from other societies will open our eyes to needed improvements in our own. They are truly helpful, though, only when they are adapted to an indigenous Canadian conception of the proper structure and mission of its Supreme Court.

Legal Reasoning in Our Highest Court

INTRODUCTION

In Chapter 1, I dealt with only one half of the phrase "law in courts". Although each of these elements can be fully understood only through its relation to the other, some order of exposition is necessary. Still, many readers may be troubled by the sequence I adopted. My analysis of the Supreme Court of Canada relied on the hypothesis that the structure of an appellate court will vary, depending on what is believed to be its primary function—adjudication or policy-making. The work of any such court is always some mixture of both of these functions, because an appellate court does two things at the end of a case. It grants a specific form of judgment in favour of the plaintiff or the defendant (thus resolving their legal dispute) and it writes a legal opinion justifying this decision, an opinion which is published and followed as a precedent in that legal system. The tacit assumption of my argument so far is that, in writing these opinions, judges exercise an independent influence on our law. They implement the legal policies they think are proper. Yet is this really true? Are not judges supposed to resolve these concrete disputes by applying the already established law? If that is their judicial duty, how can there be room for this independent influence on the future evolution of our legal order?

I dare say that most Canadians, including some of our judges, hold to the traditional belief that the law controls the courts rather than that the courts shape the law. There is some public awareness that the United States Supreme Court may be an exception to that rule. However, we remain comfortable in our assumption that this is an exotic case, and not one to be transplanted in Canadian soil. Most Canadian legal academics regard this belief as naive. Through close analysis of different decisions and areas of law, many scholars have shown how our judges have reached conclusions which were not compelled by conventional legal materials. No doubt they hold to a somewhat more sophisticated picture of the judicial process. Yet the pendulum may have swung too far towards the assumption of the freedom and discretion of the judge. My argument will be carried forward on both fronts in trying to sort out the degree of truth and myth in each of these opposing claims. My ultimate conclusion will be that judges do have a duty of fidelity to law, but this obligation is owed to a "law" whose nature is much more flexible and expansive than our judges suspect.

The popular view of what courts do is primarily shaped by what we may call the "easy case". Jack Jones runs into Steve Smith at an intersection. As a result, Jones is prosecuted for a traffic offence or sued by Smith for damages for his injuries. The principal task of the judge is to listen to the evidence and decide what really happened. Once he has a clear picture of the events, the judge takes the proper rule in the legal system and applies it to these facts to produce the correct legal decision. How does the judge find this legal rule? With the aid of opposing counsel, he looks it up in a statute book, or in a volume of the law reports, or in a legal text. These are the *sources* of law in which the judge can discover the valid legal rules he is supposed to apply. H. L. A. Hart coined an apt term we can use to characterize the judicial technique. In any mature legal system, there is a complex "rule of recognition" which lawyers and judges can use to test whether a rule has actually obtained membership in that legal system.

The point of this assumption can be better understood if we imagine an alternative possibility. Instead of looking back to see what rules have already been made, suppose the judge decided the instant case by selecting the rule he thought would be most useful in the future. Certainly this second judicial technique might produce more efficient and more equitable social arrangements. Yet in the popular view, this is exactly what the judge, as the impartial voice of the law, is not supposed to do. Judges should not have the freedom to choose their own rules, no matter how wisely they might choose. The test for whether a proposed standard is a legal rule should be its pedigree, not its content.

I do not deny the core of truth in this familiar notion of what judging is all about. It starts to come unravelled a little as soon as we wonder what there is to argue about in the easy case, if all the judge does is select the proper rule from the proper book. The original trial presents no problem; here there may be disagreement about what actually happened (did Jack Jones stop at the intersection or not?), or what the law should do about it (how much damages are Smith's injuries worth or what fine should Jones receive for his offence?). However, this answer will not do for appeals because most of these revolve around disputes about the applicable law. Often the party who lost at trial does not agree with the legal rule which the judge decided to use. If he wants to appeal this will take time and cost a great deal of money. If judicial administration of the law was as simple a process as I have just sketched—the judge looks up the established rule in the books and applies it as written—then why are there so many appeals from the legal decisions made by qualified trial judges? The staple fare of appellate courts (and, incidentally, of the academics in the law schools), are the "trouble cases". To meet the demands of this rather different kind of legal problem, a more elaborate conception of law will be necessary. [1]

The Barbara Jarvis Case

Let's examine one such appeal case in detail to see exactly what I mean. *Barbara Jarvis v. Associated Medical Services*[2] is a good example of the kind of trouble case which winds its way up to the Supreme Court of Canada because the parties are willing to expend the money and effort to see the question finally resolved.

Barbara Jarvis worked for Associated Medical Services as a Railroad Claims Supervisor. The Office Employees Union had applied for bargaining rights for the employees in the A.M.S. office and Mrs. Jarvis was active in the original organization of the unit. Some time after certification was applied for, but before the certificate was finally granted, she was promoted to her supervisory post. Still she continued to have some involvement with the union. Twice Dr. Hannah, the managing director of A.M.S., vigorously objected to such activity when it came to his attention and she reluctantly acquiesced in his instructions to stop it. However, an incident occurred on February 2nd, 1961, which culminated in her discharge.

The union and the employer had arranged a bargaining session for that day. Mrs. Whittier, the union president (who was not an employee of A.M.S.), phoned Mrs. Jarvis and talked to her at lunch hour. She asked Mrs. Jarvis to find two of the employees who had volunteered to serve on the bargaining committee, ascertain if their work was up to date, and ask if they would attend the scheduled meeting. That afternoon Mrs. Jarvis spoke to each of the women in the office about this meeting. This conduct apparently conflicted with a company notice of December 1959 which prohibited any union activity on either company time or company premises. When Dr. Hannah learned that Barbara Jarvis had conversed with these employees on company premises about this union meeting, he fired her.[3]

---

1 An earlier formulation of this theory of legal reasoning in courts can be found in my article, "Legal Values and Judicial Decision-making" (1970), 48 Can. Bar Rev. 1. Full reference to the scholarly literature will be found there.

2 The decision of the Supreme Court of Canada is reported as *Barbara Jarvis v. Associated Medical Services Inc. and Ont. Labour Relations Bd.*, [1964] S.C.R. 497, 44 D.L.R. (2d) 407; the earlier proceedings in the Board are reported in (1961), 61 C.L.L.C. para. 16, 218.

3 I should mention this further twist to the facts. Mrs. Jarvis spoke to one woman in the office during their lunch break. She spoke to the other woman in the office at 4:00 p.m., and thus before the end of the work day at 4:30 p.m. However, Dr. Hannah apparently believed that both ladies had been contacted outside of working hours, though on the company premises, and discharged Barbara Jarvis on this assumption. His mistake may have had some legal significance. A blanket prohibition of all union activities on employer premises is in violation of the Labour Relations Act, R.S.O. 1960, c. 202 [now R.S.O. 1970, c. 232], while the

I think this is sufficient factual background to understand the legal problem presented in the case. The source of law which everyone agreed must be consulted was the Ontario Labour Relations Act. There the judges could read that "Every person is free to participate in the lawful activities of a Union" [section 3], that no employer could "discharge a person" for exercising his rights as a Union member under the Act [section 50], and that the Ontario Labour Relations Board had the power to order reinstatement in employment of "the person" whom it finds was discharged contrary to the Act [section 65]. Mrs. Jarvis did apply to the Labour Relations Board for reinstatement on the grounds that her discharge was based on her exercising her right to participate in union activities. Eventually the majority on the Supreme Court of Canada held that Barbara Jarvis was not a "person" within the meaning of that Act and thus enjoyed no rights or remedies under the statute. As we delve into the intricate question of whether this conclusion can be justified, we shall gain some sense of how complex is the role of law in judicial reasoning.

The starting point need be no different than I stated earlier. The Labour Relations Act was enacted by the Ontario Legislature. The quoted provisions were placed before that body, taken through the required readings and legislative formalities, and adopted by majority vote. The clearest element in our legal rule of recognition is that what the legislature enacts as law is binding law. Accordingly, Ontario citizens became legally obligated to comply with the statute in their actions, and judges to apply it in their decisions. Yet this language will create an immediately effective legal duty only to the extent that it conveys an unambiguous meaning to the person who wants to apply it. Often it does happen that the meaning of a term in a statutory provision is clear and directs a unique legal result in a situation. Of course, these are the very cases which do not generate appeals all the way up to the Supreme Court about how the statute should be interpreted. Appeals on matters of law occur when the parties can see two plausible versions of the ambit of a legal rule and the judge must settle which of them is correct.

But how can there be any doubt that Barbara Jarvis is a "person", the critical term used in the Act? If this question is put in the abstract, certainly she would satisfy the ordinary understanding of what the term means. Yet the words in a human language do not have a uniquely-fixed meaning or precisely-defined scope. The sense they are trying to convey is heavily dependent on the context in which they are used. Here the context is a very complicated scheme to regulate the world of industrial relations. The legislature did not write this statute simply as a literary exercise. It saw pressing social problems within labour relations

---

same may not be true of a prohibition of any union activities during working time for which the company is paying. In any event, the case was argued and decided on the basis that Dr. Hannah discharged Mrs. Jarvis for a reason which normally is not permitted by the Labour Relations Act. See the account in the Labour Board's decision, cited in fn. 2, *ante*, at 980-81.

and sought to repair the deficiencies in the existing legal response. Sometimes cases arise where the literal application of a statutory provision appears incongruous within the general lines of legislation. When such a legal conclusion will not fit reasonably well within the contours of the legislative scheme, judges may begin to reflect about whether that result really is dictated by the law. This is what happened in the *Barbara Jarvis* case, and the lengthy litigation followed.

The Labour Relations Act has two primary objectives. One is to channel collective bargaining along stable and orderly paths in order to achieve industrial peace. To this end, procedures are set up whereby a union (with majority support among the employees) can receive a certificate from the Labour Relations Board entitling it to bargain with the employer towards a collective agreement. The Act recognizes that there are some individuals in the employ of a firm, in particular the supervisory staff, who would be placed in an awkward position if they were included in a bargaining unit represented by a union beholden to the employees, the very people they have to supervise. Hence the Act explicitly excludes from the category "employee" those who "exercise managerial functions". As I mentioned earlier, Barbara Jarvis was an ordinary employee within the potential bargaining unit when the application for certification was made. By the time her discharge occurred, she had been promoted to a supervisory position outside the reach of the statutory term "employee". This was the anomaly which triggered the search for the proper meaning of the term "person" within that same statute. Was it not inconsistent with the objectives of the labour legislation that an individual who was deliberately excluded from the bargaining unit should enjoy statutory protection against discharge for union activities?

This takes us to the second objective of the legislation, the fostering of a free choice by the employees for or against collective bargaining. This aim is implemented by a series of prohibitions against coercive activities by either union or management which might interfere with the voluntary decision of the employees. The Labour Board was empowered to grant certain remedies in case an offence was committed against this part of the Act. The legislature consistently used the term "person" in these provisions, rather than the term "employee" with its several exclusions. Of course, the union argued vigorously that this very difference in language reinforced its position that Barbara Jarvis was a "person" entitled to protection against employer unfair labour practices. The company responded that the operative section of the statute prohibited discrimination against "a person in regard to employment" and provided for remedial action "with respect to the employment of such person". If "employment" is given the same narrowed statutory scope as "employee", then the term "person" must be restricted to those individuals whose "employment" falls within the statutory definition. Why would the legislature have selected the different term "person" instead of "employee"?

The reason is that it wanted to prohibit illegal coercive actions taken against persons who sought but were denied employment. To cover this conduct against individuals who had never become employees, the statute required a broader term. This legislative objective would still be accomplished by interpreting the term "person" in a way which did not encompass supervisors like Mrs. Jarvis.

Barbara Jarvis presented a typical dilemma in the appellate court interpretation of a legal rule. The surface language in which the rule was expressed did not provide the answer. On its face this language prescribes various standards of behaviour. It may tell private citizens not to engage in conduct which is harmful to others (*e.g.*, discharge of employees on account of their union membership). It may tell government officials what benefits or remedies they should grant individuals (*e.g.*, certification of a union with majority support among the employees). However, the terms in which these legal standards are expressed always have an open texture. The body which created the rule may not have envisaged clearly all its potential applications. The words it selected may not convey those original intentions precisely.

The language used is still important. It starts the enquiry on its way and sets the outer bounds to the interpretations which are permissible. For instance, it was clear that the deliberate legislative choice of two words, "person" and "employee", required that a wider scope be given to the former. Yet, as we saw, both the union's and the employer's arguments presented plausible alternatives about how this scope should be defined. Selection of the correct alternative is the essence of the art of appellate court judging.

The judge will not find the solution in the bare words of the statute book, no matter how long he stares at the page or how many dictionaries he may consult; the answer is not there. This does not mean that a court is lost in a sea of legal uncertainty. Judges simply must recognize that there is more to a legal rule than its linguistic expression. Every legal rule has a hidden dimension, an underlying structure. The rule prescribes a standard of conduct in order to achieve some social objective within an over-all statutory scheme. The aims of the legislature have an equal claim on the title "law" as do the words chosen to express this aim. The reasons why a judge is supposed to respect the language of a legal rule equally demand fidelity to its purpose. As the passage of time throws up marginal and unanticipated cases to an appellate court, faithful interpretation of the rule requires that the judges discern this hidden reality of legal policy and draw out its implications for the case at hand.

In some respects, the judge's enquiry resembles that of the detective in the classic mystery story. The legislature has provided important clues in the standards of conduct it has consciously adopted and clearly expressed. The judge's task is to reconstruct the concealed pattern which produced these clues. With this key, he can unravel the legal puzzle which triggered his quest. Yet the analogy is imperfect. Someone *did* commit the crime which the detective is investigating, but only too often the nerve of the problem of statutory interpretation is that the legislature *did not* provide a standard of conduct for the novel situation. The court must complete the story on its own but in a way which fits coherently into the tale the legislature did not quite finish.

When we penetrate the linguistic surface of the Labour Relations Act, we still find two plausible reconstructions of the pattern. Viewing the situation from the standpoint of Barbara Jarvis, the primary reasons for excluding supervisory personnel from the actual bargaining unit do not require the same exclusion from the protection against unfair labour practice. Indeed, there are vital reasons why a member of management may positively need such protection. The line between "employee" and "managerial" status is a fine one, and individuals shift readily from one category to the other depending on the level of production in the firm. (The truth of this observation could be verified in the factual situation of the *Barbara Jarvis* case itself.) To protect themselves, lower echelon supervisors will continue to maintain their union membership. Because they are likely to be veteran employees of the firm, their continued interest and involvement in union activities is probable. To permit the employer to discharge a person for such membership or activities may be both unfair to the individual and chilling in its effect on the free exercise of collective bargaining by other employees.

This was the argument for an expansive interpretation of the term "person". There was also a defensible argument for the restrictive interpretation sought by A.M.S. In order to foster free collective bargaining by employees in unions which are truly independent of employer domination, the Act makes some other provisions. Unions which are aided by the employer shall not be certified; dissident employee petitions which are sponsored by employers shall not be recognized; employers who become involved in the union or its activities are penalized. Ordinarily an employer acts through members of its management, including a supervisor such as Mrs. Jarvis. In order to protect itself from possible liability under these provisions (which were designed to eliminate such historic evils as "company unions", "sweetheart agreements", and "union busting"), an employer should be entitled to prohibit its supervisors from having any involvement with the union. If the supervisor persists, discharge should be permitted. To provide room for this legislative objective, the scope of unfair labour practices had to be restricted by defining the term "person" so as to exclude managerial personnel.

The *Barbara Jarvis* case went through four levels of decisions extending from the Ontario Labour Relations Board right up to the Supreme Court of Canada. Sixteen different decision-makers analyzed the question; six adopted the argument for Mrs. Jarvis and ten concluded in favour of A.M.S. On balance, I find the union position more persuasive. The legitimate employer concerns could have been achieved by permitting discharge of supervisors only when motivated by *bona fide* concerns for an improper involvement of the employee in the affairs of the union. The evidence did not permit such a finding in this case. The total exclusion of everyone outside the statutory definition of "employee" from the protection of the Labour Relations Act was much too drastic a step for that purpose.[4] The Ontario Labour Relations Board took this view but was eventually overruled by the majority of the Supreme Court of Canada. After three years of litigation, Barbara Jarvis's discharge stood.

In this chapter I am not going to undertake any detailed critical assessment of the actual holding in *Barbara Jarvis*. My point in discussing it was to display a more faithful picture of the actual role of law in judicial reasoning. What tentative conclusions might we draw from the analysis to this point?

In appeals focused on questions of law, a judge can rarely rely on a clear legal standard which he finds already ensconced in the law books. The layman's view of the easy case is not an appropriate stance here. In order to resolve individual disputes presented for adjudication, a court must work out independently the boundaries of any such rules it can find. Just because the law is unsettled and unclear, the judges cannot throw up their hands and say they do not know what to do. They have to meet the responsibilities of their office and decide where this case does fall within the ambit of the present legal system. When the Supreme Court of Canada held that Barbara Jarvis was not afforded protection by the Labour Relations Act, it established the legal prescription for this problem (as it would equally have done had it reached the opposite conclusion). *Barbara Jarvis* was only one of thousands of such appellate court decisions in Canada that year. When we look at the total sweep of Canadian law, we find that a substantial portion is the product of just such judicial elaboration of existing legal materials.

If judicial influence on the evolution of our law is an inevitable feature of the adjudicative role, a second conclusion follows. Courts must be vitally concerned about the policy embodied in the legal standards they do adopt and use. Judges cannot hide, ostrich-like, behind the myth that the answers are provided in the statute book, ready-made. As we have seen, the legal decisions which have already been made will be of help to a court in delineating the social objectives it should strive to achieve. Still we need judicial imagination in building on this foundation and judicial sensitivity to the quality of the legal product our courts project into the future. A major theme of this book will be the question whether the Supreme Court of Canada displays sufficient appreciation of its own significant impact on the growth of Canadian law.

---

4 I should mention the further complication that there were several other statutory exclusions from the term "employee" which did not involve supervisors and there was no good reason at all why they should not enjoy protection against discharge for union membership.

Barbara Jarvis is fairly representative of appeal court decisions which settle uncertain legal situations. However, some of its features will not be reproduced in every such case. The Supreme Court was able to focus on a specific rule dealing with unfair labour practices. It was not a situation of a gap in the law or of a conflict between two or three rules pointing in different directions. Moreover, the rule in question was part of a comprehensive regulatory statute enacted by the legislature which had undoubted jurisdiction in the area. Despite these features, the case still posed a difficult problem of interpretation within the penumbra of the one legal rule. *A fortiori,* judicial creativity will be necessary in those cases where one or more of these conditions is absent.

I should add a word about one of these complicating features, the problem of legal authority. There was no doubt in *Barbara Jarvis* that the Supreme Court was constitutionally required to recognize the wishes of the Ontario Legislature as law, at least to the extent that its meaning was clear. In many cases it is precisely these lines of authority which are ambiguous and this aggravates the unsettled character of our law.

The best example is the "common law" constructed from the long history of judicial opinions written to decide individual cases. By comparison with statutes, it is even more difficult to extract and interpret a rule from the discursive prose of these opinions. Even worse, the courts are constantly faced with the further question of whether and to what extent these rules are authoritative. With some constitutional exceptions, this is not a problem with statutes. Judges are supposed to obey the legislature. But when is one court required to obey another court?

For example, what judge-made law is the Supreme Court of Canada obliged to follow?[5] Surely it is not bound to comply with the wishes of a trial judge in British Columbia or an appellate court in New Zealand. It is reasonable to assume that a court will only be bound by the decisions of another court of at least equal legal rank. Yet, as far as Canadian law is concerned, there is no court equal in authority to the Supreme Court of Canada which is at the peak of our judicial hierarchy. Only the earlier precedents of the Supreme Court itself can be binding at that level. Judgments of all other courts can be of persuasive value only. Lawyers will put them forward for consideration but the Supreme Court need adopt just those which appear proper.

This legal distinction between binding and persuasive precedents appears neat on paper but does not always work out in practice. In the first place, the rules laid down by the earlier decisions of the Supreme

---

5 The best extended treatment in Canadian jurisprudence is MacGuigan, "Precedent and Policy in the Supreme Court" (1967), 45 Can. Bar Rev. 627. The most noteworthy development since then occurred in the decision of *Peda v. R.,* [1969] S.C.R. 905, 7 C.R.N.S. 243, [1969] 4 C.C.C. 245, 6 D.L.R. (3d) 177, in which the Court hinted strongly that it no longer felt absolutely bound to follow its earlier decisions.

Court are not absolutely binding. We shall encounter some of the devices the Supreme Court uses to sidestep decisions it finds uncomfortable. There are recent hints from some of its members that the Court will frankly overrule precedents that are no longer acceptable. Secondly, there is a real "pecking order" in the value of precedents from other courts. Any experienced reader of our Supreme Court Reports knows that when the House of Lords arrives at an important new legal judgment this will be persuasive indeed in urging our highest court to rethink its own apparently binding precedent. Thus the common law presents a very disorderly picture when looked at by a final court of appeal. There are so many decisions coming from the large number of judicial sources, and such a variety of conventional techniques for rearranging them, that it is rare indeed that a judge at that level will find a common law rule dictating his conclusion.

THE VALUE OF LAW

In my analysis of *Barbara Jarvis* I have tried to portray the room a legal system inevitably leaves for judicial development of the law. Appellate court judges cannot evade their personal responsibility for the quality of the legal rules they use to adjudicate the controversies before them. For good practical reasons, those appeals on questions of law which wend their way to the Supreme Court of Canada will turn on issues for which the law is unclear and must be judicially settled. Recognition of this fact must not obscure the truth that these are marginal situations which emerge in the interstices of a law that is clear and has already been settled.

The Ontario Labour Relations Act speaks to most of the human conduct which it regulates in terms that do not permit much judicial influence. Even in a trouble case which has been appealed, the court will consider itself obliged to comply with the central core of established law controlling almost all the potential legal issues in any concrete situation. Only if there really is a legal puzzle will the judges adopt a creative stance. Because judges consistently follow this practice of obeying the law as it has been laid down, rather than their personal views of what the law should be, the parties to a dispute will find it worthwhile to isolate only the doubtful issues on the appeal. If judges did not consistently apply the law when it was clear, a party who suffered under any established rule would have no reason to leave the matter dormant. He might just as well argue that the earlier rule was a poor one and this court should ignore it. If judges continually accepted this invitation, then they would settle disputes on the basis of pure policy without any law, a very different practice from the one we now have.

Needless to say, almost everyone thinks it a good thing that our courts follow the law to the extent they are able. Analysis of the arguments that might support this premise will not significantly strengthen popular conviction. Yet the exercise is still worth while. Only if we understand the reasons why the courts should arrive at their decisions within a legal framework can we talk intelligently about how they should do so, especially in the difficult cases on the periphery of existing doctrines. An alternative premise is easy to imagine. Suppose in the area of the common law,[6] our courts did not believe that the rules laid down in earlier cases were precedents and at least presumptively binding in law and instead decided each dispute in the light of current views of social welfare and equity, not by following the views of the judges in some previous case. Put thus baldly, the alternative is rather appealing. After all, these are supposed to be the primary ends of government. Why should the judges let the established law impede their own pursuit of these objectives?

The case for government by law is more complex than it might at first appear because there are several distinct levels of human behaviour at which it appears. To sort them out I will use the example of traffic control at a busy intersection. In this situation there are important interests—the prevention of injuries, the settlement of disputes, and so on—about which a government has to be concerned. It cannot simply rely on voluntary acceptance of informal standards of courtesy and good sense. These must be crystallized in clear and enforceable directives. There are two basic mechanisms for achieving these regulatory objectives, and we are familiar with both in this very context. A police officer can be assigned to the intersection to control traffic by giving specific orders and signals to individual motorists. This officer is given discretion to adjust the traffic flow as he judges best in changing conditions at the intersection. The alternative device is the formal announcement of general standards of behaviour; a typical example is: "a person must come to a full stop before making a right turn at a red light." These standards are to be used by motorists in orienting their own conduct—as they approach the red light, for instance—and the citizen is threatened with a penalty if he is found to have violated them. This is the method of law, the subjection of human conduct to the governance of rules. The problem, then, is why we might find the rule of law more attractive than official discretion, and what this preference has to do with the action of courts.[7]

---

6 Statutory law involves the complicating factor of the relationship between an elected legislature and an appointed judiciary. I shall deal with these institutional considerations in the next section. Here I shall focus on the values of law as such and ask why one judge should follow rules just because they were previously laid down by another judge.

7 In arguing for the value of "law", I do not mean to foreclose critical assessment of the desirability of any particular law. This latter enquiry would turn primarily on the substance of the policy embodied in the law in question. For purposes of my discussion I assume that a government has only the one policy objective in mind and must choose between these two relatively feasible mechanisms for securing it. What are the advantages it might see in law, rather than discretion?

From the point of view of the government, law is a much more efficient mechanism for securing citizen compliance with its regulatory policies. There are simply too many instances of human activity to permit face-to-face official approval or direction of more than a tiny fraction. The authorities can place police officers at the busiest intersections during rush hour, but traffic control must be achieved primarily through individual adherence to general legal rules. From the point of view of the governed, the value of law may be more subtle, but perhaps even more important. This form of official intervention in human affairs is much less intrusive on our sense of individual freedom. Rather than facing us with directly coercive commands, the government announces general and impersonal standards and then trusts that its citizens will decide to comply with them. In a real sense these standards become part of the natural environment to which we adjust our behaviour. In any successful legal regime the vast majority of these voluntary adjustments respects the claims of the rule.

But no legal system is totally successful. Motorists do violate highway traffic laws and cause automobile accidents and personal injuries. The remedies attached to the legal rule, whether civil or criminal, must now be utilized. Again we can see two basic alternatives. The government can require that each case be presented to an official who alone can finally dispose of the problem. On occasion we do preserve this official discretion where we perceive a possibility of a serious and irreversible impact on the interests of others. A couple cannot simply put into effect their private agreement to terminate their marriage by divorce; they must go to a judge for approval. Still our preference is private negotiation and settlement of the dispute within the framework of established legal rules (and the trend is in this direction for divorce in at least childless marriages).

Much the same reasons support this judgment. Private citizens should be permitted to resolve their problems on the basis of their own appreciation of the merits of the case, rather than take the risk of some outsider making an authoritative but mistaken judgment. Officials must be allowed to ration their time efficiently by concentrating attention on the few disputes which are left unresolved by private means, rather than spreading themselves thinly over all of the disputes which did occur. In automobile accident cases, for example, something over 95% of the claims are settled without a judicial decision and we are trying to find ways of eliminating the remaining 5%. In criminal cases we also find a large percentage of convictions produced by private plea bargaining leading to a guilty plea. Here there is much sentiment for reform in exactly the opposite direction that we encounter in the divorce area. Many now advocate some form of public judicial supervision of the considerations leading to a plea of guilty. This is one of the exceptions which help illuminate the rule.

Exactly what does this analysis of private behaviour and negotiations have to do with judges? Even if we prefer a system of self-applying rules for those decisions which do not go to court, there will always be some unsettled disputes that a court must decide. Why should we not leave the judge a discretion to look at all of the facts of the case before him and try to discover the individual disposition which will be most equitable and helpful to all concerned? The answer is very simple. If the government wants to use the device of law to channel private behaviour, it must commit itself to comply with this same law in later official assessment of that behaviour. If the government has announced certain traffic rules that it wants its citizens to obey, whether in their driving or in settling disputes about accidents that do occur, its judges must accept and apply these same rules in resolving the cases which do filter through to court.

This is the reason for the policy of *stare decisis*, the practice of judges following earlier precedents. When a court resolves a concrete dispute, it renders a decision about events that occurred considerably earlier. If it justifies its conclusion by adoption of a new legal policy which it now believes is more desirable, the court will frustrate the expectations of the party who relied on the earlier standard and believed he was secure (and law-abiding) in so doing. If it became common practice for judges to ignore or overturn established rules in disposing of new cases, private adherence to these rules would lose its meaning. Suppose it was an unpredictable matter of chance whether obeying the rule of the right of way at an intersection would exclude civil or criminal liability in a later judicial proceeding. The influence of the law as such on this private conduct would be reduced to the vanishing point. Judicial compliance with the established law is an essential condition for the success of the legal enterprise. If we value the rule of law as a mechanism through which the government can regulate private behaviour and enhance individual freedom, then we must accept the restraints this implies for judicial freedom.

There are further internal advantages to judicial settlement of disputes through the application of law. The successful operation of the judicial process itself requires an effective legal framework. Like any organization, the judiciary is a complex and enduring structure whose members are continually being recruited and replaced. It is unlikely that they will naturally share an informal consensus about what is the right and equitable result in a concrete case. The only way to minimize the influence of personal background and attitudes and achieve some uniformity in judicial response is to have available a set of official standards which all of the judges are supposed to apply.

Why is uniformity desirable? It avoids the constant re-arguing of old questions as new judges appear. It eliminates the incentive for litigants to "jockey" a case before a judge who has the right attitude. It minimizes the likelihood of a judge deciding a case on the basis of prejudice or emotion. Most important it satisfies a minimum claim to fairness; different legal conclusions must be based on the merits of the cases, not the accident of the judges who happen to decide them. These are not simply abstract evils I am talking about. There are graphic, real-life examples of what happens in a full-blown system of judicial discretion. Perhaps the best known such practice is the sentencing of the criminal offender. Gradually we have abolished almost all legal restraints on the "individualization" of the sentence. This may or may not be a good thing on balance. An inevitable cost in this effort is the pervasive risk of each one of these pathologies of personal discretion.

These are considerations which apply to any official body charged with the task of settling private disputes. Our judicial process has a further distinctive characteristic which itself requires the use of legal rules. As I noted in Chapter 1, judging in Canada is carried on within an adversarial system.[8] The parties to the litigation take the initiative in preparing factual evidence and legal argument for the adjudicator.[9] However, adjudication is a meaningless façade unless the parties (through their counsel) can rely on certain established criteria as the bases for the judge's decision. Suppose we return to our traffic example for a moment. Private counsel have to gather the relevant evidence, organize their witnesses, and prepare their arguments. Although each does this job independently of the other, we want them to join issue at the heart of the dispute between them, and present all the material necessary for a rational decision by the judge. This intricate process can be successful only if the lawyers have access to public standards which a judge will apply. If the judge they happen to draw intends to reach his decision on the basis of his personal feelings about equity and social welfare which have not yet crystallized in legal doctrine, then he will have to make an independent quest for the data and analysis he needs for an intelligent conclusion. In the absence of legal standards, the judicial process must inevitably move from the adversarial to the inquisitorial model.

I do not mean to suggest that this is an unthinkable prospect. Even now most official decisions in Canada are made through an investigative mechanism (although we do reserve the more critical questions involving an individual's freedom or well-being for the adjudicative procedure). Suppose we were prepared to sacrifice the values of private participation in the judicial process in order to improve the quality of the policies that are applied; I think we would find that abandoning *stare decisis* would not be conducive even to this goal. It is true that if a judge follows a rule laid down in a precedent, this may serve only to perpetuate an

---

8 An analysis of the pros and cons of the adversarial format for the judicial process can be found in my "Two Models of Judicial Decision-making" (1968), 46 Can. Bar Rev. 406 at 412-16.

9 I might add that the rationale for adversial adjudication as the model of official dispute settlement is the same distrust of governmental control of an individual's choice about how his affairs and interests are to be protected.

earlier error. It is equally true that a later revision can produce a poorer solution as well as a better one. Against the chance of improvement in the quality of the law, we must weigh the certainty that legal and judicial time will be used in the constant re-argument of earlier decisions. What happens if we hold to *stare decisis* so that litigants and judges can rely on legal authority settling previous issues? As new cases come forward, the participants can concentrate their efforts in devising the best solution for the novel legal issues it raises. This new rule is inserted into the legal system and becomes part of the framework for isolating further marginal questions and thinking them through in painstaking detail. In the long run the practice of following precedent may produce the highest quality of law through this case-by-case, incremental approach.

The cumulative force of these arguments persuades me that there are important and enduring values behind the obligation of judges to respect the legal framework in resolving concrete disputes. Accordingly, I do not advocate any unrestrained policy-making discretion for the Supreme Court of Canada. Yet we must take a pragmatic, hard-headed view of judicial fidelity to law. It is not a self-evident or self-applying formula. Judges must apply the established law rather than their own views of desirable social policy because, in the long run, this is the necessary vehicle for that society achieving its policies. In any interdependent community, the avoidance of conflict and the attainment of co-operation require that one person be able to rely on his expectations of another's behaviour. In many areas of human conduct such reliance can best be achieved by the creation and predictable application of legal rules. In turn, the successful operation of a system of legal rules requires judicial acceptance of these same standards in later appraisal of that private behaviour, even though the judge himself may not like the policy embodied in the rule he is required to follow.

From this vantage point, several caveats follow. If judicial compliance with legal rules is justified because of the good it accomplishes, there will certainly be occasions where the underlying reasons for the practice admit of exceptions. There will always be cases like *Barbara Jarvis*, for which there is not a firm and predictable rule on the precise point at issue. Sometimes the consequences of judicial reversal of a precedent may not be very serious (perhaps it deals with an area of human behaviour where there is little reliance on legal doctrine), and these will be outweighed by the good consequences of a change in the policy of the law. Finally, it is often the case that reliable legal standards are secured only through doctrines that embody reasonable policies. Outmoded legal rules may receive only lip service in their operation because judges are tempted to draw artificial distinctions to avoid patently unjust results. We shall encounter several instances in which the Supreme Court of Canada could best have promoted a truly predictable legal system by quick and clear surgery on a legal anachronism. I shall elaborate on each of these qualifications at various points throughout this book. Suffice it for now to say that, while judicial adherence to the law is important, it does not relieve appellate court judges of their responsibility for the policies embedded in the rules they use. This is especially true in those trouble cases which typically appear before our final court of appeal.

THE COURT AND THE LEGISLATURE AS VEHICLES FOR LAW REFORM

These legal values of predictability, regularity, and objectivity place significant restrictions on a full-fledged judicial pursuit of the most rational governmental policies. They would do so even in a society where there were no other lawmaking institutions. Of course we do not live in such a society. We have legislatures of various kinds, agencies of government whose primary role is making and remaking the law in accordance with changing public needs. Should our judges not confine themselves to their own primary task of administering the law as it is and leave it to the legislature to reform the law in the direction in which it ought to go? Not only the values of law but also the values of democracy seem to tell against judicial innovation within our legal system.

There is a large kernel of truth concealed in this traditional refrain against judicial "activism". Courts do have a distinctive structure which equips them to perform some tasks well, but renders it advisable that other jobs be left to the legislature. However, when we lay open the elements of this argument it does not serve as a bar to all judicial action; instead it serves as a warning against judicial over-reaction. In the previous chapter I described in detail the important components of the Supreme Court of Canada. I shall now trace the implications of the judicial structure for an appropriate and realistic division of labour between the Court and Canadian legislatures in the ongoing renovation of our legal system.

The clearest distinction between a legislature and a court is that judges are appointed with tenure while legislators are elected as our representatives. Political parties compaign on a programme and answer in an election for what they have done in power, precisely because we want them to be responsive in their decisions to the voting public. By contrast, our judges are deliberately exempted from a campaign for office founded on the policies they might promise to implement in their decisions (e.g. a "hard line" in criminal cases). Courts are insulated from partisan politics because we want an impartial arbiter to apply impersonal legal principles in a concrete case, no matter what passions and biases such cases can generate (as in the several F.L.Q. trials). No human institution can be totally successful in this quest but can there be any doubt that our judges are more judicious than our elected politicians?

This virtue has its corresponding limitations. When we staff a court with an elite group of elderly lawyers who only by chance share the changing values and aspirations of the public, we are naturally distrustful of such a body initiating major changes in social policy. Take the issue of tax reform which has so exercised Parliament and the public in the last decade. Surely a Supreme Court which need answer only to its own conscience would be an unlikely institution to select among the many proposals with their varying impact on the critical interests of different groups and regions in Canada.

This line of argument, while valid to this point, should not be taken too far. There are many anomalies and injustices in our law around which no political campaign would ever be fought. They survive with no defensible rationale either because of simple legislative inaction or because some narrow interest group can exert just enough pressure to diffuse the efforts of those who advocate reform. The protection which automobile drivers have enjoyed against "gratuitous passengers" is a good example of the injustice an insurance lobby can perpetuate against a long series of unlucky victims, because of a rule founded on the most spurious of arguments. Just because it must be elected, a political party must concentrate its efforts on issues of high visibility affecting large voting groups. There are many archaic legal doctrines which do not make headlines and do not find their way into the political arena. Cumulatively, they can have a serious impact on the quality of our legal justice. Judges are constantly happening upon such doctrines in the course of litigation. They have the opportunity to do something about the injustice quickly and quietly. It is this same sheltered characteristic of our Supreme Court—the unhurried, rational atmosphere of adjudication—which makes it a valuable forum for testing specific doctrines in the light of basic principles and smoothing off the rough edges which may be found.

A second institutional difference affects the judges' awareness of the "policy facts" which should be the underpinning of any intelligent reform of the law. Judicial innovation takes place in the course of a lawsuit whose record is devoted to evidence about "adjudicative facts"—who did what to whom in the immediate situation? However, any new legal rule should be founded on an appreciation of the recurring social issues raised by this kind of case and the typical long-run consequences the rule will produce. Examination and cross-examination of witnesses is not a very helpful tool in penetrating the amorphous fog of the social sciences to reach a firm footing in the kinds of social trends upon which one wants to base a law. Indeed, there is a recurrent danger that a court, whose members are uniformly lawyers, may get a very distorted picture of the underlying social reality from the way an effective counsel can paint the equities in his client's situation.

A legislature calls on much more effective techniques of fact-gathering, ranging from departmental investigations through committee hearings right up to full-scale enquiries by a Royal Commission. In any one of these settings, expert knowledge can be presented and sifted in its full complexity and then assessed by legislators who have varying backgrounds and experience and represent many different constituencies among the public. Surely this kind of forum, and not a judicial hearing, was the preferred vehicle for a realistic appraisal of the dangers of drug use, to take another recent example of a Canadian socio-legal controversy.

Yet we must not leave the portrait drawn in such a one-sided manner. Many doubtful legal doctrines do not reflect complicated social undercurrents beneath the facts of the immediate adjudication. Judges do acquire a first-hand acquaintance with the real-life situation for which they are devising a new legal rule. Over a period of time the law reports compile a sizeable record of the many concrete examples of a general problem, and each of these is depicted in its human detail. Even where there are complex issues to which scientific expertise may be relevant, the material prepared for legislative change can also be made available to the courts. Royal Commission reports have a history of being placed on the legislative shelf, unopened or at least not acted upon, but there is no reason why our judges cannot read them. To be sure, our courts may have a somewhat limited legal background in appraising these findings, but then every proposed law reform has a legal dimension about which the bench and bar are the experts. In many cases this dimension is predominant, whether it be the technical lawyer's law of the rule against perpetuities or enduring principles of our civil liberties such as natural justice.

This brings us to a third feature of the judicial structure. Not only are courts heavily dependent on the quality of the materials presented by individual counsel but they are also dependent on the assertion of a concrete claim as the occasion for judicial innovation. Judges do not have control over their own law reform agenda. A legislature can decide that the time has come for a systematic review of a whole problem area, for example, occupier's liability in tort, and can draft a scheme for reform which fits together in a coherent way. A court is limited by the accidents of litigation and the fragmented view it gives of an area. The total dimensions of the problem can emerge only after a long succession of cases, and these will be heard by many different panels of judges.

Yet this characteristic of adjudication has its compensations. As I said earlier, a judge always sees legal injustices in the concrete and he can perceive the human implications of any legal changes he proposes to make. Moreover, he can commit himself to a new rule for only that narrow situation in which he has to decide, and leave to "elucidating litigation" the mapping of the terrain he is now entering. Because judicial law reform is incremental, step-by-step, the damage from any one judicial error is limited. When the imperfection is spotted after a time, it need not be a major undertaking to have it refined.

47

Finally, courts suffer somewhat in the number and quality of the legal instruments which they can use to pursue their objectives. A legislature can create new offences, it can appropriate revenues, and it can create official agencies to administer its schemes. Judges are largely confined to authorizing private damage suits, extending the reach of legislative schemes for which the means of enforcement are already established, or denying access to the courts to those actors (including officials) of whose policies the court disapproves. But there is one important device which judges, and not legislators, are entitled to use—the retrospective operation of the legal innovation. When a felt injustice is seen in a number of cases and triggers a statutory reform, this operates only for future cases. If a "one man lobby" goes to court and persuades the judges to bring the older law into line with the contemporary sense of justice, he gets the benefit of the reform to remedy the harm he has already suffered. When this "lobbyist" asks the court to do something, it cannot just refuse to listen as our politicians often do; the judges must write a public, reasoned opinion about what, if anything, should be done about the case.

When we reflect on these several differences in the institutions, we can delineate a rough division of responsibility between court and legislature in improving the quality of Canadian law. A legislature should be allowed to concentrate on major reviews of an area of law, through which it explores all the available expert knowledge, works out compromises between important competing interests, and develops a systematic scheme for reform, which it implements through the sophisticated techniques it is able to devise. In order to preserve its time and energies for this vital task, the legislature should be able to rely on the judges to work out the implications of established values in our society (especially those expressed in major legislative innovations) and smooth the anomalies and injustices in the law that must be applied in concrete litigation. The court engages in incremental law reform, operating at retail, and dispenses the results of its work to individuals in our society when they really need it.

Ideally, the relationship of legislature and court should be understood as a law-making partnership. Undoubtedly the legislature will be the dominant architect of our legal system. Without its vision, imagination, and energy, we will have a very shaky and uncomfortable structure. This does not mean the legislature would work best if it had to work alone. The overall design will be much better if we utilize the craftsmanship of the judges working in the field. Courts see the problems early, at first-hand, and have a distinctive perspective from which to offer a solution. It is true that they will sometimes err in their judgment. So will the short-stop who makes a gallant try for the tough fielding chances. When errors are made in the open in front of an audience, it is only natural to want to leave the play to a team-mate, especially if he is more skilled. But surely we are better served by the person who tries to make that extra contribution and thus gives himself a chance to succeed a good part of the time.

And we should remember that in the case of judicial errors, the legislature is always there to back the court up and mend any damage that may occur.

THE ROLE OF PRINCIPLE

It is a basic feature of an appellate process that the judges write a reasoned opinion justifying their legal conclusions. We can now see how much more complicated this reasoning is than the layman's view of what is involved in the easy cases. To be sure, courts are supposed to adjudicate the concrete cases before them by fitting them within the legal system. Important legal values such as predictability, efficiency, and impersonality support this demand for judicial adherence to the established law. Yet the dictates of this law are not unambiguous in the typical case which reaches a final court of appeal. As we saw in *Barbara Jarvis*, the language used in a statute will not clearly tell the judges what the legislature has prescribed for the issue at the heart of the appeal. That ingredient of the legal system will be firmly settled for the first time by the opinion of the court adjudicating the immediate lawsuit.

Since this is the inescapable responsibility of the judicial role, we shall naturally prefer a style of legal reasoning which appraises the fitness of the rules that are available and anticipates the policy results of the one that is selected. Only in this way can the judicial contribution to the law that governs us exhibit decent workmanship. Yet we rightly deplore too free-wheeling a stance in our judges. Even a final court should not have complete discretion to look at any policy factors its members consider relevant or take the law in any direction they believe desirable. A detached view of the judicial institution raises some qualms about the wisdom, the coherence, and the popular acceptability of judge-made law. Judicial creativity is a necessity and can be a virtue, but it must have its limits. Can we say anything useful about where these boundaries are located?

There is a legal instrument which summarizes and integrates the thrust of these many factors lurking in the background of any judicial decision. This indispensable weapon in the judicial armoury is the *legal principle*. A principle is a very different kind of legal doctrine than a rule. A rule is applied directly to a fact situation in order to prescribe a specific legal result. A principle is an argument which is appealed to as a justification for the adoption of such a legal rule in the trouble case where this is necessary. I shall talk of several examples later on in the book but a brief sketch of one illustration may help clarify the distinction now.

In Canadian law if a person is in possession of a substance which is an illegal drug (such as heroin) but which he honestly believes is an innocent substance (like powdered milk), he is not guilty of the offence of possession of a narcotic. This doctrine is a legal *rule* which was firmly

49

settled in our law by the Supreme Court of Canada's decision in *Beaver*.[10] When applied to any such situation, the rule prescribes acquittal. The Supreme Court reached its conclusion in *Beaver*, in the hitherto uncertain state of the law (and in the face of a vigorous dissent) by relying on the principle of *mens rea*—a person should be excused for his criminal conduct if he does not have a guilty mind. This doctrine does not prescribe a legal conclusion for every situation it covers. There are exceptions to the principle of *mens rea*: in the more recent case of *Pierce Fisheries*[11] the Supreme Court held that a person with undersized lobsters in his possession should be convicted of this offence notwithstanding his honest belief that all his lobsters were of legal size.

The significance of the principle is that it points to the adoption of a legal rule because it embodies the values and social policies which ought to influence the direction in which the courts take our law.[12] The doctrine is a weighty argument whenever a criminal defendant advances a novel excuse and will often be followed as it was in *Beaver*. The argument is not irrefutable, and the principle is not automatically applied in every such case. When a judge examines the policies which underlie the principle, he may find them of lesser weight in the circumstances of his case and hold that an exceptional rule is justified by countervailing arguments.

All of this may be true but what exactly is its significance? Am I just repeating my earlier conclusion that judges should appeal to social policies and values in justifying the adoption of new legal rules and these will tilt the balance sometimes in one direction, sometimes in another? The intriguing issue is why one might describe such an argument as a *legal* principle.

Let us return for a moment to the analysis of *Barbara Jarvis*. There we saw that any legal rule has two sides. On its surface the language in the statute prescribes a legal result. Sometimes puzzlement about exactly what legal result is prescribed will lead a court to probe the depths of the rule: there it should find a social value judgment as the underside of the law. The legal prescription was written to remedy a social problem and achieve a public goal. When a court undertakes the task of fleshing out the legal rule, it is supposed to reflect on the implications of these underlying social policies and elaborate the law in a way which respects the integrity of that hidden policy dimension.

---

10 *Beaver v. R.*, [1957] S.C.R. 531, 26 C.R. 193, 118 C.C.C. 129. This case, as well as *Pierce Fisheries*, fn. 11, *post*, is analyzed in some detail in Chapter 4.

11 *R. v. Pierce Fisheries*, [1971] S.C.R. 5, 12 C.R.N.S. 272, 12 D.L.R. (3d) 591, [1970] 5 C.C.C. 193.

12 There are several such policies underlying the principle of *mens rea* — enlarging individual freedom, protecting the innocent from criminal punishment, economizing in the use of the criminal sanction, etc. I just mention them here by way of illustration because I shall review these decisions and policies in detail in Chapter 4.

My preliminary examination of legal reasoning in the context of *Barbara Jarvis* may have conveyed a slightly misleading impression of the process. The case does show how a legal purpose can be enacted as authoritatively and followed as carefully as the verbal expression the legislature adopted for it. However, one should not picture the legal provision under immediate investigation as having its own unique and sharply distinct social policy.

Any area of social life presents a series of interlocking human problems. Each type of situation will require its own legal prescription but the same strands of public policy will run throughout the area. If the law is to intervene successfully, it must mount a co-ordinated assault on this constellation of specific issues. One can easily see this in the case of a statute such as the Labour Relations Act which purports to subject collective bargaining to comprehensive regulation. The legislature's policies with respect to certification must mesh sensibly with the scope of its protection for union organization. The same should be true of the rule adopted by the Supreme Court in *Beaver* to the effect that honest mistakes may excuse the possession of heroin. We have any number of crimes created by many different statutes, and for each such offence a variety of excuses may be advanced (*e.g.*, mistake, accident, insanity, drunkenness, etc.). Just as in the case of collective bargaining law, the decision to adopt a rule allowing an excuse in one case reflects a value judgment about the competing policies which are threaded through all of these human situations. If the whole point of legal intervention is to achieve certain public objectives, it is only natural to expect that the policy preference at any one point will fit reasonably well into the set of similar judgments and rules within the whole area of regulation.

Now the point of *legal* principles can be seen. Judges must develop and settle the law in the light of the policies believed appropriate for that area. However, these value judgments need not simply reflect the personal attitudes of the judges who happen to sit on that appeal panel. Instead, the court should be able to discern a series of policy judgments already embodied in existing legal standards. The judges must articulate a theory which explains how these many judgments form a systematic whole, a theory which is summarized in the legal principle. The principle expresses the theme by which a society has gradually resolved the competing interests and values which are the common strands of this area of life. Once such a theory is articulated, it may become the fundamental reality of the law which governs the judges. If a new question arises, a court can and should appeal to this principle to justify its new legal rule. If one of the existing rules seems incompatible with the thrust of the law's evolution that same principled argument will justify a revision.[13]

---

13 In this chapter I have emphasized the scope for judicial creativity in areas where the existing legal materials are ambiguous or even silent. The thrust of my argument has been the delineation of the considerations and criteria which should shape judicial reasoning in these trouble cases. However, there are also many

The concept of a legal principle is the linch-pin of my definition of the proper scope of judicial law-making. I do not mean that such a tool is a necessary feature of every judicial kit. Unfortunately, it is only too easy for a nation's judiciary to view the legal system as a series of unconnected legal rules whose only common denominator is that they were all enacted by recognized law-makers. In such an environment a judge can fill the unavoidable legal gaps only through the exercise of his personal discretion. What I do suggest is that this expanded concept of law is both viable and desirable. Legal principles are a worthy, though not an inevitable, judicial instrument. Our judges can and should work out coherent views of the underlying structure of different areas of the law, founded on a theory of how the relevant values and interests are meshed and compromised. This theory should be the touchstone by which judicial innovation is carried on, both in creating new rules and in altering or abolishing the old ones.

Why should our judges operate with this picture of the role of law in courts? The reason is that this concept best does justice to all of the factors which should shape judicial reasoning. It recognizes the inevitability of judicial creation of new legal rules in the course of administering any legal system in a changing world. Hence judges are turned to reflection on the policies which should inform their decision; this can only enhance the quality of the judicial product. Yet legal and institutional values caution against any freedom for the shifting members of an appellate court to revise the law in accordance with their purely subjective views. Instead of a predictable, orderly, and impersonal *legal* system, we would be governed by an erratic and idiosyncratic judicial discretion. These dangers are largely avoided in a judicial institution which requires its members to defend their legal innovations by principled arguments that are visibly shaping the evolution of that whole area of the law.

These principles are located in much the same public sources of law as the bare rules which are conventionally supposed to control our judges. The professional legal audience can view the theory as it develops over a series of judicial opinions and test whether it is a satisfactory rationale of the many legal doctrines in the area. Once the lawyers understand this theme, they can participate in that same process of legal reasoning and anticipate where it will take the law in the future. Lawyers will do this at the stage of counselling the private citizen about action he can

---

situations in which a court will find a rule that is clear in meaning but unreasonable in result. The original legal judgment may have been unwise from the beginning or may have become outmoded by changing social conditions. A court has an equal responsibility here to engage in creative renovation of such anachronistic doctrines and the argument of this chapter should tell judges how this duty may be discharged. Strange though it may sound at first, the implication of my position is that a court can be under a legal obligation (founded on principle) to overturn a hitherto binding legal rule. At the opening of the next chapter I shall describe a case, *Fleming v. Atkinson*, [1959] S.C.R. 513, 18 D.L.R. (2d) 81, which illustrates precisely what I mean.

safely take, negotiating pre-trial settlements of disputes that have already arisen, and preparation and participation in adversarial litigation. Judicial innovation can be kept decently restrained by scholarly criticism of opinions within a common framework of legal argument.

In sum, if an internal logic is visible in the existing structure of the law, the legal community should be able to sense, at least within a reasonable margin, the scope for judicial creativity in the immediate future. In fact, I believe that legal argument in terms of principle is not only a necessary avenue towards a better quality of legal *justice*, it is the primary source of the stability and predictability of a legal *order*.

CONCLUSION

It should be clear by now that the picture I drew of the two basic judicial functions was too much a contrast of black and white. There is no sharp dichotomy between adjudication of concrete disputes within the law and adoption of general policies for the law. The reality that we see is a gradually changing shade of grey, reflecting the mix of appellate court tasks.

Canadian judges are naturally reluctant to admit, even to themselves, the truly creative role they play in composing the legal system which they administer. But the age of judicial innocence is long past. No one can deny the inescapable influence of a court which makes authoritative legal decisions and then publishes its opinions to be followed by other judges. What a timid court can do is deliberately keep to a minimum the occasions when it disturbs the existing language of the law. Or a court can move near the other end of the spectrum. Having tasted the heady wine of judicial power, it can become ever bolder in renovating what it sees as an unsteady legal structure. Yet even this body will ultimately be brought up short by the barriers that its adjudicative arrangements place in the path of judges trying to have their way in the real world.

The task for legal philosophy is to carve out a viable balance between these persistent temptations. I do not mean that we can locate an ideal stance at any precise point. The best hope we can envisage is a sense of the proper judicial mood. Our judges must utilize all their opportunities to rework and refine the legal standards they use; in doing so they must respect the limitations inherent in the judicial position which creates the opening for their power.

There is a great deal more that could be added to a theory of law in courts. I have not talked about the many technical factors in the construction of statutes, the analysis of precedent, or the interaction of legislation and the common law. The heart of a position in any one of these technical areas of jurisprudence is a tacit assumption about the proper scope and method of judicial innovation. I have dwelt somewhat on the concept of a legal principle which I believe is the key to the

53

most fruitful grasp of this enduring dilemma. Certainly this notion is not a sufficient answer in all cases nor an easily-used instrument in many. There is no uniquely correct solution to this complex equation of social policies, legal values, and institutional responsibilities.

I suggested in Chapter 1 that the work and structure of appellate courts in different societies will be a function of the manner in which other law-making institutions in those societies are discharging their obligations. In the rest of the book I shall try to show how the basic stance of a court in one society—the Supreme Court of Canada—can and should vary sharply in different areas of law. The view that I take of the logic of legal reasoning is a pragmatic one, heavily dependent on those features of the legal environment which I have pointed to in this Chapter. In the next section of this book I will try to put more flesh on the theory and test its implications through a detailed examination of the work of the Supreme Court of Canada in five different areas of its jurisdiction.

PART II

Recent Law from the Supreme Court:

An appraisal

The Architect of the Common Law

3

THE SUPREME COURT AND TORT LIABILITY IN CANADA

*"Mastering the lawless science of our law,
That codeless myriad of precedent,
That wilderness of single instances...".*

(Tennyson, Aylmer's Field)

I shall begin my analysis of the role and performance of the Supreme Court of Canada by reviewing some of its decisions in the area of tort liability for personal injuries.[1] Perhaps some students of the judicial process will ask why bother with these rather insignificant cases? Let's get on to the attention-getting constitutional or civil liberties decisions. However, there are several reasons why I think tort law is a good starting point. First, we can fully understand much of the contemporary character of the judicial process only if we see how it is directed at the adjudication of private law disputes between one individual and another. Moreover, most of this area of law is almost totally judge-made, the *common law*. Our Supreme Court is a useful vehicle for reflecting on the true range and complexity of the judicial function precisely because of the breadth of its jurisdiction. The Court regularly handles the garden variety tort case as well as the newsworthy public law dispute. We must not miss the opportunity to appraise the exercise of judicial creativity in a private law area where the Court is not distracted by the involvement of other institutions, whether legislative or administrative. Finally, as I shall try to demonstrate, these attitudes concerning the private law role of the Supreme Court of Canada are wrong. Tort cases do raise important issues of public policy, and it is critical that they be settled intelligently.

---

1 A review of all of the Court's work in this area since 1949 can be found in my article "Groping Towards a Canadian Tort Law: The Role of the Supreme Court of Canada" (1971), 21 U.T.L.J. 267.

Let us start with a typical motor vehicles action which reached the Court, and produced a not-so-typical response.[2]

THE CURIOUS DOCTRINE OF CATTLE TRESPASS

One sunny summer afternoon, Floyd Atkinson was driving a jeep along a gravelled country road in a farming district in Ontario. Suddenly, upon reaching the brow of a hill, he was confronted with a herd of cows belonging to a farmer named Leo Fleming. Although he applied his brakes and steered past some of the cows, Atkinson's jeep eventually struck three of the animals, killing two, and causing serious injuries to his own knee. The driver sued the farmer for his personal injuries and the latter responded with a claim for his two dead cows. Apparently Fleming took the attitude that he could let his cows wander where they wanted and they customarily pastured on the highway, strolling back and forth across the road. The trial judge found this to be negligence on his part and, given a certain lack of due care on the driver's part also, apportioned the relative responsibility 60% to the farmer and 40% to Atkinson.

This would seem to be a relatively straightforward case and easy to resolve in terms of the ordinary doctrines of negligence law. Unfortunately, hidden away in the nooks and crannies of the common law was a legal rule which absolved the farmer of any duty to prevent his cattle from straying on the highway and endangering its users. This rule owed its origin to two factors: (1) when highways were first created at the end of the medieval period in England, land was dedicated by the adjoining landowners subject to their own right of passage for their animals; (2) for a very long time this created no risk of danger from domestic animals such as cattle because traffic was so slow moving that the animals could easily be avoided. With the advent of automobiles, this factual situation was radically changed. However, the House of Lords, in its 1947 decision in *Searle v. Wallbank*,[3] declined an invitation to revise the legal duties of the farmer to bring them into line with modern needs, and the Ontario Court of Appeal felt compelled to respect the authority of this common law precedent in its 1952 decision in *Noble v. Calder*.[4] The true wishes of the Ontario judges were expressed in these concluding passages from their own opinion in *Fleming v. Atkinson*:[5]

> I do not want to part with this case without expressing the hope that it may draw attention to the present unsatisfactory state of the law in this

---

[2] *Fleming v. Atkinson*, [1959] S.C.R. 513, 18 D.L.R. (2d) 81.
[3] [1947] A.C. 341, [1947] 1 All E.R. 12.
[4] [1952] O.R. 577, [1952] 3 D.L.R. 651 (C.A.).
[5] [1956] O.R. 801, [1956] 5 D.L.R. (2d) 309 at 323 (C.A.).

province as to civil liability for injuries sustained due to the presence on our public highways of straying domestic animals. *The Courts cannot change the law; the legislature can.* The common law as applied by the House of Lords in England to the highways there is not adequate here, and yet the Courts of this province must follow those decisions. I am certain that a jury would be astounded at being told that the owner of a horse or cattle beast who allowed it to stray on King's Highway No. 401 would, as the law now stands, not be civilly liable to others using that highway for the damage caused by its presence there . . . In my respectful opinion the law should be uniform throughout the province. All this can be accomplished by legislation that empowers the Court to determine, as a question of fact, having regard to all the circumstances including the nature of the highway and the amount of the traffic that might reasonably be expected to be upon it, whether or not it would be negligent to allow a domestic animal to be at large upon it . . . [emphasis added].

When the case reached the Supreme Court of Canada, one judge, Mr. Justice Cartwright, agreed that the English common law, as reflected in *Searle*, defined the duties of the cattle owner until and unless they were changed by legislation. In his view it was not the function of the judges to alter a legal doctrine when it no longer reflected reasonable social policies. Fortunately for Canadian law, and for Floyd Atkinson, Mr. Justice Judson for the majority took a wider view of the judicial mission. He did not consider himself bound by an English doctrine which originated in features which are not part of Canadian society and which was reiterated in a heavily-criticized House of Lords decision. The decision of the Supreme Court in *Fleming v. Atkinson* is important because it clearly expressed our judicial independence of the House of Lords, especially when that body adheres to such an irrational legal anomaly.[6] It is even more important as an example of the style of legal reasoning which a truly independent Supreme Court, at the top of our judicial hierarchy, must exhibit.

A rule of law has, therefore been stated in *Searle v. Wallbank* and followed in *Noble v. Calder* which has little or no relation to the facts or needs of the situation and which ignores any theory of responsibility to the public for conduct which involves foreseeable consequences of harm. I can think of no logical basis for this immunity and it can only be based upon a rigid determination to adhere to the rules of the past in spite of changed conditions which call for the application of rules of responsibility which have been worked out to meet modern needs. It has always

---

6 Under the traditional doctrine the farmer was liable to the adjoining landowner for damage caused by his straying cattle, as well as to the owner of the highway for damages to the latter; he was liable to users of the highway if he negligently drove his cattle for passage on the highway and they were injured; the only immunity was the one applicable to this case, where the cattle were allowed to stray on the highway and thus cause injury to the user.

been assumed that one of the virtues of the common law system is its flexibility, that it is capable of changing with the times and adapting its principles to new conditions. There has been conspicuous failure to do this in this branch of the law and the failure has not passed unnoticed. It has been criticized in judicial decisions (including the one under appeal), in the texts and by the commentators.... My conclusion is that it is open to this Court to apply the ordinary rules of negligence to the case of straying animals and that the principles enunciated in *Searle v. Wallbank,* dependent as they are upon historical reasons, which have no relevancy here, and upon a refusal to recognize a duty now because there had been previously no need of one, offer no obstacle.[7]

Judson's opinion is almost a textbook illustration of the conception of legal reasoning I proposed in the preceding chapter. Judges should not just blindly follow a legal rule because it has been recognized in the law for a long time. If the rule appears to require unjust results in the immediate situation, the judge must ask why. He should have a sense of unease when asked to use a rule that does not fit comfortably into the basic principles of tort responsibility which condition a lawyer's perception of the area. Perhaps there will be come good reasons for this exceptional doctrine: on investigation of the cattle trespass rule, its only support turns out to be ancient history. In such a situation the legal obligation of a judge is clearly the forthright elimination of the legal anomaly which produces that kind of injustice.[8]

---

[7] [1959] S.C.R. 513 at 535.

[8] I mentioned earlier that the Supreme Court of Canada is technically bound by the decisions of no other court. *Fleming v. Atkinson* [*ante,* fn. 2] is the best authority for that proposition. For a long time the Supreme Court of Canada was thought to be subject to the law laid down in precedents of the House of Lords. This position was understandable in view of the fact that the Privy Council — the House of Lords in another guise — was our final court of appeal. In 1949, the Canadian Parliament removed this possibility of appeal of individual decisions of the Supreme Court of Canada. The Court completed the journey to judicial independence when it held, in *Fleming v. Atkinson,* that it was no longer restricted by the British version of the common law as propounded by the House of Lords.

This still leaves open one question about the place of precedent in the Supreme Court. The Court is not bound by decisions of any foreign tribunals (such as the House of Lords in *Searle v. Wallbank* [*ante,* fn. 3]) or other Canadian courts (such as the Ontario Court of Appeal in *Noble v. Calder* [*ante,* fn. 4]). Is the Court bound by earlier decisions of its own? In the case of *Stuart v. The Bank of Montreal* (1909), 41 S.C.R. 516; affirmed [1911] A.C. 120, the Supreme Court held that it was. This may have been an appropriate attitude for an intermediate court of appeal, but hardly for the body which now has ultimate judicial responsibility for the evolution of Canadian law. We do not have a clear expression of a change in attitude as we find in *Fleming v. Atkinson* about House of Lords decisions. However, there are fairly strong hints in *Peda v. R.,* [1969] S.C.R. 905, 7 C.R.N.S. 243, [1969] 4 C.C.C. 245, 6 D.L.R. (3d) 177, that the

THE NEED FOR
JUDICIAL RENOVATION

What are the lessons we can draw from *Fleming v. Atkinson* about when and how the Court should respond in the common law? The case is certainly an unprepossessing factual situation with which to lead off a detailed assessment of the work of the Supreme Court across the spectrum of Canadian law. The question of whether the farmer or the motorist should bear the losses caused by a cow does seem to be of a somewhat lesser order of importance than constitutional disputes, issues of civil liberties and due process, problems of administrative regulation of the economy, and other such issues which regularly appear before the Supreme Court. The legal situation in the *Fleming* case is typical of the private law disputes which still constitute the bulk of the Court's work and which many now advocate deleting from its jurisdiction. I will leave my assessment of these proposals for later when we have a more detailed view of the kinds of problems involved in these cases. For the moment we must recognize that there was an issue of general law to be resolved in the case and that the Supreme Court of Canada still has final judicial authority in this area. As is typical of a great many private law doctrines, tort liability for escaping cattle will not affect very many people but when it does arise, the question of whether damages can be collected will be of vital importance to the person involved. There are many legal doctrines with precisely this impact and the cumulative quality of their policies tells a lot about the justice afforded to the individual in our society. Up to now, the judiciary has been primarily responsible for their development in Canada It behooves us then to enquire into the Court's performance in this area and to suggest the standards by which it should govern itself.

As Mr. Justice Judson stated in *Fleming v. Atkinson,* there is a general *principle* of law firmly established in this area. A person is required to take reasonable care in his behaviour when it creates the risk of physical injuries to another. If he does not take care and his faulty behaviour causes losses to another, the law requires that he assume responsibility for payment of damages to make whole the innocent victim.[9] This legal

---

Supreme Court judges do not consider themselves absolutely bound by their own precedents, even very recent ones.

We shall encounter several tort cases where the earlier decisions were ignored, though none where they were explicitly overruled.

9 This legal doctrine is founded on the basic moral value of fairness. Everyone is supposed to shoulder the burden of careful foresight to protect the interests of his neighbour and can expect reciprocal consideration from others. If one person does not conform to this standard in his behaviour and causes harm to an innocent victim, there is nothing the law can do at that point to undo the harm. However, it can translate the injuries into a rough monetary figure and decide who should ultimately bear it. Given the choice of the responsible actor and his unfortunate victim, the reason for the established principle is clear. The claims

principle had been clearly and authoritatively established in the general law of torts in the case of *Donoghue v. Stevenson*,[10] but had become embedded in the motor vehicle area some time earlier. Appraised in the light of this theory of liability, the special immunity for "cattle trespass" was an historical anomaly. As Judson J. showed in his opinion, there may have been some rationale for its original adoption in England several hundred years ago but there certainly was no valid argument which could be made for its retention in contemporary Canada.

Mr. Justice Cartwright's dissent did raise some doubt whether the Court should leave it to the legislature to administer the *coup de grace* to the doctrine. To adopt the framework of analysis I sketched earlier, assuming there are good policy reasons for tort liability in this situation, are there countervailing legal values which should make a court wary of itself abolishing the immunity? In my view, the *Fleming* case is significant because when we assess in a realistic way the arguments against judicial innovation, they seem largely inapplicable here. In this respect *Fleming* is typical of tort law and, indeed, of much of the private law area.

What about the argument of predictability in the law and the possibility that judicial elimination of the immunity will defeat the expectations of those who relied on it being the law? Did the farmer rely on his immunity from tort liability when he failed to take reasonable care to control his cattle? If he did, is this the kind of expectation the legal system should be concerned to satisfy? Simply to ask these questions is to answer them. In tort law, at least as regards accidental injuries, the reliance interest of possible defendants enters primarily at the point of insurance planning against liability for the risk. Studies have indicated that special rules of tort immunity such as this one, especially when they are hedged in by equally anomalous exceptions, are irrelevant to insurance decisions. Indeed, if there are any reasonable expectations which will be frustrated in a situation similar to that of the *Fleming* case they will be those of the injured motorist when he consults his lawyer and finds that the farmer is protected by a special rule dating back to

---

of this moral judgment may be a little strained when a venial fault on the part of the defendant has caused massive harm to one or more blameless victims. The law has produced a host of doctrines limiting the extent of tort liability for these situations, but I cannot delve into them here. A more radical objection has been lodged against this theme in our current tort law. While few argue that fault is not a sufficient reason for shifting accidental harm through tort liability, many voices contend that it is not a necessary reason. In a time of widespread insurance, governmental welfare schemes, large business enterprises, and so on, the law need not confine itself to a choice between the immediate actor and the person who has been injured. I shall return to this issue later. I have reviewed the issues and literature in this debate about the fundamental problem in tort law in my article "Defamation, Enterprise Liability, and Freedom of Speech" (1967), 17 U.T.L.J. 278. See especially 289-310.

10 [1932] A.C. 562 (U.K.).

medieval England. If the farmer's lawyer (or that of his insurer) has any understanding of this whole area of tort law and the rationale for its evolution, he can estimate the shakiness of the farmer's immunity and anticipate its probable removal. For these reasons, the Supreme Court in *Fleming v. Atkinson* could quite confidently ignore the argument about the damage to the predictability of the law.

What about the competence of the Court to make an intelligent change in the law? The possible defects in judicial law reform seem irrelevant to this actual problem. There is no need for lengthy investigations, social science research, expert testimony, and so on, to decide about change. The issue is basically one of esoteric "lawyer's law" which can be resolved by careful analysis of the implications of the basic legal principles underlying the area. If the legislature were moved to reform in this area, it would have to rely on the same sort of appraisal and it would find it in the textbooks and law review articles which are equally available to the courts.

In fact, the "cattle trespass" rule is one in which the resources of the judicial forum are especially valuable. The issue is narrow in compass, occurs infrequently, and is only one of a very large number of such relatively independent tort problems. Yet there are a lot of judges in a lot of courts hearing such cases all the time. Each judge sees the human implications of the issue vividly portrayed in the concrete dispute before him. On the basis of the research and arguments prepared for him by opposing counsel, he can work out the solution which seems most rational in the light of the basic policies in the area. This proposed rule, when reported, can become a piecemeal addition to the evolving common law of torts. The legislature seems much too bulky and unwieldy an instrument to solve the problem of cattle trespass. It operates at the wholesale level while so much of our private law requires retail treatment.

But at least the legislature is elected, one may suggest. Should not changes in the law be made by a representative body, rather than the appointed and tenured court? We must turn to the reasons for our qualms about judicial innovation and take a realistic view of their relevance to particular cases. The problem in *Fleming v. Atkinson* is not one which will figure in an election campaign. It is inconsistent with democratic values (though not always illegitimate for this reason) for a court to intervene and impose its own policies in an area where the popular will has been expressed in the political arena. If the legislature were moved to reform in this esoteric problem area, it would merely be ratifying a proposal worked out by an equally unrepresentative Law Reform Commission at as invisible a level as would be a judicial innovation.

Once more we find that not only is there no real argument against a judicial initiative, but there are positive reasons in favour of such an active role. Private law doctrines such as this often lead to a distortion of the legislative process. Pressure for reform is very diffuse and unorganized. There is no lobby of accident victims petitioning the government. Instead, there is usually only an academic who has shown how some legal relic is working a real injustice on the very few people who run afoul of it. However, there is often a narrow interest group which might be somewhat harmed by the change. The farmer's insurance premiums will go up a bit and he may have to answer for his negligence in a lawsuit. A politician might be a little worried about the farmers' votes if their organizations object, especially if there is no countervailing lobby pressing for the reform. It is extremely unlikely he would be moved to *create* the cattle trespass immunity, but he might be loath to come out in the open and remove it entirely. The safest course in his eyes is to "let sleeping dogs lie", allow the proposal to die on the legislative order paper, and rationalize this inaction on the grounds (often valid) that he is busy on too many other problems.

By contrast, the Supreme Court was duty-bound to reach a positive conclusion about this legal problem in order to resolve the concrete dispute between Fleming and Atkinson. It had to hear the arguments from both sides, decide which position was most persuasive, and justify its conclusion in a written opinion which is reported for others to see and criticize. If judges within such an institution are willing to exercise their power to develop our law in a rational way, then we can provide the individual litigant who has been hurt with a forum to which he can come as a one-man lobby looking for legal justice. There is something to be said in a democracy for an institution which will resolve such disputes on the basis of the quality of the arguments presented, rather than the number of votes represented.

On just about every dimension then, these legal or institutional values seem to favour *judicial* initiative in this area, and they certainly do not warn against it. In order to complete this picture, let me give an example of a tort law reform I do not think a court is entitled to make, even though the judges may be convinced of its substantive desirability. The basic principle underlying our current law of torts, the one appealed to in *Fleming v. Atkinson,* is that negligent fault is the basis of liability. More and more voices contend that this is too narrow a criterion. Especially in the motor vehicle accident area, we hear proposals for a legal doctrine of strict liability, founded on policies of risk distribution, market deterrence, etc. I think we are going to see some such doctrine adopted in Canada shortly but this reform should be the work of the legislature, not the court. Why is this so?

In the first place, this will produce a very substantial change in the incidence of legal liability and it may require substantial increases in the premium level. To the extent that insurance companies have charged lower premiums in reliance on the fault doctrine, they can claim that this justifiable expectation should not be frustrated by retrospective judicial alteration of the law. I am not sure myself how compelling this argument is. It depends on the degree of increased recovery in the new system and the ability of the insurance industry to finance the extra payments for past losses out of future premiums.

The real point is that the court could not likely estimate this either, which brings us to a second and major objection against judicial adoption of strict liability. The court simply is not competent to set up a complete new scheme for compensating automobile accident victims. This is not a simple matter of eliminating an irrational anomaly like the cattle trespass doctrine and applying the established principle of fault. The objectives of a strict liability scheme require a complex series of adjustments in the kinds and level of damages recoverable, the relationship of tort liability to various other forms of disability compensation, the nature of the insurance which is to be used, and even the forum in which claims are to be made. To perform this job, we want royal commissions, legislative committees and research by a battery of experts. We cannot rely on the efforts of a few Supreme Court judges sitting in their chambers in Ottawa.

Finally, the Court does not have the authority to adopt such a scheme into law. Let us suppose that a Royal Commission had been appointed, had laboured for several years examining the issues and the various alternatives, and then worked out a detailed scheme. The expert work has been done but the legislature, for various reasons, has not gotten around to acting on it. Should the Court decide to implement this new scheme in substitution for the common law of fault-based tort liability on the assumption that it is indeed a better system? In my view, the answer is still no! As anyone who reads Canadian newspapers will realize, the desirability of compensation without fault is a matter of sharp political controversy in several Canadian provinces. It has figured prominently in several election campaigns and governments have teetered on the edge of defeat in trying to get schemes enacted. The various plans present important and ambiguous value judgments about such matters as social welfare, compulsory government insurance, administrative agencies, and the responsibility of the dangerous driver. The place where these controversial issues should be aired and inevitable compromises worked out is the public legislative arena where the participants can be held responsible for their judgments. The last place in which we would want the decision made is the sheltered, closed world of the judges who are in the process of resolving a private lawsuit.

THE TANGLED WEB OF
OCCUPIER'S LIABILITY

There is a whole area of tort law which is shot through with such irrational rules as the cattle trespass doctrine. This is the law of occupier's liability. In the course of resolving the action in the English case of

Indermaur v. Dames in the year 1866, Mr. Justice Willes used the following language to state the reason for his decision for the plaintiff.[11]

> The class to which the customer belongs includes persons who go not as mere volunteers or *licensees*, or guests, or servants, or persons whose employment is such that danger may be considered as bargained for, but who go upon business which concerns the occupier, and upon his *invitation*, express or implied.
>
> With respect to such a visitor, at least, we consider it settled law that he, using a reasonable care on his part for his own safety, is entitled to expect that the occupier shall on his part use reasonable care to prevent damage from *unusual danger* which he knows or ought to know; and that . . . whether such reasonable care has been taken (by notice, lighting, guarding, or otherwise) and whether there was contributory negligence in the sufferer, must be determined by the jury as matter of fact. . . . (emphasis added).

This was a perfectly adequate formulation of the doctrine needed to deal with the facts of that case. Unfortunately, lawyers have treated his words with a reverential attitude appropriate, if at all, only for Holy Writ. It is said[12] that Willes J. was a judge whom "the Muse has inspired, perhaps as the reward for his stricter meditation". Because of the "learning, care, and skill" he applied in formulating the duty, "he who alters one word of it does so at his peril."

The natural product of this kind of attitude is a rigid body of law which tries to pigeonhole different situations and then ordain a precise legal result for each. As the dean of Canadian tort law scholars waspishly remarked: "Here, truly, we have departed little from the methods of the Middle Ages".[13] This process of artificial categorization reflected the infancy of torts when each calling such as innkeeper, carrier, blacksmith, doctor and contractor had its own special form of legal duty. Legal developments in the 20th Century gradually altered this picture, culminating in a coherent theory of tort liability for carelessly injuring one's "neighbour". Unfortunately, the law of occupier's liability has remained a prominent holdout against the tide of legal evolution in the direction of this principle. Some adventurous lower court judges have tried to move the law in this direction but have immediately been slapped down by the higher courts. The Supreme Court of Canada is not alone in this supine attitude towards 19th Century concepts, but that certainly does not excuse its very clear failures.

A great many occupier's cases have reached the Supreme Court of Canada since it became Canada's final court of appeal in late 1949. Because I can deal with only a few, I have selected one area in which

---

11 *Indermaur v. Dames* (1866), L.R. 1 C.P. 274 at 278.
12 Griffith, "Duty of Invitors" (1916), 32 L.Q.R. 255 at 256 and 267.
13 Wright, "The Law of Torts" (1948), 26 Can. Bar Rev. 46 at 82.

there are two pairs of cases aptly illustrating the deficiencies in the typical style of reasoning of our Supreme Court. The defendant occupies premises in which he carries on some business or undertaking. The plaintiff is lawfully on these premises with the permission of the defendant and is injured by reason of some allegedly dangerous condition of the building. If we assessed this problem in terms of the general principles of tort law, we would ask if the occupier had reason to be aware that the visitor might be endangered by the condition of his premises and whether he could reasonably be expected to take some steps to prevent such an accident materializing. No such straightforward process of analysis is permitted in the current state of occupier's liability law. Instead, the rules require that we first characterize the status of the plaintiff vis-à-vis the defendant as an invitee or a licensee, and then label the condition of the building which triggered the accident as a trap or an unusual danger. Only then can we address ourselves to the nature of the obligation the occupier may owe his visitor.

What is the criterion for distinguishing between a licensee and an invitee? The first few cases in which the distinction was used had a sensible difference in mind, between the situation of the social guest accepted into the home and a customer or client invited to use a place of business. It makes sense to require a higher standard of care of someone such as a storeowner, who is running a business for profit and inviting the general public to use it for his own economic benefit, by contrast with a person who invites a guest into his home for social reasons and can expect the latter to take the same risks from the condition of the building that the occupier and his family do. These are certainly relevant factors in deciding what is the reasonable standard of behaviour in the circumstances. However, when they are hardened into two exclusive and exhaustive categories, we find a large number of intermediate cases which do not fit comfortably into either. Judges are forced to ask questions which do not admit of sensible answers. Perhaps we should not be surprised when the course of their decisions seems incoherent.

Take the very common situation of a person who is visiting a tenant in a building and is injured by the condition of the public areas which are still occupied by the landlord. In the *City of Ottawa v. Munro*,[14] the municipality operated a public housing project in which a flat was leased to the plaintiff's grandmother. The plaintiff, Joey Munro, was a four-year-old child living with his grandmother. Each floor had a common washroom for all of the tenants and this area was still under the control of the landlord. The child was injured when he climbed up on a counter for the sink and fell out the adjacent window. The superintendent of the building had previously been warned of this situation and, although a guard had been put on the window in another part of the project, he refused to place one on this floor. A key element in the de-

---

[14] [1954] S.C.R. 756, [1955] 1 D.L.R. 465.

termination of the case was a decision about the plaintiff's status. The Supreme Court, following some heavily criticized decisions of the House of Lords, held that the plaintiff was only a licensee and in no better position than a social guest in someone's house. This meant that liability required a finding that the condition in the washroom was a "trap", a place of concealed danger. Obviously, it was not such a danger to an adult tenant but the answer would be quite different if the law required the landlord to so maintain his premises as to afford protection to children. In language which I find incredible in the second half of the 20th century, the Supreme Court of Canada decided that there should be no such duty. Rand J., as usual, is not content with the authorities and states quite clearly the rationale for his decision. It was obvious that there was no danger to an adult and the tenant here was an adult. Should the landlord have to alter his premises to protect the child? Here is his answer:

> Is the child in any better position? The only ground upon which this can be suggested is that what is apparent to the tenant may be a trap or an allurement to the child. Apart from the fact that the child is brought on the premises by his father it would be a strange proposition that a landlord be bound to alter his premises in order to make them safe for the child when they are unobjectionable as to his tenant. The answer to be given the tenant is simply that if the premises are not fit for his children he should look for others. Now that may appear to be a cold answer when premises are at a premium; but if through stress of circumstances the tenant and *a fortiori* a tenant's licensee, must live where he can, then any special accommodation necessary for the needs of his children must, in some manner, be provided by himself. Of course not all tenants have children and children may arrive in the family at any time and it would be a *reductio ad absurdum* that the duty of the landlord in relation to the structure of his accessory accommodation should depend on such happenings. On long leases of, say apartments, safe today they would become dangerous tomorrow as and where and when children happened to be added to a family.[15]

This is a "cold answer" indeed for little children living in public housing provided by our governmental authorities.

A very different response occurred in the next case, *Hillman v. MacIntosh*.[16] The plaintiff here was a C.N. Express driver who was in the defendant's office building to collect parcels from one of the tenants. He was injured when he rang for the elevator, opened the elevator door and walked in, only to find that the elevator was not at that floor. Without even referring to its earlier decision in the *Munro* case, the Supreme Court found that Hillman was an invitee and thus was owed the higher

---

15 [1954] S.C.R. at 761.
16 [1959] S.C.R. 384, 17 D.L.R. (2d) 705.

duty of care by the defendant. Two possible grounds have been suggested for the distinction between these two situations. One accident occurred in a residential apartment building while the other occurred in a commercial office building. However, this is no reason for different legal duties for an owner who operates both buildings for a profit and who increasingly is placing the two types of building in the same complex. Another suggested rationale is that the visitor should have the same status vis-à-vis the landlord in the landlord's part of the building as he bears to the tenant in the tenant's portion. Munro was a licensee in his grandmother's flat (a social guest), while Hillman was an invitee when in the tenant's office. On further reflection, this distinction also appears spurious, as this example will demonstrate. Two people are injured by a defect in the elevator of an apartment building. One person is going to a party in an apartment, the other to deliver a package. Is there any possible justification for allowing one person to collect damages from the landlord and not the other?

The consensus of most analyses of this situation is that, even within the peculiar logic of the law of occupier's liability, the plaintiff should be characterized as an invitee in both these cases. If the rationale for requiring a higher duty of care from the occupier is that he derives some material or economic benefit from the plaintiff's presence on his property, then there is such a benefit in this type of situation, albeit an indirect one. The landlord operates the building so that he can lease portions of it and make his profits from the rent. He could not lease this space if he did not provide means of access to the apartments or offices which were available both to the tenant and those people who will be visiting the tenant. When the visitor is on the elevator, he is not there with a view to providing any direct benefit to the landlord. However, the provision of the elevator, and the permission given to all visitors to use it, is a necessary means for the landlord making a profit from the building: thus he should be required to take the higher degree of care to see that it is safe.

Hence the process of application of a common law rule—here distinguishing between "invitee" and "licensee"—in novel situations is essentially the same as we saw earlier in *Barbara Jarvis* with regard to a statutory rule distinguishing between a "person" and an "employee". The answer cannot be plainly read on the verbal face of the rule. The judge must try to understand the underlying purpose or rationale of the doctrine and then exercise his best judgment about how this objective will be served in the novel case. Unless the Court in each case tries to give some kind of reasoned elaboration of its doctrine, the law will eventually become a collection of discrete and incoherent holdings such as we see in *Munro* and *Hillman*. We will find many more instances of this same tendency in our examination of the work of the Supreme Court of Canada, all basically attributable to the same source.

There is another important reason for preferring this same judicial style. If a court continually decides how a situation should be legally treated only by first asking why the law would want it treated that way, then it is able to subject to continual, critical re-examination the specific policies the law has previously adopted in response to the question why. A multitude of examples have occurred which testify to the very tenuous character of the distinction between invitee and licensee, even when understood in the light of the basic rationale I have described. How do we classify situations such as the building inspector in a home, the child in a school, the person using a phone in a store, and many other marginal cases? Continued reflection on such examples should eventually have persuaded our courts that the original distinction is not a sufficient criterion for arriving at a duty of care in all cases, however plausible it looks in the most obvious situations. As we saw in *Fleming v. Atkinson,* when the court becomes convinced that a judge-made common law rule is irrational if examined in the light of basic principles, it can overturn it. Our courts have consistently missed the opportunity in the area of occupier's liability.

I don't mean to say that the Supreme Court should, out of the blue, declare the whole law of occupier's liability to be repealed forthwith. Judges would be extremely uncomfortable with the notion that they could eliminate at one stroke as extensive, complicated, and deeply ingrained a set of legal doctrines as are involved here. If we examine these qualms realistically, there isn't that much of substance behind them. It is extremely unlikely that occupiers have relied on their special treatment in the law in charting their behaviour, though there is some possibility that insurors have adjusted their premium levels for property owner insurance to take account of the lesser incidence of liability. Running counter to this is the popular expectation of most of us that occupiers of property will take reasonable care for the safety of their premises before inviting us on to them, or pay damages if they do not, an expectation that will often be frustrated by the existing law. The other factors relevant to judicial innovation—the competence of the courts to recognize the irrationality of the existing law and devise a wise solution and the legitimacy of their intervening in a relatively non-political problem and bringing existing doctrines into line with basic principles already established in tort law—tell as equally in favour of judicial creativity as they did in *Fleming v. Atkinson.* And the injustice which is constantly being worked by the legal system (as in the *Munro* case, for example) is much more widespread.

The virtue of the common law process is that it will permit judicial revision of this area of law without a sudden and total break with the past. Judicial rationalization of the law of occupier's liability can be undertaken incrementally, piece by piece. As long as a court understands the direction in which the law should be moving, a view which it can discern from reflection on the themes of the law of torts generally, it can begin to rework each of the special doctrines as they are brought up in a particular case and gradually bring them into line with the overall drift of tort liability. After the judicial system has had sufficient experience with this effort, the groundwork will be laid for the adoption of the basic principles of negligence law, without any offence to important legal values.

There is a very good example of how such a process could and did begin in the Supreme Court of Canada in the case of *Campbell v. The Royal Bank of Canada*.[17] Unfortunately, there is an equally good example of how the process can be aborted, as occurred in the next Supreme Court decision, *Brandon v. Farley*.[18] Each of these cases dealt with the same problem of the judicial role in defining the duty of care owed to invitees. Once we have decided to categorize the plaintiff as an invitee, we must next ask the question whether there was an "unusual danger" on the premises against which the occupier was obliged to protect his visitor. This phrase was included in the language of Willes' judgment quoted earlier and was innocuous enough when offered as a reason for resolving the dispute in that case. Unfortunately, it has proved very detrimental to the growth of our law when later courts lifted it out of the context of his opinion and read it as though it were part of a carefully drafted and binding statutory rule. This has given rise to countless arguments in the cases about whether or not different situations constituted an *unusual danger*. Not surprisingly, we find a long string of Canadian cases asking this question about snow and ice conditions in our winter. *Campbell* and *Farley* were two such cases which reached the Supreme Court of Canada.

Mrs. Campbell, a 51-year-old woman, walked into a branch office of the Royal Bank on a snowy day in Brandon. She was not a regular customer of the bank but wanted to have a cheque cashed. While walking from the teller's cage to the accountant's desk to have the cheque initialled, she slipped and fell, suffering a fractured hip that permanently disabled her. The cause of her fall was a film of water which had accumulated on the floor; apparently the snow carried in on the boots of customers melted while they were in the bank. The majority of the Manitoba Court of Appeal and the dissent in the Supreme Court of Canada held that this was not an "unusual danger", a not implausible conclusion. If the purpose of this category is "to exclude the common recognizable dangers of everyday experience in premises of an ordinary type" (to use the language of Mr. Justice Ritchie's dissent), then surely nothing can be less unusual than this watery condition in a Manitoba bank in the winter.

However, Mr. Justice Freedman of the Manitoba Court of Appeal (who is recognized as one of Canada's finest judges) made an ingenious

---

17 [1964] S.C.R. 85, 46 W.W.R. 79, 43 D.L.R. (2d) 341.
18 [1968] S.C.R. 150, 63 W.W.R. 116, 66 D.L.R. (2d) 289.

argument against this conclusion which was adopted by the Supreme Court majority in an opinion written by Mr. Justice Spence. After all, what is the practical effect of a finding of no "unusual danger"? It means there is no obligation on the occupier to protect his entrants against injury from such a danger. It is precisely here that this special doctrine of occupier's liability deviates from the principles of tort law. Every other defendant is under an obligation to protect his neighbours against all dangers, even ordinary ones, if and to the extent this is reasonable. Sometimes, of course, this may not be reasonable, but the decision of whether it is "unusual" will not settle that question. In fact, it often may be more reasonable to guard against usual dangers, simply because they are more frequent and more easily recognizable than other, more far-fetched occurrences. On the other hand, the fact that they are usual may indicate the common judgment that they are not very serious risks and are customarily tolerated because the chance of any important injury is slight.

The critical element in this judgment, and the one which is left out by the traditional analysis of unusual danger, is the ease and economy with which the familiar risk, viewed in terms of the frequency and severity with which it may occur, can be eliminated. This is the element which Freedman J.A. on the Manitoba Court of Appeal and Spence J. on the Supreme Court of Canada inserted into their analysis of the concept. They suggested that in the bank, where many people congregated, it was reasonable to expect some protection from the slippery walking surface since this was readily available (e.g., from matting placed on the floor or occasional mopping up by a janitor). It would not be reasonable to expect a municipality or a homeowner to put such a surface on its sidewalks, because there is no such point of concentrated activity. Because it was reasonable to expect the danger to be eliminated in the bank, its presence could legally be termed "unusual". The significance of this analysis is that the duty of the occupier to his invitee is now basically indistinguishable from that expected of everybody else, and this without any need for major surgery on the legal doctrines.

Unfortunately, these expectations were dashed by the next such case which reached the Supreme Court, *Brandon v. Farley*. For many years, Farley had carried on the business of purchasing water from the city for sale to farmers in outlying areas. He used a truck with a 500 gallon capacity which he filled at the fire hall with a hose. On the day in question, Farley also ran afoul of the Brandon winter. The weather was cold and snowy and the door sills were covered with accumulated ice caused by the spillage from the hose when it filled the tanks of other trucks. Farley slipped and fell and was seriously injured. The trial judge found that the employees at the fire hall were negligent in failing to remove the ice or put sand on it as they had been instructed to do. Mr. Justice Freedman for the Manitoba Court of Appeal allowed Farley recovery explicitly on the basis of the reasoning in the *Campbell* case. Because the dangerous icy conditions could and should easily have been remedied by the occupier, they constituted an "unusual" danger. Unfortunately, Mr. Justice Ritchie, who had dissented in *Campbell*, now persuaded his fellow judges, including Spence J., to retreat from this view.

The alleged basis for distinguishing the earlier case is that Farley was not simply a member of the general public but rather one of a distinctive class whose business could lead him to expect freezing water. Hence, as to Farley, the danger was not unusual, and the city owed him no duty of reasonable protection. Even within the tortured logic of this area of law this distinction is irrational. Though Mrs. Campbell was a member of a more general class of bank customers, surely the danger she encountered was no more unusual for her than the special danger which Farley encountered. More important, the factual distinction between the cases is simply irrelevant to the consequential legal difference, that is the denial of any protection against injury to those people whose business exposes them more frequently to danger, no matter how easy it is for the occupier to minimize the danger. The contrast in the results in *Campbell* and *Farley* is equally as indefensible as the contrast in *Munro* and *Hillman*: the failure of our Supreme Court to ask the simple question "why *should* this be the conclusion of our law?" worked a real injustice on two unfortunate claimants.

There is a special irony in the reasoning of the Supreme Court of Canada in these cases. Not only has the Court not taken the opportunity to be creative and improve our law of occupier's liability (as I suggest a realistic analysis of its institutional resources would require), but it has actually imposed some of the more rigid and anomalous categories in recent decisions where there were no precedents of its own to restrict it. The primary source of its arguments were decisions of the House of Lords in the 1950's[19] which had been even more severely criticized than the decision of *Searle v. Wallbank* (which the Supreme Court did refuse to follow). These decisions of the House of Lords triggered so much dissatisfaction with the law that the British Parliament was moved to abolish the special categories of occupier's liability and subject it by statute to the law of ordinary negligence. One would think that if a Canadian court, legally free to move Canadian law in one direction or another, were to look to the United Kingdom for guidance, it should follow the judgment of the House of Commons, rather than the House of Lords. Unfortunately, in the peculiar wisdom of the common law, exactly the opposite inference is drawn. If the decisions of the House of Lords were so bad that Parliament had to revise them by statute, then this proves these decisions really did express the common law, and our courts are bound to follow them. "Judicial reversals avowedly based

---

[19] In particular, *London Graving Dock v. Horton*, [1951] A.C. 737, [1951] 2 All E.R. 1 and *Jacobs v. London County Council*, [1950] A.C. 361, [1950] 1 All E.R. 737.

upon the social inexpediency of the earlier conclusion stifle its germinating powers, but the same sober judgment of a representative assembly merely adds virulence to the poison of judicial unwisdom. Indeed, at times, the process portrays a fantasy more than fit for a new Erewhon".[20]

POLICE USE OF
DEADLY FORCE

The factual situations which gave rise to the cases I have discussed up to now presented primarily *remedial* problems to our law. An accident has occurred, serious personal injuries have been inflicted, and the question asked is how we should allocate this loss. The broad categories of negligence law have relatively little influence at the earlier stage of human activity in determining the way the motorist, the farmer, or the occupier of land will behave in order to prevent the accident occurring in the first place. Appraisal of the content of tort doctrines in this area is directed primarily to the issue of whether a fair conclusion has been reached about who should bear the loss after it has occurred: the victim who has suffered the injuries or the defendant who is asked to pay for them? My criticism of the Supreme Court's work is that too often it reaches decisions which seem patently unjust and that the doctrines it lays down permit very subjective and irrational differences in legal results for very similar situations.

There is a significant realm of human behaviour where the doctrines formulated by the courts in resolving tort actions can channel the private conduct itself. Indeed I believe it is here that we will see the future thrust of tort law. Much of the traditional task of adjusting the impact of accidental injuries after they have occurred will be taken over by various forms of compensation or social security schemes administered outside the courts. If the law of torts is to have any future vitality, it will be found in the control of organizational power, whether public or private. Police forces effect arrests and newspapers publish critical stories. These customary patterns of behaviour create a recurring risk of injuries to innocent parties. Tort litigation is a common reaction. The availability of the tort remedy can help shape the behaviour of the police officer or the newspaper editor in the direction the courts believe is desirable. How sensitive has the Supreme Court of Canada been to the competing values involved in this conduct when it defined the limits of tort liability in these two areas?

The first situation with which I will deal involves the use of firearms by police officers in effecting an arrest. A pair of cases reached the Supreme Court dealing with this issue, *Priestman v. Colangelo, Shynall*

---

20 Landis, "Statutes and the Sources of Law" (1965), 2 Harvard Journal of Legislation 7 at 23-24.

and Smythson in 1959, and *Beim v. Goyer* in 1965.[21] There was a marked similarity in the events giving rise to the two accidents. Smythson, a 17-year-old in Toronto, and Beim, a 14-year-old in Montreal, each stole new cars, apparently to take "joy rides". Each was spotted by police officers in their vehicles, Smythson by Priestman and Beim by Goyer. When the boys refused to stop, the police gave chase at dangerous speeds along the city streets. There the situations diverge. Priestman aimed his gun at the tire of Smythson's car as he was reaching a busy intersection, in order to stop him. Just as he fired, his arm was bumped and the bullet accidentally struck Smythson in the neck, rendering him unconscious. The car went out of control, ran up on the sidewalk and killed Columbo Colangelo and Josephine Shynall who were talking quietly while waiting for a bus. By contrast, Beim, the driver of the stolen car in the other case, collided with a parked vehicle and thus stopped himself. He hopped out of his own car and fled across a deserted, snowy and rocky field. Goyer gave chase with his gun in his hand. He fired two warning shots in the air and he also fell twice while crossing the field. Unfortunately, when he tripped and fell a third time, the gun went off and the bullet hit Beim in the neck, paralyzing him.

One may be struck by the remarkable coincidence that twice a police officer was bumped as his gun went off but the bullet found its way into the neck of the fleeing suspect. Anyone familiar with the reported cases, however, will understand that this is not an unusual occurrence. Be that as it may, let us speculate on the possible pairs of decisions that might arise in lawsuits brought by the victims against these respective police officers. The basic setting and sequence of events in each case is quite similar. One could understand a legal doctrine which allowed recovery in both cases or denied it to both plaintiffs. Yet there are some important differences. Priestman *intentionally* fired his gun in a crowded city area and as a result injured two completely innocent bystanders. Goyer's gun went off *accidentally* while he was running across a deserted field and as a result injured the escaping offender. Surely it would be reasonable for the court to apply a legal doctrine which held Priestman liable and exonerated Goyer. Only the fourth logically possible pair of decisions, making Goyer pay but not Priestman, strikes us as incongruous. Sadly, this is the combination our Supreme Court decided upon.

The key legal element in the decision was section 25(4) of the Criminal Code which reads:

> A peace officer who is proceeding lawfully to arrest...any person for an offence...is justified if the person to be arrested takes flight to avoid arrest in using as much force as is necessary to prevent the escape by flight, unless the escape can be prevented by reasonable means in a less violent manner.

---

21 *Priestman v. Colangelo, Shynall and Smythson*, [1959] S.C.R. 615, 30 C.R. 209, 124 C.C.C. 1, 19 D.L.R. (2d) 1; *Beim v. Goyer*, [1965] S.C.R. 638.

The question for the Court was whether this provision, enacted by Parliament under its criminal law powers, absolutely entitled a police officer to effect an arrest at all necessary cost, including the risk of harm from his gun if this appeared necessary, and left him free of any liability in tort. The majority on the Ontario Court of Appeal in the *Priestman* case held that the further obligations of the civil law of negligence still limited the exercise of police powers. Mr. Justice Cartwright, dissenting in the Supreme Court of Canada, agreed with this position only insofar as it preserved the rights of innocent third parties. He believed the law must be read as allowing the use of deadly force against juvenile offenders like Smythson and Beim if this is necessary to arrest them for an offence for which they would likely receive probation if caught. With this limitation, he would require police officers to exercise reasonable care in their decision about whether to try to make an arrest if a gun were needed. In this "calculus", the importance of apprehending an armed bank robber who might well kill someone on his next attempt would justify the use of somewhat riskier measures than in apprehending offenders like Smythson and Beim.

The Supreme Court majority, in an opinion written by Mr. Justice Locke, thoroughly disagreed. The flavour of its views may best be conveyed by direct quotation.[22] The basic premise, expressed in Latin, was that *salus populi est suprema lex*. Locke J. understood this to mean that there is "an implied agreement of every member of society that his own individual welfare shall, in cases of necessity, yield to that of the community; and that his property, liberty, and life shall, under certain circumstances, be placed in jeopardy or even sacrificed for the public good". Turning to the precise issue before him, he heartily disagreed with the view, expressed in some lower court opinions, that "shooting is the very last resort and that only in the last extremity should a police officer resort to the use of a revolver in order to prevent the escape of an accused person who is attempting to escape by flight." Instead, as he stated, "police officers in this country are furnished with firearms and these may, in my opinion, be used when, in the circumstances of the particular case, it is reasonably necessary to do so to prevent the escape of a criminal whose actions, as in the *present case*, constitute *menace* to other members of the public" (emphasis added). On the basis of this analysis, his conclusion that Priestman was entitled to use every means necessary to arrest Smythson was inevitable.

Given this expression of views by the Supreme Court majority in *Priestman*, the reversal of direction only six years later is unexpected. It surprised both the majority of the Quebec Court of Appeal in *Beim v. Goyer* and the dissenting members of the Supreme Court of Canada, who thought that if Priestman was exonerated from liability then, *a fortiori*, so should Goyer have been. Unfortunately, while the result in *Beim*

---

22 *Priestman v. Colangelo*, [1959] S.C.R. 615 at 623, 624-25 respectively.

may be laudable, the manner in which the Court reached it is not. The majority simply adopts a dissenting lower court opinion without even a gesture of response to the arguments of its own dissenting members. It is assumed that a distinction may be drawn between the cases, considering Priestman's intention to fire at the tire and Goyer's intention to fire in the air, but the logic of this point quite frankly escapes me (since in both cases the fact that a person was hit was quite accidental). *Beim* is another example of our present Court's unhappy tack of trying to "have its cake and eat it too" to reach the fair result in the immediate case and yet avoid the responsibility for openly overruling earlier decisions it believes were wrong. We are left with one more instance in the pattern of pairs of decisions which simply are legally irreconcilable.

I do not mean to suggest that the Court's task was an easy one in these cases. The clash of social interests is apparent. Police officers face the unhappy lot of having to use coercion and force to deal with offenders who would harm the rest of us. To this end, Canadians allow their police to use dangerous firearms. Maybe we should have followed the British example, but we did not. Guns are such an ingrained part of the police function here that no court could properly forbid their use. However, we do not want to empower our police to run amok and cause more harm in enforcing the law than they prevent from others breaking it. The law must strike a balance between these competing interests and express its conclusions in guidelines which are clear and meaningful to the officer on the street.

The answer of the Canadian parliament is contained in the language of section 25(4) quoted earlier. This judgment stems from a time when serious offences were all punishable by death after conviction and society was thus not so concerned with limiting the use of deadly force before arrest. The course of lower court decisions in recent years indicated that this early, open-ended grant of discretion to the police was no longer consistent with contemporary Canadian values. The language and legal context of section 25(4) was sufficiently vague that further limitations could legitimately be placed on police use of firearms in dangerous situations, as the Ontario Court of Appeal did in the *Priestman* case. Then the Supreme Court of Canada entered the fray to give its authoritative construction of the law for this problem by its majority decision in *Priestman*, only to summarily reverse itself in *Beim*. Yet both of these decisions, on their face, remain part of the law of Canada. This simply is not good enough for the policeman who must decide whether to use his gun, the citizen who may be injured, and the lower courts which must resolve the ensuing litigation. In this area, as in all too many others, the actual role of the Court has been to sow confusion in our law, rather than to clarify it.

These contrasting pairs of cases I have been reviewing illustrate a general problem in judge-made law. The precedents which comprise the basic elements of the common law are often composed of several lengthy opinions discussing and justifying the decision to be made about the particular litigation. Not everything a judge says in his opinion can become law. As usual, we have Latin phrases to express the distinction between the *ratio decidendi* and the *obiter dictum* of a case. Only that part of the opinion which was necessary for the particular decision has authoritative force; remarks which are made by the way have only persuasive value, if that. This characteristic of the common law has led some to describe the common law as "unwritten", by contrast with statutes in which every word used by the draftsman has direct legal force.

A great deal of jurisprudential ink has been spilled over the issue of what precisely is the distinction between the *ratio decidendi* and the *obiter dictum* in a judicial opinion. It is easy to grasp the underlying point of the distinction. We want to confine judicial law-making to those issues which are graphically presented to the court by the factual dispute before them and which will be illuminated by the arguments of opposing counsel who are immediately interested in winning that particular case. We do not want to allow judges to lay down a set of general rules which will govern situations that were not before them, which they could not anticipate, and which the resources of the adversary process will not help them resolve. For logical reasons which I cannot go into here, there is no formula into which this objective can be translated. There is no rule which enables a later court to decide automatically whether the binding *ratio decidendi* of an earlier case is applicable to its own situation. Sometimes there are *relevant* factual differences between the two cases, and sometimes there are not. The decision requires a constant exercise of judgment by later courts trying to follow earlier precedents.

This ambiguity creates the possibility of such pairs of decisions as *Munro* and *Hillman, Campbell* and *Farley,* and *Smythson* and *Beim,* each a pair of decisions from the same Supreme Court, dealing with the same basic problem, and delivered within five or six years of each other. Sometimes the Court will simply ignore the earlier decision, as it did to *Munro* when it decided *Hillman.* More often, it will point to some factor it believes distinguishes the cases, as it did in *Farley* and *Beim,* the later cases in the other two pairs. Given the doctrine of the *ratio decidendi,* the tactic is quite legitimate in principle. In my view, however, the actual use of the doctrine in the way seen in these cases is completely inconsistent with the function of precedents.

What happened in each of these situations? The later panel of Supreme Court judges found a factual distinction between its own case and the earlier precedent and used this to support a difference in legal result, even though there was no sensible justification for the different legal conclusions. There is no possible reason why the law *should* give

Beim greater protection from police firearms than it did Colangelo (and surely the same conclusion is true for the other pairs). What I think happened in these, and so many other cases, is that the later panel did not like the decision in the earlier case and did not want to follow it. Because the Court felt constrained by the doctrine of *stare decisis* not to frankly overrule the precedent, it chose to "distinguish" same on the facts.

The lesson to be drawn from these cases is that this judicial attitude is self-defeating. Instead of having one case which frankly overruled the earlier one, we are left with two decisions, both apparently binding precedents in our law. Because there is no intelligible rationale for a legal doctrine which reaches these two incompatible results, it is almost impossible to know how to apply the doctrine in any new case which again will have some different shading in its facts. The result is that the application of the common law becomes an unpredictable and subjective process, "a wilderness of single instances" which gives judges a façade of legal authority to justify whichever contrasting result they may want to reach. But as we saw earlier, the whole point of the doctrine of precedent is to minimize the unpredictable and subjective application of the common law. If this is what we are trying to achieve through a doctrine of precedent, then the failure to candidly overrule *Smythson* in *Beim*, for example, is counter-productive.

The objectives of the doctrine of *stare decisis* can only be attained by treating it as a *principle* of judicial behaviour, allowing for exceptional overruling of a precedent where this is necessary. If we treat the doctrine as a binding *rule*, which never permits such a reversal, we drive the judicial impulse to do justice underground, from whence it will surface in an unpredictable and tortured use of the concept of the *ratio decidendi*. The critical lesson we see here, and one which I will reiterate throughout this book, is that we cannot really have law, without having reasonable law.

NEWSPAPER CRITICISM OF PUBLIC FIGURES

I must not leave the impression from my review of some of the tort law work of the Supreme Court of Canada that that body is always as ambivalent in its judgments about important legal problems as it has been in the last several cases. This is certainly an endemic problem in the Court's work. However, there are also areas where the Court has taken a single-minded view of what the law should be and pursued this policy consistently over a series of decisions. A very interesting example is the problem of the legal basis of liability for defamatory comments in a newspaper. Here we have a very clear idea of what the law is and we can concern ourselves with the more important question of whether the law is as it should be.

I should state immediately that, in my view, the law as developed by the Supreme Court of Canada is based on a mistaken order of priority among social values. One of the factors producing this law is a fallacy which is almost an occupational hazard of lawyers. For historical reasons, defamation evolved as a distinct cause of action, with doctrinal categories that are peculiarly its own. Once lawyers and judges become accustomed to thinking of a set of legal problems as unique and distinctive, because after all they are grouped under a different name, they fail to integrate that area of law into the changing patterns and principles which pervade the rest of the law of torts. The lessons that are learned as the legal system deals with its typical problems are not transferable to deal with very similar problems in an esoteric field which seems to have a logic all its own. In contrast with some of the other examples we have considered, the deviation in defamation has been in the opposite direction, toward greater liability, not less.

As a bridge to this discussion and to illustrate what I mean, let us look at an intermediate example. *Guay v. Sun Publishing Co.*[23] was a case which reached the Supreme Court of Canada in 1953. Apparently Mrs. Guay, a resident of Vancouver, had become estranged from her husband who was living with their three children in Ontario. The Vancouver Sun printed a story in one issue that both husband and children had been killed in an automobile accident. The story was completely without foundation and was the result of a vicious practical joke played by someone who concocted the tale and gave it to the paper. However Mrs. Guay bought the paper, believed the story, and became very distraught, eventually requiring medical treatment. She sued the paper for damages and the trial judge found in her favour, applying the ordinary principles of negligence to conclude that the newspaper was careless in not checking the details of its informant's facts. The British Columbia Court of Appeal reversed the trial judge on the grounds that the ordinary law of negligence did not apply in this case and that a tort action required proof of intentional malice or fraud. The majority of the Supreme Court of Canada upheld the Court of Appeal and produced a miscellaneous set of reasons.

It is not my purpose to discuss in any detail the merits of this specific problem. Suffice it to say that there are real legal problems in finding liability in cases in this area. Moreover, in my view, there are good, practical reasons for this reticence of the legal system, quite unlike some of the cases I have already discussed. There are two distinctive features of a claim such as that of Mrs. Guay: the conduct she complains of is negligent speech and the harm she has suffered is primarily emotional distress. The law is very dubious about each. What are the relevant differences between words and deeds? In ordinary life, we expect somewhat greater care in conduct that might harm others (such

---

23 [1953] 2 S.C.R. 516, [1953] 4 D.L.R. 577.

as driving a car) than we do in what people say. Moreover, harmful talk may cause ever-expanding damages as the words are repeated and relied on several times over. What about the distinction between the harm of emotional distress and more tangible injuries to the person or property? Injured feelings are very difficult to identify accurately, and it is even more difficult to estimate their subjective magnitude, especially since both judgments must be made some months later. All that the law can do is award money damages as a consolation, and how exactly does one go about translating emotional distress into monetary terms?

Analysis of the *Guay* case furnishes a good illustration of what I mean about negligent fault being a *principle* of liability, rather than a definite *rule*. When we find that someone's carelessness has caused another person injury, this is always a persuasive argument for recovery, and it finds substantial legal weight in the example of what the law does in so many other areas. However, if there are sensible, pragmatic reasons in the features of the immediate situation, our courts are entitled to create a legal exception to the scope of liability. I do not mean to suggest here that these reasons should, in fact, have been decisive for rejecting Mrs. Guay's claims. Perhaps they do not have sufficient weight to overcome the principle of fairness that the person who is at fault should compensate the innocent victim for the injuries he has inflicted. The point that I want to make is that the bias of the law in such situations is heavily against recovery, and not unreasonably so.

Now let us contrast the typical defamation action. It contains basically the same constituents as *Guay*. The defendant has uttered words which are untrue, this time misrepresenting something about the plaintiff personally, and these detract from the plaintiff's reputation. Sometimes this will cause financial harm (and I am not directly concerned about those cases), but most of the time the plaintiff's real injury is his distress, embarrassment or anger at the impression conveyed to others about his character. Contrary to what I just said about the basic attitude of the law to these situations, when the lawyers and judges name an action as one of *defamation*, the legal response is the opposite. The defendant is liable for damages even if there is no fault at all, unless there is a special legal privilege. As I said earlier, this anomalous rule exists due to purely historical causes. No one has ever offered a valid practical reason why a person who carefully drives an automobile but gets in an accident permanently disabling another should be free of liability but a newspaper which prints a defamatory story which it believes to be true and which it has carefully checked out should have to pay for the injury to the plaintiff's reputation.

This anomalous approach was embedded in the common law of defamation long before the Supreme Court of Canada assumed final judicial responsibility for our law and, while this fact does not justify the inaction of our judges, it may excuse it. However, there are some exceptions to this doctrine of strict liability where our own Court has had some real influence. If there is a genuine need or interest in publication of a statement, the defendant will be held entitled to do so free of liability for an honest mistake. This is called a "qualified privilege". An example is the case of employee references. A business may write the former employer of its prospective employee to find the reason he left his job. It is clear that the person seeking the information has a valid interest in it and thus the person supplying it has a privilege protecting him against mistakes which may harm the employee's reputation and even lose him the job. The vital area of Canadian defamation law which was left unsettled until recent years was whether there was a similar qualified privilege for statements made in newspapers to the public in such matters of general interest as a political campaign. Was there a legal privilege for accidental defamation in the "public interest", as there already was in the "private interest?" The Supreme Court of Canada gave us the answer to this question in one of the more fascinating sequence of cases in recent Canadian law.

There are two facets, in particular, which make these cases interesting. First, many of the important defamation cases in Canadian law have involved prominent political figures and emerged from election campaigns. Our politicians show no reluctance to remove their disputes to the courts. Secondly, Mr. Justice Cartwright played a dominant role in settling the course of Canadian law, by his involvement in all of these cases. The sequence opened with two cases brought in Ontario courts near the end of World War II. In *Dennison v. Sanderson*,[24] a group of C.C.F. candidates for municipal office in Toronto in 1943 sued for a libellous advertisement in the Toronto Globe and Mail which, among other things, labelled them as card-carrying Communists. One of these candidates, William Dennison, was until very recently the Mayor of Toronto. Only two of the fourteen plaintiffs were successful and they won damages from the jury of only one penny each. They all appealed on the grounds that the trial judge erred in ruling, *inter alia*, that there was a qualified privilege to publish in a newspaper materials about a candidate in an election which were believed to be true. Mr. Justice Cartwright, who was then a very prominent counsel, argued the appeal unsuccessfully for the plaintiffs. In the next case, *Drew v. Toronto Star*,[25] George Drew, the Premier of Ontario (and later leader of the federal Progressive Conservatives) sued the Toronto Star for editorial comment in the 1945 provincial election campaign which alleged that his government maintained a "secret police" or "Gestapo" (repeating the charges of Mr. Jolliffe, the Ontario C.C.F. party leader). Again the trial judge held that this was an occasion of qualified privilege; again Mr. Justice Cartwright, as counsel, argued the appeal for the plaintiff. He was successful

---

[24] [1946] O.R. 601, [1946] 4 D.L.R. 314 (C.A.).
[25] [1947] O.R. 730, [1947] 4 D.L.R. 221. Affirmed [1948] 4 D.L.R. 465 (Can.).

on this appeal, but only on the grounds that the factual basis for the privilege had not been established because of the procedure at trial.

These two cases indicate that there was a plausible legal argument to be made for the "public interest" privilege. Two lower court judges believed in its existence and there was some prior Canadian authority in support of it.[26] There certainly was no firm Canadian, or even British, authority against the privilege. The Ontario Court of Appeal did not agree or disagree with the trial judges as to the question and neither of these cases proceeded on to the Supreme Court of Canada. However, Mr. Justice Cartwright did make his personal way to the Court, when appointed at the end of 1949. Here he was more successful in implementing his views than he had been as counsel.

In 1952, the Supreme Court of Canada was presented with the case of *Douglas v. Tucker*.[27] This was a suit by Tucker, the leader of the opposition Liberal party, against Tommy Douglas, then Premier of Saskatchewan and leader of the provincial C.C.F. party (and later first leader of the national N.D.P.). In the 1948 election campaign, one of the key issues was the alleged C.C.F. policy of "socialization" of farm land. This led to some discussion of Tucker's personal involvement in the 1930's with an investment company which loaned money to farmers at 15% interest and then foreclosed on mortgages when the money was not repaid. Eventually Douglas made a speech which was reported in the papers charging that Tucker was being sued for fraud in connection with one of these transactions. This charge of fraud was the basis of a libel action by Tucker. Writing for a unanimous Supreme Court, Cartwright J. held that there was no qualified privilege to make such comments about an election rival, if they were to be published in a newspaper. He appeared to have his way in settling the Canadian law for this issue.

Yet the reasoning in his decision was sufficiently ambiguous that an Ontario trial judge, Mr. Justice Spence (who was soon after appointed to the Supreme Court himself), did not follow it in two libel actions over which he presided, *Banks v. Globe and Mail* and *Boland v. Globe and Mail*.[28] The first involved editorial comment about the role of the plaintiff, Hal Banks, in a lengthy strike on Canadian ships. The second suit was about a Globe and Mail editorial which charged Mr. John Boland, an independent Conservative candidate in the 1957 federal election, with "shabby, McCarthy style tactics" in trying to show that the Liberals are "soft on Communism". The change from the *Dennison* case in the attitude of the Globe and Mail and the public about what kind of charge is defamatory is striking. In the *Boland* case, Mr. Justice

---

26 *E.g., Showler v. MacInnes*, [1937] 1 W.W.R. 358, 51 B.C.R. 391.

27 [1952] 1 S.C.R. 275, [1952] 1 D.L.R. 657.

28 *Banks v. Globe and Mail Ltd.*, [1961] S.C.R. 474, 28 D.L.R. (2d) 343; *Boland v. Globe and Mail Ltd.*, [1960] S.C.R. 203, 22 D.L.R. (2d) 277.

Spence placed squarely on the record his rationale for preferring the view that there was a privilege:

> Therefore in my view we have two judges of this Court who have found that the publication of comment in newspapers as to candidates for election to public office, and made during the course of an election campaign, are uttered on occasions of qualified privilege and the opinion of neither one of those has been disturbed on appeal.... Surely no section of the public has a clearer duty to publish, for the information and guidance of the public, during a Federal election in Canada than the great Metropolitan daily newspaper such as the Defendant. Just as certainly the public, every citizen in Canada, has a legitimate and vital interest in receiving such publications. At this point I do not intend to deal with either the bona fides of the publication or with the alleged over-extension of the publication thereof, to both of which I shall refer later, but only with the question whether the occasion was one of qualified privilege. I have come to the conclusion that a Federal election in Canada is an occasion upon which a newspaper has a public duty to comment on the candidates, their campaigns and their platforms or policies, and Canadian citizens have an honest and very real interest in receiving their comment, and that therefore this is an occasion of qualified privilege.[29]

Both of these cases reached the Supreme Court of Canada and Cartwright J., again writing the only opinion for the Court, reversed Spence J. and clearly implemented in our law his preference for the opposite policy:

> To hold that during a federal election campaign in Canada any defamatory statement published in the press relating to an candidate's fitness for office is to be taken as published on an occasion of qualified privilege would be in my opinion ... harmful to that "common convenience and welfare of society" which Baron Parke described as the underlying principle on which the rules as to qualified privilege are founded.... It would mean that every man who offers himself as a candidate must be prepared to risk the loss of his reputation without redress unless he be able to prove affirmatively that those who defamed him were activated by express malice ... so wide an extension of the privilege would do the public more harm than good. It would tend to deter sensitive and honourable men from seeking public positions of trust and responsibility and leave them open to others who have no respect for their reputation....
>
> It is said that it is for the interests of society that the public conduct of men should be criticized without any other limit than that the writer should have an honest belief that what he writes is true. But it seems to me that the public have an equal interest in the maintenance of the public character of public men; and public affairs could not be conducted by men of honour with a view to the welfare of the country if we were to

---

[29] Quoted by Cartwright J., [1960] S.C.R. at 206.

sanction attacks made upon them destructive of their honour and character, and made without any foundation.[30]

In a final case, *Jones v. Bennett*,[31] decided just before he retired, Cartwright J. embedded these conclusions even more firmly in our law. Mr. W. A. C. Bennett, the Social Credit Premier of British Columbia, was sued for remarks he made at a Social Credit dinner meeting about a senior civil servant whom he had just had retired amidst a great deal of controversy. Cartwright C.J. had no doubt that Mr. Bennett was not privileged to make these remarks "to the world", through the newspaper reporters whom he knew were at the meeting. In fact, he was dubious about applying the privilege to speak freely and honestly at a political meeting if there were no election campaign in progress. Fortunately or unfortunately, depending on one's point of view, he did not need to commit himself or the Court in deciding the case in favour of the plaintiff.

We have here a situation where the Supreme Court of Canada clearly and authoritatively laid down the rules relating to this important issue of public policy. It did so on the basis of the judges' preference for the value of the reputation of public officials over the value of the freedom of the press to present criticism of these officials to the public, at least freedom to do so without fear of substantial damage awards if the critics are unable to prove to the satisfaction of a court the truth of what they said. I certainly do not disapprove of the Court adopting such a rule on the basis of its views about the proper order of priority between these two competing interests. It had to adopt some rule to adjudicate the private lawsuits brought by Banks and Boland against the Globe and Mail. In this area, as in so many areas of tort law, the Court has no logical alternative. Whichever way it decides, and it must decide, the opinion it writes will define our law of newspaper comment in a form which embodies a preference for one policy or another. The criticisms which can be brought against the Court are directed at the policy which it consciously adopted.

Let us consider the background of legal principle to this issue. In the ordinary law of torts, if, for instance, an insured driver strikes and permanently disables a pedestrian, he will be liable only for negligent fault. In the special cases where the conduct consists of negligent words, or the only injury is emotional distress, the law is loath to allow recovery even within the basic principle of tort liability. These defamation cases involved incorrect statements causing some form of emotional distress (if that). Where there is some private business interest in the communication, the law encourages it by establishing a privilege to publish it honestly, even if the speaker turns out to be wrong. Let us look at the vastly different message the Court has sent out to newspaper editors

---

30 *Ibid.*, at 208.
31 [1969] S.C.R. 277, 66 W.W.R. 419, 2 D.L.R. (3d) 291.

and publishers. "Our politicians have very thin skins. They will be severely distressed by critical comment which harms their reputation. Indeed, this may even deter some good men from entering the political arena. As a result, you publish anything defamatory of these people at your peril. You will be safe if your statements are true (and you can prove it some months later to a jury). However, you take the risk that your facts may turn out to be wrong. No matter how honestly you believe in your story and how much care you have taken in researching it, you must accept strict liability for any mistakes, and pay damages set at the discretion of the jury (and in our cases, damages ranged from $.01 in the *Dennison* case to $15,000 in *Jones v. Bennett*). No doubt this may result in ultra cautious self-censorship on the part of newspapers, and a less than frank and robust exchange of public views about the qualifications of our candidates and officials. However, the public interest in freedom of speech and the press must take second place to minimizing the risk of sullying an individual's reputation."

Let's contrast the similar judgment the Court had to make about the legal sphere of action of police officers in arresting escaping offenders (in the course of another private tort action of 1959, brought against Priestman. The signal to the police was blurred somewhat in *Beim v. Goyer*, as the Court may have had second thoughts, but this earlier decision has not been overruled). What was its message to the police? "Don't be afraid to use your guns if this is necessary to arrest any offender, no matter what the crime is. The public interest in the enforcement of the criminal law requires that you be given great latitude in performing your police duties. No doubt, the exercise of your discretion may result in serious physical injury to some innocent bystanders but we will protect you from tort liability should this occur. The innocent victim must simply recognize that individual sacrifices are necessary to achieve the public good." Again the Supreme Court had to make the law to adjudicate the tort action; yet what kind of law did it make? After contrasting the two judge-made policies, I suppose any further comment on my part is superfluous.

THE PRIVATE LAW ROLE
OF THE SUPREME COURT

Let us step back now from the details of individual tort problems and consider the question of the proper role for the Supreme Court of Canada in the area. Perhaps we can do this best by appraising a concrete proposal which has been put forward by several people in recent years. They argue that the area of private law should be removed from the jurisdiction of the Supreme Court. There is more to private law than torts, but I believe it fair to say that those are the cases they have primarily in mind. What are the reasons for the proposal? What light does analysis of these reasons throw on the problem of judicial involvement in tort law?

A primary factor, though usually left in the background, is the view that tort cases deal with relatively trivial issues. Why should the time and attention of the highest court in the land be wasted on a dispute between a pedestrian and an insurer? As Peter Russell has said:

> The federalist grounds for this reform are reinforced by the widespread view that the Supreme Court spends a disproportionately large part of its time and energy on trivial private law cases. . . . Most of these do not involve matters of any great importance; more often than not they are cases governed by laws subject to provincial legislative authority. Adjudication of these cases by the Supreme Court constitutes an extravagant misuse of the Court's energies. . . . A further appeal to the national Supreme Court should be only where the decision in question raises some issue of importance to the nation.[32]

In one sense, there is validity to this view, but in another there is not. Too many of the tort cases which reach the Court involve primarily questions of judgment about "the facts". Was the defendant at fault? How much damages should the plaintiff collect? Was there contributory negligence? The remedy for this problem is to remove the appeal as of right from the jurisdiction of the Supreme Court and give the Court discretion to allow appeals where it believes the case raises an issue of law of some importance. Is it not true that the private law issues in tort cases are fairly unimportant and we might as well remove them from the Court's jurisdiction completely? In my view the answer is, most emphatically, no!

If we confined Supreme Court involvement to only those cases which present real questions of law, then I believe the kinds of cases I have reviewed in this chapter are important and worthy of the Supreme Court's deliberations. There are several distinctive traits which contribute to this significance. First, the immediate dispute may be vital to the interests of a particular individual. Whether the pedestrian injured by a motor vehicle, or a visitor injured on the occupier's property can collect their damages may be one of the most important decisions to affect the person's life. To be sure, the significance of the rule which settles this is quite different from constitutional doctrines, for example, which lay down the boundaries for governmental action that quite conceivably can affect the interests of millions of citizens. Tort law doctrines dictate the results in cases which are quite self-contained and may not recur very often (e.g., *Fleming v. Atkinson*). There are a great many such rules, and, taken cumulatively, they determine the degree of justice meted out by the legal system to individuals who have been harmed.

---

32 Russell, "Constitutional Reform of the Canadian Judiciary" (1969), 7 A.L.R. 103 at 126.

Second, some of these tort law decisions are the vehicle for resolving complex value conflicts. The Supreme Court in *Smythson* or *Douglas,* for example, established the policy of our law in fields where there was a clash of important individual and social interests. Some of the more celebrated civil liberties cases to reach the Supreme Court—e.g., *Roncarelli v. Duplessis*[33]—involved tort claims. The tort action can be a vehicle through which an individual who has been harmed can obtain redress from the oppressive action of a public official. The availability of the same kind of award can be used as a threat to silence public comment in areas of controversy. The courts play a significant role in these cases in determining the kinds of public behaviour which will be encouraged or discouraged by these apparently private law claims. Hence, there is a public interest in the quality of many of the legal rules defining the availability of tort actions.

Thirdly, private law cases are important because they permit *judicial* influence on the law. Not only is it vital that the substantive rules be wise, but the court is the institution which must take primary responsibility for their quality. Unlike the fields of public law, where there are legislatures, administrative agencies, and public officials making decisions, we must rely on the courts for much of the inevitable reform of tort law. For the reasons I have outlined, I believe judicial innovation to be unambiguously desirable here. If the Supreme Court of Canada is, or at least should be, the best court in Canada, then its leadership in the area of private law is important. Tort law is not too trivial to occupy some of the Court's docket.

There is a second and better argument which can be made for the proposal. This is based on considerations of federalism. If there is to be legislative action in the area of tort law, it would be within the jurisdiction of the provinces over "property and civil rights". If this is our constitutional arrangement, why should this rationale not be equally applicable when the action is *judicial?* Let the courts of appeal sitting in each provincial capital have the final say about the law of torts within their respective jurisdictions, rather than letting the Supreme Court of Canada impose a national solution from Ottawa. While recognizing that the cases do raise important questions of legal policy, and that the Supreme Court of Canada may be able to do a better job, the federal principle dictates elimination of this jurisdiction from the Supreme Court's work. "Always, when autonomy confronts control, the choice at its starkest becomes that between the competing values of self government and of better government, and so here."[34] Indeed, in recent years, the performance of the Supreme Court leads one to believe the choice may not be that stark.

---

33 [1959] S.C.R. 122, 16 D.L.R. (2d) 689.

34 Abel, "The Role of the Supreme Court in Private Law Cases" (1965), 4 A.L.R. 39 at 45 and 47 respectively.

This argument is very persuasive when one recognizes the fact of judicial power. Judges do have real influence on the content of our law. The Court's judgment about the way the law of defamation should develop, for example, was as decisive as would have been the case if the legislature had made this decision. Why not leave this judgment to the court of the individual province? "The primary advantage is the greater responsiveness of the law to the differing needs or sentiments of the provinces." We must be primarily concerned with the "functional aspect (of the law) as an instrument of social accommodation" and this will be enhanced "by the greater familiarity of local judges with the relevant social context. . . . One gets a feel for these matters only by living in a community. No amount of learning or intellectual acuity is quite a substitute."

The argument is attractive. There is a real resemblance between the legislative and judicial influences on the evolution of our law. If we have made and still enforce a distribution of legislative power on federal terms, why not apply the same principle to the use of judicial power? This may not have been required in our original constitution because in 1867 the reality of judicial law-making was not easily perceived in the prevailing judicial climate (and, in any event, there was a further appeal to the one Privy Council). If I am right in my analysis of the impact of the Supreme Court on the law in the cases I have reviewed in this chapter, and if these are a fair sample of the judicial role in tort law, we cannot hide from the fact of judicial creativity any longer. Why not abolish appeals to the Supreme Court on such private law cases, not only under the Quebec Civil Code (which has triggered the original interest in the question) but under the law of any province?

Analysis of this federalism argument heightens our appreciation of the important fact that the Supreme Court has the responsibility of shaping the growth of tort law. When we reflect, again, on the institutional basis of this responsibility, we should also see the limitations on the federalism analogy. The Court creates legal rules in resolving concrete disputes, but does so by reasoning from established legal principles. In tort law (at least outside Quebec), these principles underlie the common law of the English-speaking world and are based on precedents that often antedate the very existence of some of the provinces. Perhaps legislatures might introduce specific variations based on an appreciation of peculiar local needs or a distinctive interest in the community. Maybe one province, dominated by farming interests, would prefer to retain the cattle trespass immunity. I wonder if judges are institutionally equipped to be sensitive to such factors. Do they really get a feel for these matters because they live in a province? Are not Canadian appellate judges pretty well drawn from the same narrow stratum and background? It is unlikely that the adversary process is an adequate mechanism for educating the court about relevant provincial oddities. Granted that local

89

autonomy is a desirable objective, does insulation of the provincial courts of appeal from further review contribute much to their achievement?

The federalism argument, while attractive at first, is not totally compelling. Judges do make law, as do legislatures, but then they do so in a different way, within a more limited scope, and pursuant to more restricted considerations. The decision about whether the jurisdiction of the Supreme Court should be federalized is one which must be made after a full analysis of the dimensions of *judicial* creativity, not by a simple analogy with the legislature. This requires an appraisal of such competing factors as the conflict of legal uniformity and experimentation, the likely distribution of technical judicial talent and the scope for judicial recognition of local needs and interests, and so on. It is not my purpose here to enter fully into this controversy. My reason for raising the question is primarily to illustrate the significance of both the fact and the manner of judicial innovation in the common law which I believe can be seen in the tort cases I have reviewed.

The Oracle
of the
Criminal Code

4

MENS REA IN THE
SUPREME COURT[1]

*"Judges march at times to pitiless conclusions under
the prod of a remorseless logic which is supposed to
leave them no alternative. They deplore the sacrificial
rite. They perform it, none the less, with averted gaze,
convinced as they plunge the knife that they obey the
bidding of their office. The victim is offered up to
the gods of jurisprudence on the altar of regularity."*

(Mr. Justice Cardozo)

The role of the Supreme Court in Canadian criminal law is more
intricate and delicate than it is in tort law. The reason is that the
criminal law is largely defined by a crisply worded statutory provision
of the kind we saw in *Barbara Jarvis* in Chapter 2. On the surface this
would appear to place significant restrictions on the scope for judicial
creativity. The freedom of a court in the face of an earlier legislative
judgment is rightly more circumscribed than is the case with purely
judicial authority. Yet, on further investigation, we can discern important
similarities in the part played by our judges in the growth of each of
these areas of law. The basic criminal law is expressed in a Code, a
legislative enactment to be sure, but one intended to summarize the
results of several centuries of common law development. The common
law of both torts and crimes stemmed historically from the same source,
the writ of trespass, and only gradually was differentiated in line with
the differing objectives of the two kinds of legal remedy. This important
judicial influence, both historical and contemporary, can be seen in a

---

1 A review of all of the Court's work in this area since 1949 can be found in my
article "The Supreme Court of Canada and the Doctrines of Mens Rea" (1971),
49 Can. Bar Rev. 281.

great many corners of the vast and complex structure of our criminal law. I can deal with only one, the doctrine of *mens rea*, summarizing the various excuses for criminal behaviour.

ADHERING TO PRINCIPLE IN THE WAR ON DRUGS

A natural starting point in examining the contribution of the Supreme Court of Canada is the decision in *Beaver v. R.*,[2] a case I mentioned earlier, and an important event in the evolution of the Canadian law of *mens rea*. Louis and Maxie Beaver were convicted of the possession and sale of heroin in a factual situation which alone would make me want to talk about the case. A Constable Tassie of the R.C.M.P., going under the alias of Al Demeter in his role as an undercover narcotics agent, was introduced to the Beaver brothers by one Montroy, a drug addict. At that meeting Montroy told the Beavers that Demeter wanted to buy some heroin, and eventually the defendants agreed to sell the agent a half ounce of heroin for $400. That afternoon, Louis and Maxie picked up Demeter in their car and drove to a point where Maxie got out, went to a lamp post, and picked up a parcel which he gave to Demeter in return for the $400.

Eventually the undercover agent surfaced, the Beavers were charged, and these facts emerged undisputed at trial. It is sufficient for our purposes to focus on the possession charge. The Opium and Narcotic Drug Act, R.S.C. 1952, c. 201, prohibited "possession" of heroin without a licence and prescribed penalties for the offence. There was no doubt that the Beavers were in actual possession of heroin and thus committed what the law calls the *actus reus* of the offence. If one believes this conduct is harmful and should be prohibited, then the defendants in fact engaged in unlawful, harmful behaviour. If they did this, why should they not be convicted? The reason is that there was further evidence in the case which the Beavers contended should be a legal excuse for their conduct.

Louis Beaver testified that the day before the meeting with Demeter and the sale of the heroin, Montroy had come to him and talked about Al Demeter. Montroy said that Demeter had double-crossed him in some way and that he wanted to get even. He proposed that Beaver should agree to sell Demeter heroin but in fact deliver him a package of powdered milk, which would look exactly the same as the drug. Beaver would get the $400 and pass it along to Montroy who would have his revenge. Beaver said that he agreed to this scheme because Montroy had done several favours for the two Beavers while they were in the penitentiary. However, someone must have slipped up in the plan to

---

[2] [1957] S.C.R. 531, 26 C.R. 193, 118 C.C.C. 129.

substitute the powdered milk for the heroin under the lamp post. When it turned out to be heroin instead, the Beavers were just as surprised as anybody.

Anyway, this was the story put forth by the defence. The Ontario trial judge did not put it to the jury and ask them whether they believed the Beavers (or at least had a reasonable doubt). Instead, following a decision of his own Court of Appeal, he held that a mistake as to the nature of the substance was not a defence to a charge of possession of a narcotic. At the time this case was appealed to the Supreme Court of Canada there were conflicting decisions about the issue in several provinces but no earlier decisions of its own. Nor did the legislation speak explicitly to the problem, although narcotic offences were created and defined by a fairly comprehensive statute. Section 4 of the Opium and Narcotic Drug Act prohibited the bare "possession" of a narcotic; it did not affirmatively require that this possession be "knowing" nor did it exclude this kind of excuse. The fact that the legislation was silent about the legal validity of such a mistake is as good an index as any that the legislature had never focused on the problem.[3] The Canadian law for this problem would be settled by the Supreme Court of Canada in disposing of the Beavers' appeal. In a split decision the Court held in favour of the excuse.

Both the majority and the dissenting opinions began with the same legal assumption. The criminal law presumed that a person could not be convicted of a criminal law offence unless he had a wrongful intent. Like so many legal principles, this has a Latin phrasing: *actus non facit reum nisis mens sit rea*. The majority opinion of Mr. Justice Cartwright cites several authorities to this effect, which make the point that the doctrine is designed to protect the liberty of the citizen and to prevent punishment of the innocent. In the case of statutory offences, this doctrine can be over-ridden by a contrary legislative expression which the courts would be bound to follow. Judges have also allowed themselves the option of excluding *mens rea* in certain cases where this seems appropriate from the subject-matter of the statute. It is this rather vague doctrine which leaves the matter open for the judgment of the court and whose application generated the real controversy in this case.

First of all, Cartwright's majority opinion dismissed the authorities for strict liability in the criminal law as not really analogous to this situation. Those cases dealt basically with such offences as a butcher

---

[3] There was some discussion in the opinions about a prosecution argument based on the provisions of section 17. The latter defined a form of constructive possession which could be excluded by affirmative proof of lack of knowledge. It was suggested that the absence of such explicit language in section 4 showed a legislative wish to exclude any relevance of knowledge or mistake. For various reasons, I think that the implications of section 17 for this issue are equally as ambiguous as the bare language of section 4 itself.

selling unwholesome meat, or a trader having imprecise scales. Here we have a very serious offence, the character of which is set by the fact that there is a minimum mandatory jail sentence of six months (plus a minimum fine). One senses that Cartwright's defence of the principle of *mens rea* in this case is very sketchy just because he believes the answer is obvious. He simply will not impute to Parliament the "monstrous intention" to impose a minimum sentence of six months on a defendant who is deemed to commit an offence if someone else gives him heroin when he honestly believes the substance to be baking soda. The elements of the case for *mens rea* can be discerned very dimly in this opinion which is the major effort of the Supreme Court in the area of so-called serious or "real" crime. It is rather unfortunate for the general development in this area of the law that the existence of this rare mandatory jail sentence relieved the Court of the need to articulate better arguments against the very powerful dissent of Mr. Justice Fauteux.

Fauteux J. starts with a rather different perception of the "subject-matter" of this Act:

> The plain and apparent object of the Act is to prevent, by a rigid control of the possession of drugs, the danger to public health, and to guard against the social evils which an uncontrolled traffic in drugs is bound to generate.

When he reviews the statutory scheme to discover the setting in which his judgment is to be made, he again interprets the attitude of Parliament very differently from the majority.

> The enforcement sections of the Act manifest the exceptional vigilance and firmness which Parliament thought of the essence to forestall the unlawful traffic in narcotic drugs and cope effectively with the unusual difficulties standing in the way of the realization of the object of the statute.[4]

This view was based on the existence of a great many sections in the Opium and Narcotic Drug Act which reversed traditional criminal law doctrines to ease the path of the police and prosecution even at the expense of the liberty of the citizen. More particularly, there were extension of police powers of search of both person and premises, by day and by night (section 19), the use of writs of assistance to avoid the necessity of individual search warrants (section 22), the alleviation of the burden of proof of the Crown and inroads on the presumption of innocence (sections 6, 11, 13, 16, 17 and 18), the creation of minimum mandatory sentences (sections 4 and 6), the mandatory deportation of convicted aliens (section 26) and the extension of the Identification of Criminals Act, R.S.C. 1952, c. 144 even to summary offences under the statute (section 27). "All of these provisions are indicative of the

---

4 *Beaver v. R.*, cited in fn. 2, *ante*, at 546, 547 and 554 respectively.

will of Parliament to give the most efficient protection" to the public from the use of heroin. In this setting, Fauteux J. reasons, why should judges be loath to create a similar exception in the traditional protection of the doctrine of *mens rea* which is their responsibility? He argues that the various provisions of the Act are,

> indicative of the intent of Parliament to deal adequately with the methods, which are used . . . to defeat the purposes of the Act, ingenious as they may be. That enforcement of the provisions of the Act may, in exceptional cases, lead to some injustice, is not an impossibility. But, to forestall this result as to such possible cases, there are remedies under the law, such as a stay of proceedings by the Attorney General or a free pardon under the royal prerogative.

He concludes by holding that the bare language of the section creating the offence must be read literally, the conduct alone of possession of heroin is an offence, and no further requirement of knowledge of the nature of the substance need be proved.

THE VALUE AND THE BURDEN OF MENS REA

Beaver is a very interesting case to me because we see exposed on the face of the opinions the two contrasting perspectives on the criminal justice system—which have been named the "crime control" and "due process" models. The confrontation between these two attitudes has shaped the evolution of the criminal law generally, and certainly determined the character of our law of *mens rea*. The ultimate positions are implicit in the opinions of Fauteux and Cartwright JJ. respectively. Fauteux J. states that the "efficient" achievement of the objectives of the narcotic laws will be furthered by the exclusion of legal excuses such as mistake. Cartwright J. states that the law must make these excuses available in order to protect the innocent. Each then focuses on the relevant elements in the setting of the narcotic laws to try to show that his preferred goal is more important. We must understand the rationale for each of these judicial starting points in order to appreciate the problems in the cases I will discuss in this chapter.[5]

How would this kind of legal doctrine—one which allows Beaver to excuse his possession of heroin on the grounds he thought it was powdered milk—interfere with the efficient enforcement of the narcotic laws? After all, what is the point of convicting and sentencing someone who is not aware that his conduct is criminal? The particular defendant has not shown himself to be dangerous and in need of individual

---

[5] A somewhat more extensive discussion may be found in my article, cited in fn. 1, *ante*, at 284-291.

correction. Potential offenders who are in that stage of ignorance cannot be deterred by the threat of criminal punishment because they are not aware they are committing an offence. However, every time you permit a defendant to advance a new excuse which is available as a matter of law to those who merit it, you create the possibility of misuse of the doctrine by those who are not really entitled to it. If the law creates exceptions and qualifications in its general prohibitions in order to take account of the equities of individual situations, it creates loopholes whose existence may lessen the deterrent influence of the law on those who really are guilty.

This concern is particularly applicable to the requirement of a "wrongful intent". To decide at a trial some months later what a person thought is a much more tenuous matter than establishing the external, objective and verifiable facts of what he did. In both cases, the Crown must prove the element in the defendant's legal guilt beyond all reasonable doubt. Proof of *mens rea* is not impossible: we know that from the many convictions that are obtained in areas where it is required. However, prosecutors and police are always worried about such rules which permit defendants to dream up an ingenious excuse (and *Beaver* looks like a beautiful example of this) and hope it will have some plausibility for an inexperienced jury. The defendant has nothing to lose, and he merely has to be convincing enough to raise a reasonable doubt. Those who are primarily worried about crime control have an understandable concern about the impact of the doctrine of *mens rea*.

The defenders of *mens rea* are not willing to allow the objective of efficient enforcement of the criminal law to justify the sacrifice of certain unlucky individuals who do have a valid excuse. It is inevitable that some people will engage in criminal conduct accidentally or by mistake. To deny such a person his defence because of the dangers of creating a loophole for the guilty will involve very harsh consequences for an innocent person. This is most blatantly the case in *Beaver*, where his conviction would lead to a mandatory sentence of at least 6 months in jail. Even in the ordinary run of the criminal law, where his excuse might get him a suspended sentence, to suffer a conviction and a criminal record after a public trial is a very serious disability and harm. The point of the doctrine of *mens rea* is that we convict only those who have voluntarily chosen to commit an offence and so deliberately exposed themselves to the risk of punishment. Suppose that someone has not decided to forfeit his immunity by knowingly engaging in criminal conduct. To subject him to the grossly unequal treatment of the criminal process simply for the more efficient protection of the rest of us is offensive to the principle of justice. It also entails a substantial loss in individual freedom from the state. A major point of the concept of *mens rea* is that it permits us to choose a way out of the clutches of the criminal law. If we eliminate it, we have no way of protecting ourselves against accidental involvement with the police, prosecutor, trial, etc.

We are all subject to the risk that the unlucky defendant, singled out by fate, will be one of us.

The proponents of "crime control" respond that all of this concern is purely hypothetical. Police and prosecutors also care about these values of freedom and equality and they have enough good sense to proceed against only those defendants who have fabricated their excuses. They will informally dismiss those who are truly innocent of any "wrongful intent". If they don't, and a case of injustice does come to light in court, there is an opportunity for a discretionary pardon afterwards (as Fauteux J. pointed out). It is precisely here that the advocates of "due process" join issue. They don't really trust the officials administering our criminal justice system. They do not want to rely on the exercise of discretion by a prosecutor, who operates at a low level of visibility, and who is basically involved in one side of what he may see as the "war on crime". The thrust of the doctrine of *mens rea* is to allow the excuse as a matter of legal right, on the basis of evidence and arguments presented in open court, with conflicts resolved by an impartial judge or jury. If this requires some sacrifice in efficiency of enforcement, then so be it.

The *Beaver* case is a microcosm reflecting this basic confrontation in the criminal law between these two contrasting attitudes. Our criminal law treats neither objective as an absolute value. It assumes that without an effective criminal sanction, we will not have a viable society preserving the due process objectives of freedom and equality, but that there is also no point in permitting the criminal law to offend against the principles of the very society it is trying to protect. A workable compromise is necessary. We must look at different situations pragmatically, assessing the weight of the claims of each in concrete situations. This is what the Court did in *Beaver*, and it reached the conclusion we have seen. In a recent decision in *Pierce Fisheries*,[6] it reached the opposite conclusion, but again on a similar pragmatic basis.

THE PUBLIC WELFARE EXCEPTION

Pierce Fisheries is an instructive contrast with *Beaver* because there was such a marked similarity in the surface legal elements of the situation. The accused firm was charged with the offence under the Fisheries Act, R.S.C. 1952, c. 119, of having undersized lobsters in its "possession". Apparently some 50,000 to 60,000 lbs. of lobster had been delivered to the plant that day, by truck or boat, and the inspector found 26 undersized lobsters. There was no evidence that any of the officers of the

---

6 *R. v. Pierce Fisheries Ltd.*, [1971] S.C.R. 5, 12 C.R.N.S. 272, 12 D.L.R. (3d) 591, [1970] 5 C.C.C. 193.

responsible employees of the defendant firm knew of their size, and the firm had instructed its employees not to purchase lobsters which were in breach of the Regulations under the Act. As in *Beaver*, the term "possession" was not qualified by any reference to knowledge or intention, but again there was another provision of the same statute which did advert to this element. The question, then, was how the Court should construe the immediate offence in the light of this ambiguous direction from the legislature, read in the light of the basic principle of *mens rea*. Cartwright J., in a lone dissent, remained intransigently in favour of the position of the accused.[7] He argued that *Beaver* laid down a binding legal rule for the construction of criminal offences—even conduct "not involving grave moral turpitude"—based on the activity of *possession*: "in a criminal case there is in law no possession without knowledge of the character of the substance." Perhaps the basis of his conclusion appears in a passage at the end of his opinion where he asks whether it may be in the "public interest" to allow absolute liability only where there are specific and unequivocal words from the legislature to that effect.

Mr. Justice Ritchie's opinion for the majority agreed that there was a common law presumption of *mens rea* as "an essential ingredient of all cases that are criminal in the true sense".[8] However, he held that there is no such presumption for a "wide category of offences created by statutes enacted for the regulation of individual conduct in the interests of health, convenience, safety and general welfare of the public". The key to this category is that they "are not criminal in any real sense, but are acts which in the public interest are prohibited under a penalty". The Court must always ask whether it is faced with a "new crime added to the general criminal law", or "an act of a truly criminal character" for which a "stigma" attaches to any person convicted of it. In *Beaver*, the Court had found that it was a "*serious crime* to possess or deal in

---

7 Interestingly enough, Mr. Justice Fauteux was equally intransigent in the earlier decision of *R. v. Rees*, [1965] S.C.R. 640, 24 C.R. 1, 115 C.C.C. 1, 4 D.L.R. (2d) 406. The defendant here was charged with "*knowingly* or wilfully contributing to juvenile delinquency" under section 33(1)(b) of the Juvenile Delinquents Act, R.S.C. 1952, c. 160. His defence was that he honestly believed the girl to be older than the statutory age limit of 18. Working with this pretty explicit statutory language, the Supreme Court held that this was a valid excuse for the offence. Fauteux J. wrote a lone dissent holding that a mistake as to the girl's age should not be considered a defence to this charge, even though it is a critical element in the illegality of the conduct in question. The diametric opposition of Justices Fauteux and Cartwright in criminal cases stretching over a period of 20 years is one of the most striking examples in Canadian law of the influence of a judge's personal attitudes on his course of decisions, at least if scaling of judicial votes is indicative of the real judicial attitudes motivating a decision. See the position of Cartwright and Fauteux JJ. on the *mens rea* scales in my article, cited in fn. 1, *ante*, at 294-299 and on the general criminal law scale in Peck, "The Supreme Court of Canada 1958-66" (1967), 45 Can. Bar Rev. 666 at 716.

8 *R. v. Pierce Fisheries*, cited in fn. 6, *ante*, at 13, 14, 16, 17, 22, and 23 respectively.

narcotics", as indicated also by the mandatory jail term. This Court could find little resemblance to the offence of possession of undersized lobsters, and did not believe the latter was a serious crime to which any stigma attached. Ritchie J. was concerned here that "if lack of knowledge by a responsible employee constituted a defence for a limited company ... it would in many cases be virtually impossible to secure a conviction". The Court could not apply the doctrine of "evil intent" because then "the statute, by which it was obviously intended that there should be complete control without the possibility of any leaks, would have so many holes in it, that in truth it would be nothing more than a legislative sieve".

The *Pierce Fisheries* opinion creates the impression, even more pronounced than was the case with *Beaver*, that while a decision may be right, no satisfactory rationale is provided. Mr. Justice Ritchie simply states that conviction for this offence is very different than it is for possession of heroin, and that the difficulties created by the *mens rea* doctrine could render the statute an unenforceable sieve. He may be right but he doesn't explain why. This pair of decisions is not like some of the horrible examples I described in the tort area of a legal distinction without any functional difference at all. There are plausible reasons for characterizing the *Beaver* offence in one way and the *Pierce Fisheries* offence in another. However, a final court has a duty to do more than reach the correct result in individual cases on an intuitive basis. It must articulate the reasons for its different conclusions in a way that gives meaningful guidance to the lower courts which must deal with this same problem recurring in so many different guises. Anyone who reads the flow of cases in this area will know that lower court judges have not been able to find such guidance in the decisions of the Supreme Court.

What are the distinctive characteristics of these "public welfare" offences, of which the regulation in *Pierce Fisheries* was representative, which could reasonably support a different conclusion as to *mens rea*? There are several reasons for believing that it will be much more difficult to prove knowledge or intent and, contrariwise, that it will be much easier to fabricate these excuses. The particular offence is merely one instance of a large number of similar transactions (28 lobsters out of over 50,000 lbs. that day); there is a fine line between legal and illegal situations (3 3/16 of an inch for a lobster); and because many different individuals in the firm or organization participate in the activity, it is hard to single out the one responsible. Management can just post signs in the area and then deny knowledge of what happened. I should note that these very same factors are also good reasons for believing that there will be many offences committed through legitimate mistakes. This must not obscure the fact that it is a lot more difficult for a court to separate the valid from the invalid excuses than in a case like *Beaver*, where a person is in the rather unusual situation of being in possession of and selling heroin.

This is merely one side of the equation, the problem of the prosecution. It is easy to see a similar shift on the other side, regarding the interests of the accused. Just as the Supreme Court judges, we all recognize, when we see it, the difference between conviction for possession of heroin and for possession of undersized lobsters, though we cannot always explain it. There are several factors in the background. Public welfare offences regulate conduct that is a considerable distance removed from any harm to any individual, and thus the retributive urges in the area are muted. The conduct is prohibited by laws of relatively recent origin and there is a relatively artificial line between illegal behaviour and legitimate business dealings. Hence, there is much less of an aura of popular moral attitudes surrounding the offence and little likelihood of public stigma in a conviction. This is reflected in the fact that the almost invariable sentence for the offence will be a fine imposed on the firm, not a jail sentence on an individual. The firm has chosen to engage in the business where these regulatory laws apply. It can be required to treat the amount of these fines as a cost of doing business and made to adjust its affairs accordingly. The values of liberty and fairness to the individual, which underlie the principle of *mens rea*, are of considerably less weight for these offences while, as we saw before, the claims of crime control are much more insistent than for the unusual and isolated criminal conduct of *Beaver*. If we consider the doctrines of the criminal law as an expression of a pragmatic compromise between these sometimes competing objectives, then the different results in *Beaver* and *Pierce Fisheries* can be understood, and perhaps justified.

THE JUDICIAL FUNCTION WITHIN OUR CRIMINAL LAW

Let us turn for the moment from analysis of the substantive issues in the Supreme Court decisions to the more basic questions of the proper judicial role in this area. As we have seen, the Court has a great deal of legal flexibility in deciding whether particular statutes create strict liability or *mens rea* offences. I will discuss some cases which show how the Court must make similar judgments about the quality of *mens rea* for those offences for which it is required. What are the implications of *mens rea* for such distinct situations as drunkenness, insanity or duress? By what justification or authority does the Court have such a decisive impact on the character of this vital area of our criminal law?

First of all, there is the unusual circumstance that the Criminal Code provides an explicit legal source for the division of labour between legislature and court in developing our criminal law. By section 8 of the Code, common law offences are abolished. The legal values I sketched in Chapter 2 speak especially firmly in favour of the legislature as the *sole* source of new criminal offences. The legislature enacts its rules in definite language and through public procedures and makes them effective as of a fixed date in the future. This may reduce to some extent the elasticity of the criminal law and allow some ingenious individuals to find loopholes in the existing offences which enable them to achieve their dubious ends. However, to quote from the original Royal Commission Report which is the source of our Code, it is "better to run the risk of giving a temporary immunity to the offender than to leave any one liable to a prosecution for an act or omission which is not declared to be an offence by the...Code itself or some other Act of Parliament".[9] Perhaps judges can develop new torts; they must not create new crimes. Society takes the risk that a few evil-doers may escape punishment when a new situation arises, and until legislation can be enacted, in order to avoid the unfairness of convicting those who thought they were behaving in an acceptably legal way but will be caught by the retrospective law-making of the judges.

The attitude of the Code is very different when it comes to the "defences". Section 7(3) reads:

> Every rule and principle of the common law that renders any circumstance a justification or excuse for an act or a defence to a charge continues in force and applies in respect of proceedings for an offence under this Act or any other Act of the Parliament of Canada, except in so far as they are altered by or are inconsistent with this Act or any other Act of the Parliament of Canada.

In this the Code again reflects the views of Mr. Justice Stephen and the Royal Commissioners who stated:

> In our opinion the principles of the common law on such subjects, when rightly understood, are founded on sense and justice . . . It is, if not absolutely impossible, at least not practicable, to foresee all the various combinations of circumstances which may happen, but which are of so infrequent occurrence that they have not hitherto been the subject of judicial consideration, although they might constitute a justification or excuse, and to use language at once so precise and clear and comprehensive as to include all cases that ought to be included, and not to include any case that ought to be excluded.

Hence, we have an authoritative statement in the Code of the view that the evolution of the law of *mens rea* should continue to be the work of the judicial process even though the rest of the criminal law was largely reduced to statutory form. What are the institutional factors which might justify this conclusion?

First of all, the defences are not matters of high political visibility and content, in contrast with definition (or repeal) of offences. The question whether an honest mistake should be an excuse for the posses-

---

9 Report, Royal Commission, Criminal Code (1880), pp. 10 and 11 respectively.

sion of drugs is of a qualitatively different order than the question of what, if any, criminal offences we should have to deal with the problem of drugs. Secondly, most of the issues raised with respect to *mens rea* do not require detailed expertise or scientific research which may be needed for many other areas of criminal law reform. This is not universally true, as the example of the insanity defence demonstrates. However, even here much of the available research has been canvassed and appraised in ways which are usable by courts as well as legislatures.[10] Moreover, a court has resources in the area which are not available to the legislatures. As we shall see, some of the key issues of *mens rea* require reflection on the implications of the basic values of the criminal law for very unusual situations. The legislature would not likely anticipate such cases in drafting and enacting general language; courts see the problem dramatically presented in a concrete, human context. Finally, the significance of "due process" for judicial reform of the criminal law is very different here than it was for the definition of new crimes. When a novel defence is raised, we cannot refuse to apply a new rule until the legislature gets around to adopting it. In the interim the innocent individual who should be excused because he was blameless will suffer the harsh injustice of criminal punishment. It is precisely because a court can and does make law retrospectively that the defendant should be able to appeal to it for a new rule to be applied to the old facts of his case.

These are the practical institutional factors which support the judgment that our law has made in favour of an active judicial role in developing criminal defences. Their operation, I suggest, is based on the assumption that the doctrine of *mens rea* is an established "legal principle" shaping this area of the law. Earlier in this book, I used this doctrine as an example of the concept of a legal principle when I was trying to show the significance of this instrument in my preliminary statement of the role of law in courts. Now that we have some appreciation of the content and use of the doctrine of *mens rea* itself, I can expand somewhat on what I mean by a legal principle.

Translated literally, *mens rea* means a "guilty mind". Obviously, there are innumerable sets of circumstances which could be relevant to the final judgment about whether the defendant's criminal conduct was as a result of a "blameworthy state of mind", an "evil intent", or whatever other synonym we can think of for the Latin phrase. Some have argued that the legal requirement of *mens rea* means that the judges or juries in the instant case should be asked to find whether the defendant was

---

10   The reasoning and findings of the English Royal Commission on the insanity defence were heavily relied on in the striking judicial reform of the American law in the Durham case. More recently, American courts have used not only the research of the American Law Institute but even its precise formulation in the Model Penal Code, to revise the traditional legal standards. I cannot think of any sensible reason why such public materials should not be utilized by lawyers in courts when they are acceptable for lawyers in the legislatures.

blameworthy, taking into account all of the facts in the immediate situation, without any further legal precision. This is certainly conceivable and practical; after all, that is how the law now deals with the defendant in a negligence action. Liability in tort depends upon the court's view as to whether the defendant showed reasonable care or was at fault in all of the circumstances of the accident. If the criminal law took a similar tack, the doctrine of *mens rea* would be a legal standard, not a legal principle. As stated earlier, principles are used in argument about the proper rules to be applied to the facts. However, for several reasons, the law has not conceived of the requirement of "blameworthiness" as a general standard to be applied directly to the events in an individual case. There is a greater need for precision, predictability, and even-handedness in the administration of the criminal law, and perhaps the controversial character of the issues generates greater emotional involvement about a situation than is common in tort law. Accordingly, the established scheme of our criminal law requires specific rules defining the various excuses, telling us for what offences they are available and the relevant facts in a situation for their application. The rules established in *Beaver* and in *Pierce Fisheries* are an example: we know that mistake as to the nature of a drug is an excuse under the narcotics laws but that mistake as to the size of one's lobsters is not an excuse under the Fisheries Act.

However, this branch of the law is not just a miscellaneous and apparently incoherent collection of such rules. The rules are developed primarily by the courts in adjudicating particular cases, and the judges do have some reasons for what they are doing. What is the role of the principle of *mens rea* in this process? I think it can be sketched in this way. In the early, formless state of the criminal law, the courts will be presented with the most obvious excuses for the infliction of criminal harms. The defendant may claim that he inflicted injuries on another through pure accident, or perhaps as a result of self defence. Acting on the commonsense view that it is unfair to convict someone in a situation where he has shown himself no worse than persons who have complied with the law, judges begin to acquit the defendants. Reflection on the reasons for these decisions will suggest arguments to lawyers for the development of similar excuses for analogous but more difficult cases (such as insanity). Gradually a theory is articulated which shows how these various doctrines implement certain basic values of criminal justice. With a sharpened realization of the objectives that the law has been intuitively pursuing all along, the courts are ready to refine their doctrines to take account of unusual variations in the situations, or even to overturn earlier rules which appear no longer compatible with the overall thrust of the law (e.g. drunkenness). The fact that there is such an underlying theory in the law, based on the acceptance of certain values, is expressed in the legal principle of *mens rea*. Two final points may be made. First, it is in the relationship of rule and principle that we find "the genius of the common law". Because the process requires the judges to turn from immediate facts to basic theory and then back to the facts, the law can be kept pragmatic, functional, and oriented to the sense of the situation. It admits of exceptions to the availability of excuses (as we saw in *Pierce Fisheries*); it can admit of many qualifications to their operation, even where they are allowed (as we shall see in some following cases). Yet there is a guiding thread to the enquiry which channels the evolution of the law. The values on which *mens rea* is based are by no means self-evident. Eminent critics of the criminal law have called for the abolition of all such concepts of individual responsibility and blame. These arguments are properly addressed to the legislature, not the courts. We have a system of criminal law into which the notion of blameworthiness has been cemented as an integral part of a very complex structure. The Court can unravel on a case by case basis the strands of the existing system and can make necessary adjustments where this appears reasonable; it cannot create a new system based on a radically different view of the function of criminal punishment. Our judges are legally *bound* by the principle or presumption of *mens rea*.

DEFINING COMMON LAW EXCUSES: INTOXICATION

With this analysis of what I believe to be the ideal scope for judicial innovation in this area of the criminal law, let us turn back to the actual performance of the Supreme Court of Canada in recent cases. The two decisions I have reviewed so far in this chapter—*Beaver* and *Pierce Fisheries*—both dealt with the question of whether new statutory offences should have read into them the requirements of *mens rea* as a necessary condition for criminal guilt. The cases I shall now consider deal with the specific quality of *mens rea* to be required in the traditional offences where there is no doubt of its general applicability. We must not forget the important relationship between these two issues; the reasons why we want *mens rea* in the first place are vital factors in determining what it should be like. However, the approach that I prefer for this area, in which an individual's blameworthiness for his criminal conduct can be excluded by the presence of any one of a number of different excuses, immediately suggests that there will be many functional and technical difficulties left in defining the legal scope of *mens rea* even after we have committed ourselves to the view that it is required. The cases that follow deal with only a small selection of this variety of legal problems, the excuse of drunkenness, the unusual case of duress, and the problem of accidental death of the victim during a robbery.

R. v. George[11] is a paradigm example of the tragedy of the criminal law. The defendant George was an Indian trapper who severely beat an

---

[11] [1960] S.C.R. 871, 34 C.R. 1.

84-year-old man named Avgeris and robbed him of $22. George had been drinking heavily all that day and while he could remember hitting Avgeris, he remembered nothing about the money. The trial judge felt there was a reasonable doubt about whether in his drunken condition George intended to steal the money and so acquitted him on the charge of theft. However, everyone at the trial forgot to consider the lesser "included" offence of common assault. When the case reached the Supreme Court of Canada, it held that George's intoxication did not excuse the assault and convicted him of that crime.

Let's first consider the technical, legal issues in the case. Both theft and assault are offences defined by the Canadian Criminal Code and each explicitly requires the presence of a mental element. However, the Code is completely silent about the validity of the excuse of drunkenness for these offences or for any other (by contrast with insanity, which is expressly defined by section 16). Perhaps the reason is that at the time the Code was drafted, there was little if any recognition of the validity of such an excuse in the common law. However, the English Courts in the early part of the Twentieth Century did develop doctrines admitting and defining the use of intoxication as a defence. The culmination of this process was the House of Lords decision in *D.P.P. v. Beard*.[12] Here Lord Birkenhead stated three rules which he believed summarized the thrust of the law as it had evolved up to then. Because of the presence of section 7(3) of the Code, our courts considered themselves capable of recognizing these new doctrines and Canadian decisions, including *George*, have uniformly followed *Beard*.

There is nothing unusual or even undesirable about this. The problem, though, is the way that our judges have approached *Beard*. They have treated Lord Birkenhead as though he were a one-man legislature writing a statute. In much the same way as happened in the area of occupier's liability with *Indermaur v. Dames*,[13] the Supreme Court of Canada has lifted one abstract passage out of the total context of the *Beard* opinion and treated that as an exhaustive statement of Canadian law. "Evidence of intoxication which renders the accused incapable of forming the *specific* intent essential to constitute the crime should be taken into consideration with the other facts proved in order to determine whether or not he had the intent". The trouble-word here is "specific". I think that Lord Birkenhead meant to attach no greater legal significance to this adjective than did Lord Justice Willes to "unusual danger". All that he meant to say was that for any offence, there is some particular mental element required and one can use evidence of intoxication to help show that it was not present in the facts of the immediate case. In *George*, though, the Supreme Court judges purported to draw a distinction between two qualitatively different kinds of intent, "specific" and "gen-

---

12 [1920] A.C. 479.
13 L.R. 1 C.P. 274.

eral". Later judges have read these opinions as tacitly assuming that only the "specific" kind of intent can be excluded by evidence of drunkenness, not the "general" kind. From this premise it is easy to conclude that where an accused is charged with an offence involving only a "general intent" he cannot advance any evidence of his drunken condition to excuse his conduct. A whole string of Canadian appeals have been generated over the issue of how different offences in the Code should be so classified.[14] After reading the thousands of judicial words expressed on the subject, I can only register my agreement with everyone else who has analyzed the problem and concluded that the distinction is totally spurious.

The irony is that the Supreme Court judges in *George* may not have intended any such peculiar legal significance to their choice of language. The B.C. Court of Appeal appears to believe that they did, and maybe they should know, because it was their decision that was reversed in *George*. However, a close reading of the Supreme Court opinions suggests that the Court assumed that intoxication might exclude even the "general intent" involved in common assault in an appropriate situation. The distinction between the two kinds of intent may have been drawn simply to help sort out the facts in *George* itself. The Court did hold that the mere fact that George was acquitted of robbery, because he was too drunk to form the intent to take the money, did not mean that he must be acquitted of assault, because he was too drunk to be aware he was beating Avgeris. The trial judge had made no explicit finding about this last issue because he did not advert to the "included" offence at all. On the evidence in the record, the Supreme Court found that George did know what he was doing to Avgeris and convicted him of assault.

The fact that the result may have been quite accidental does not excuse the Supreme Court for the tangle that its language in the *George* opinion has created in the defence of drunkenness. Its style of reasoning in this case and its other forays in the same area is directly responsible for the unpredictable and unfair doctrines that make up the Canadian law on the subject. What the Supreme Court did was extract a passage from *Beard* and then try to follow it blindly, wherever it led. What it should have done was recognize that *Beard* was only one step, albeit an important one, in the evolution of the common law, and that the opinion was written to justify a decision in the unusual facts of that case. Viewed in this context, the language in *Beard* makes sense. However, the Supreme Court of Canada has its own responsibility for elaborating on the doctrines in the area to deal with the novel situations it faces. In doing so, it must ask why we have a defence of drunkenness, what we

---

14 Apparently everyone agrees that murder and robbery involve specific intents but that manslaughter does not. The Ontario and British Columbia judges vigorously disagree about how to classify indecent assault and rape, both of which are associated with intoxication in so many situations.

are trying to achieve with it, and so on. As soon as a judge begins to reflect on these questions, he will realize that the distinction between so-called specific and general intents is meaningless. There simply is no reason for allowing drunkenness to be a defence to theft, but not to assault or rape, and nothing in the Code or the growth of the common law requires such an anomalous legal conclusion.

There are several basic options open to the law in its treatment of intoxication as a factor in the commission of a crime. It can take a nega-tive, hostile attitude and deny any validity to the excuse whatsoever (or even consider the presence of alcohol to be an aggravating factor). This attitude is based on the view that a person gets drunk through his own voluntary conduct; if he then becomes dangerous, it is his own fault and he should take the consequences. Indeed, this was the thrust of the law in the 19th Century at the time our Code was drafted and quite con-ceivably our courts could have declared their independence of later English developments and maintained that view. Instead, our courts followed the English in their adoption of the second basic option, whose lines can be clearly seen in the *Beard* opinion as a whole. A much more neutral view is taken of the fact of intoxication. If a crime requires a particular (or "specific") mental element of a sober person, then evidence of drinking may be led as one circumstantial factor to show that the defendant's mind was sufficiently clouded, confused, or inattentive that he did not realize he was committing some criminal harm. The point is that the drunk is not to be worse off than the sober person as far as establishing the ordinary legal excuses is concerned. Within this per-spective, the so-called distinction between offences of "specific" and "general" intent is seen to be purposeless. If the law admits of certain excuses of accident, mistake, etc., for murder and theft, then a person can try to prove that his drinking helped lead to the accident or mistake. If the law admits of similar excuses for offences like assault or rape, then the same avenue of defence should be open to the intoxicated person.

Reflection on the reasons why the law would want to allow evidence of intoxication would quickly show the absurdity of much of the law that has been spawned by *George*. Our judges are traditionally loath to con-sider such "policy" matters on the ground this would introduce elements of subjectivity and unpredictability into the course of decision. As this example demonstrates, it is the very failure to look for the rationale of the law which generates the kind of distorted doctrines which are neces-sarily subjective and unpredictable in their application. Judges can only implement the various legal values by a process of reasoning which goes beyond the purely formal and legalistic approach to grapple with the substantive and functional issues presented by the rules. This is a good reason for the adoption of a very different style of analysis from that used in *George*. However, it is not the only reason. Only if judges are willing to look at the sense of the doctrines they are using can the resources of the common law be brought to bear for their improvement. If the Supreme Court had tried to ask why we have a law of drunkenness, in the light of the basic values of the principle of *mens rea*, it might well have moved the law to a more adequate third option.

Drinking is an only too prevalent factor in the commission of crimes, more so than mental illness. Yet the view taken of its relevance in the legal approach described above is still rather narrow. It is true that excessive drinking may, on occasion, affect a person's awareness of the criminal character of his behaviour. However, the usual and primary effect of intoxication is to break down his inhibitions and to lessen his control of his emotions and impulses. The reason why the law allows a mistake (whether induced by alcohol or not) to be an excuse for a crime is because the person does not choose to commit an offence which he is not aware of. Thus he can't be blamed for this offence. However, intoxication may directly affect a person's capacity for choice by breaking down his ordinary resistance to the temptations of crime. George was acquitted of theft because his drunken inability to intend to steal meant that he did not choose to commit this offence. He was aware that he was beating Avgeris, though, so this form of the excuse would not avail him. Yet, suppose he could prove that he had drunk so much that his condition triggered an assault which was totally out of character for him. Why should we punish the sober George the next day for the offence committed when he was so drunk? Is this the logic of the evolution of the law of drunkenness if we consider the available evidence about its effects in the light of the basic values of *mens rea*?

The third option is to treat intoxication as a distinctive excuse in its own right, analogous to that of insanity. There are no insuperable legal roadblocks in the way of judicial creation of such a doctrine. As I said, the Code is completely silent on the subject and since it was written the courts have moved from stage one to stage two. If there are legitimate reasons for not taking the further step to stage three, they must be pragmatic, policy arguments for not accepting the implications of the principle of *mens rea*. There are such arguments available, in particular the ever-present problem of proof. As the example of insanity shows, the criminal law has always shied away from admitting excuses based on emotional, rather than intellectual, factors. How does one tell the difference between a drunken impulse that was not resistible and one that simply was not resisted? I do not propose to argue that problem here, one way or the other. My point is that this is exactly the kind of issue with which our courts have an institutional responsibility to come to grips. Following the lead of the Supreme Court of Canada in *George*, the Canadian courts have contributed nothing but confusion to the development of this area of our law.

INTERPRETING THE CRIMINAL CODE: DURESS AND "FELONY MURDER"

Some of the most difficult cases involving the principle of *mens rea* occur when there is a statutory rule apparently in conflict with it. The Court does owe a duty of fidelity to the law established by the legislature. It does not have the power to repeal earlier decisions of the legislature as I have suggested it has in the case of earlier common law precedents which are now seen to be inconsistent with the general thrust of the law. Yet a court must take a realistic view of legislative action. The Criminal Code was enacted in the 19th Century as an expression of what was thought to be the legal consensus of that time. It was recognized that not all of the problems had been anticipated or the most reasonable solutions accepted. Section 7(3) was explicitly retained to give judges the power to evolve new doctrines for the benefit of defendants who needed them. How rigidly should the Supreme Court read and apply the century-old language of the Code where it seems to work an injustice in a novel case?

R. v. Carker[15] is a classic example of this judicial dilemma. The defendant was charged with the offence of wilful damage to public property. The factual situation out of which the prosecution arose is becoming depressingly familiar. On May 10, 1964, at about 1.00 a.m., a riot began in the Oakalla Prison Farm in British Columbia. The prisoners collectively began yelling and shouting and then proceeded to smash the plumbing fixtures in their respective cells. The Crown proved that Carker had been locked alone in his cell at 11.30 p.m. and when the cell was opened at 8.00 a.m. the next morning, his basin and toilet were broken. There the case was rested, seemingly a clear-cut occasion for a conviction.

Carker's defence relied on further evidence which recent prison riots in Kingston, Attica and the like have made only too believable. When the disturbance began, the ringleaders checked to make sure that everyone was participating. In reply to a convict leader named Pombert, Carker said that he wanted no part of this "foolishness" because he was still awaiting the outcome of an appeal which might free him. Pombert replied that he would get a broken arm or a caved-in head if he did not join in. When there was no answer Pombert continued: "If you don't, I'll stick a shiv in your back when I next get a chance." At that Carker succumbed. His counsel was ready to prove that several such stabbings had taken place in prisons in Canada, including one at Oakalla, and guards were virtually powerless to prevent it. The trial judge held the excuse of "duress" inapplicable in these circumstances,

---

15 [1967] S.C.R. 114, 2 C.R.N.S. 16, 60 W.W.R. 365, [1967] 2 C.C.C. 190.

refused to admit the evidence, and after convicting Carker of the offence, sentenced him to one year further in prison.

The legal difficulty in the way of accepting this excuse is the definition of duress in section 17 of the Code:

> A person who commits an offence under compulsion by threats of immediate death or grievous bodily harm from a person who is present when the offence is committed is excused for committing the offence if he believes that the threats will be carried out. . . .

How can it be said that Carker was under a threat of *immediate* death or harm from someone who was *present* at the time the offence was committed? Carker was in one locked cell, Pombert in another, and the threat was to put a knife in Carker's back as soon as Pombert had a chance. Yet the majority in the British Columbia Court of Appeal did allow the appeal and quashed the conviction. Their decision was based on two different grounds: first, the specific offence had to be committed "wilfully", and this had connotations of an act "done by the appellant deliberately, as a free agent, and in the exercise of his own will". Second, section 17 is simply a codification of the common law at the time the Code was drafted, and section 7 of the Criminal Code could be utilized to support extensions of the excuse to closely analogous cases.

The Supreme Court of Canada unanimously reversed the B.C.C.A. and restored the conviction. In a very sparsely reasoned decision, Mr. Justice Ritchie agreed with the dissent of Mr. Justice McLean on the Court of Appeal in that the statutory definition of "wilfully" was satisfied, that section 17 exhaustively defined the excuse of duress in Canadian criminal law making section 7 irrelevant, and that section 17 was inapplicable here. To the Court it was virtually inconceivable that there could be a threat of "immediate death" to Carker when all the other prisoners were locked in their cells. Perhaps they agreed with McLean J. that "it is clear that the threat is not of immediate death, but of death at some future and indefinite time when the opportunity presents itself. All the appellant had to do was notify the guards of the threat, and his future safety could have been assured by various means".[16] It must be nice to be on the outside, taking this calm view of the situation and writing an opinion which condemns a person like Carker to another year in jail for what he was forced to do.

In my view, the principle of *mens rea* required that the Court take a more creative view of its function in order to do justice to Carker. If one reads section 17 in the abstract, as a tightly-drafted provision in a tax code, for example, the conclusion that there was no threat of *immediate* harm from a person who was *present* might be plausible. However, that is not the situation here. The Code was written to incorporate the experience of the common law in working out the

---

16 R. v. Carker, 56 W.W.R. 65 at 79, 48 C.R. 313, [1966] 4 C.C.C. 212 (B.C. C.A.).

implications of the basic principles of the criminal sanction; it should not be interpreted as freezing the development of these principles, especially in view of section 7. There are two rationales for the excuse of duress: one is that the otherwise criminal conduct and harm (here damage to government-owned toilet fixtures) is *justified* when it is necessary to avoid substantially greater harm (here a knife in Carker's back); second, even if we would prefer the defendant not to commit the offence, he may be *excused* because of a threat "which a person of reasonable firmness in his situation should have been unable to resist" (to use the Model Penal Code definition). Only a hypocritical society condemns a defendant like Carker for yielding to coercion that none of us would, realistically, have been able to withstand. On the other hand, there are dangers in an undue extension of the excuse. Not only is there the standard objection that the defence may be fabricated by two offenders to have at least one go free; even where it is valid, the excuse may facilitate the exploitation of innocent bystanders to commit offences through threats that will insulate these actors from prosecution. Hence, the law always places some limits on its availability. The policy of the restrictions we see in section 17 is to permit the excuse only in cases of an immediate threat when the accused cannot go to the authorities for his protection. In almost all cases, literal acceptance of these limitations makes sense; sometimes, though, it does not and *Carker*, I suggest, is such a case. The approach of the Court of Appeal majority is much more realistic:

> The determinative element is in all cases the belief of the person threatened that the threats will be carried into effect.
>
> The use of the words threat of "immediate" death . . . from a person who is "present" when the offence is committed, are relative terms varying in the rigidity of their meaning in the circumstances of each case, and are elements to be considered in determining the belief of the accused that the threats will be carried out. . . . A continuing threat may be an immediate menace. This was possible in this case and was for the jury to decide.[17]

In support of its admitted elaboration on the narrow scope of section 17, the Court of Appeal relied on a Privy Council decision in *Subramanian*[18] which dealt with a threat from Chinese terrorists in Malaya who melted back into the jungle but whose threat continued to be extremely credible (much like Pombert's threat to Carker). In other words, section 17 expresses a legal policy which has been adopted by the legislature and which the courts are obliged to follow. However, when a court is presented with a very unusual situation for which the policy is oblique, it should not feel constrained from appealing to its

---

17 56 W.W.R. at 74.

18 *Subramanian v. Public Prosecutor*, [1956] 1 W.L.R. 965, 100 Sol. Jo. 566 (P.C.).

power under section 7 to apply the basic principles of *mens rea* and afford an excuse to someone who merits it as much as Carker did.

No doubt many defenders of the Supreme Court will reject this view of what should have been the approach in *Carker*. They will say that the integrity of the legal system and of the relationship between court and legislature requires that the court not extend the policy of a doctrine beyond the scope of the normal meaning of the language used. A court may have this freedom in dealing with common law precedents but it does not have it with statutes. This position will have difficulty with a recent case, *Trinneer*,[19] which also involved a B.C. Court of Appeal reversal of a conviction which was then restored by a unanimous Supreme Court of Canada.

Trinneer and a friend named Frank had spent the night together out on the town, at the end of which they decided they needed a little money. Frank purchased a hunting knife and the two of them managed to get in a car driven by a Mrs. Vollett. The car was driven out of town and stopped so that Frank could take Mrs. Vollett outside while Trinneer turned the car around. Frank stabbed Mrs. Vollett several times, took her money, and the two left. Mrs. Vollett died some time within the next two hours. There was no doubt, on these facts, that Frank was guilty of culpable homicide (under then section 194) because of his "unlawful act" which "caused the death" of Mrs. Vollett. This culpable homicide amounted to murder under then section 202 [now s. 213], because Frank caused Mrs. Vollett's death while committing a robbery. He is guilty of murder whether or not he "means to cause death . . . and whether or not he knows that death is likely to be caused . . . if (a) he means to cause bodily harm for the purpose of facilitating the commission of the offence, and the death ensues from the bodily harm, . . . or (d) he uses a weapon during or at the time he commits . . . the offence . . . and the death ensues as a consequence". These legal definitions of what used to be called "felony murder" express a very simple idea; if a person commits an offence like robbery and in the course of so doing uses a weapon or causes any bodily harm, then, if death results, he is guilty of murder no matter how unintended or improbable this consequence might be. Frank was clearly guilty of the murder of Mrs. Vollett, then, under either section 202(a) or 202(d).

Trinneer's position was quite different, and he had a separate trial from Frank. Trinneer said he was in the car all the time, he did not actually commit the robbery, he did not use the knife, and he did not cause the death. The culpable homicide sections, including that of murder, are not directly applicable to him. His criminal responsibility

---

19 *R. v. Trinneer*, [1970] S.C.R. 638, 11 C.R.N.S. 110, 72 W.W.R. 677, 10 D.L.R. (3d) 568, [1970] 3 C.C.C. 289.

comes as a result of being a "party" to the conduct of Frank. Clearly he is a party to the robbery under section 21(1) of the Code:

> Every one is a party to an offence who . . . (b) does . . . anything for the purpose of aiding any person to commit it.

The question, though, is whether he is a party to the murder under section 21(2):

> When two or more persons form an intention in common to carry out any unlawful purpose and to assist each other therein and any one of them, in carrying out the common purpose, commits an offence, each of them who knew or ought to have known that the commission of the offence would be a probable consequence of carrying out the common purpose is a party to that offence.

Trinneer and Frank had the common intention of carrying out the unlawful purpose of robbing Mrs. Vollett. Frank, in the course of the robbery, committed the offence of murdering Mrs. Vollett. Trinneer would be a party to this murder if he should have known this offence was the probable consequence of the robbery.

The key legal issue in the case arose out of the instructions to the jury. The trial judge told the jury that Trinneer was guilty of murder if he should have known that Frank would probably stab Mrs. Vollett. The Court of Appeal reversed on the grounds that the vital question was whether Trinneer should have known that Mrs. Vollett would probably die from what Frank was doing outside the car. The jury did return a couple of times for instructions on this very point before finding Trinneer guilty of murder. From the account of the trial in the Court of Appeal opinions, it was pretty clear that this was a crucial instruction in the eventual verdict. After this conviction was quashed, the Crown appealed to the Supreme Court of Canada which unanimously restored the trial verdict (in an opinion written, amazingly enough, by Mr. Justice Cartwright).

Frankly, I find the legal justification for the Supreme Court's decision extremely difficult to fathom. Trinneer was charged with being a party to the offence of murder. Murder is a form of culpable homicide in which the critical element is that someone's death be caused by an unlawful act. There was no doubt that Frank caused Mrs. Vollett's death and because he did it in circumstances defined by section 202, he was guilty of murder, no matter how unexpected this consequence was to him. However, Trinneer could be guilty of being a party to murder only if this offence (death caused by the stabbing during the robbery) should have appeared as a probable consequence. This inference from the literal wording of the sections was reinforced by the course of authority. Two Supreme Court decisions of the 1950's, *Cathro* and *Chow*

Bew,[20] appeared to require these instructions, and had been so interpreted by both the Ontario and the British Columbia Courts of Appeal.

The Supreme Court's reason for rejecting this conclusion looks specious to me. The key passage in the opinion is this one:

> The offence contemplated by Section 21(2) (that is, murder as defined in Section 202(a) and (d)) was committed when Frank inflicted the bodily harm on the deceased for the purpose of facilitating the robbery or flight. *Its character was determined* when her death ensued.[21]

The distinction drawn is purely artificial. Recall, again, that Trinneer was charged with being a party to the offence of murder. In such a case, the completed offence of murder required three elements: a *stabbing* during a *robbery* causing *death*. Trinneer could only be convicted if he should have known that murder was probable. Hence, it would seem that he must have foreseen the probability of all three elements, including especially the *death* which is the crucial element in any homicide. Yet the Supreme Court held that he need have foreseen only the *stabbing* during the *robbery*. Why? Because the "offence was committed" when Frank stabbed Mrs. Vollett to carry out the robbery. Only "its character was determined when her death ensued". I can see no support at all in the Code for this novel revision of the concept of "offence" which was used to convict Trinneer of murder.

I do not mean to suggest that there is no rationale at all to what the Court was doing. In fact, I believe that the Court's intuitive view of the common sense of the situation was the primary basis of its decision. After all, Frank was guilty of murder for stabbing Mrs. Vollett during the robbery when this caused her death, no matter how unlikely a consequence the latter was. Trinneer was Frank's accomplice. Under section 21(2) he was supposed to be responsible for Frank's offence if it was a probable result of their unlawful plan. If Frank was strictly liable for the death caused by this kind of conduct, and if Trinneer should have realized that Frank would probably use his knife, why should Trinneer be any better off when death results? Chief Justice Cartwright is saying in effect that if the primary actor is guilty of murder here, then his accomplice should be held a party to that murder.

This motivation can only faintly be discussed on the face of the very formal and legalistic opinion of the Court. Maybe I am wrong in my attempt to account for the decision, although this is the only explanation I can find which makes some sense of the argument one does see.[22]

---

20 *Cathro v. R.*, [1956] S.C.R. 101, 22 C.R. 231, 113 C.C.C. 225, 2 D.L.R. (2d) 270; *Chow Bew v. R.*, [1956] S.C.R. 124, 22 C.R. 253, 113 C.C.C. 337, 2 D.L.R. (2d) 294.

21 [1970] S.C.R. at 644.

22 I should add that I am not that happy with the rationale even in these terms. Section 202 (especially its sub-section (d)) has been called a "savage and barbarous" doctrine [Willis, "Comment" (1951), 29 Can. Bar Rev. 784 at 790]. It is

The point is that the conviction of Trinneer required an even more forced interpretation of the word "offence" in section 21(2) than did an acquittal of Carker require in the interpretation of the word "immediate" in section 17. The legislature enacts the language of the Code and this places significant controls on the way individual cases can be decided. However, judges have to interpret this language in order to decide the instant case. When an unusual variation of the general problem can be seen in its immediate human manifestation, a court which is sensitive to its responsibilities can usually find enough scope in the language to do what it believes is the right thing.

LEGAL REASONING IN THE SUPREME COURT: AN APPRAISAL

This is an appropriate place to sum up my criticism of the style of legal reasoning which is now dominant on the Supreme Court. The two issues which I have looked at in some detail—the basis of liability in tort law and the status of *mens rea* in criminal law—are very similar for my purpose. The present law stems primarily from past judicial efforts and its improvement must rely heavily on future judicial creativity. The fact that the criminal law is expressed in a legislatively enacted code places some restraints on judicial freedom, but these are more apparent than real. The attention of the legislature is primarily focused on the creation of new offences and not on the further mental element necessary for conviction. The general language used in the Code leaves substantial leeway for judicial intervention (and *Trinneer* is perhaps an extreme example of this). The wording and history of section 7 of the Code is ample legislative authority for the creative activity of the courts. Hence, in both these areas of tort law and criminal law a rational division of labour leaves the courts responsible for much of the needed renovation of this part of our law.

Because of its position in Canada's legal hierarchy, the Supreme Court has the gravest responsibility. The legislatures have not acted. The highest appellate court in Canada does not feel bound by any consensus reached in the lower courts. It is not technically bound by any foreign decisions, including those of the House of Lords. There is some recent indication that it does not feel bound by its own decisions, and

---

not the kind of provision one likes to see extended by analogy, and perhaps there are good reasons for distinguishing between the primary actor and his accomplice. Moreover, the logic of the Court's argument goes much further than the Trinneer facts. If Frank carried a gun during a robbery and it went off accidentally, he is guilty of murder if someone is killed. If Trinneer, sitting in the car, should have known Frank had a gun, he is also guilty of murder; though injury, let alone death, was the farthest thing from his mind.

this merely ratifies its earlier practice of ignoring precedents (as it did in *Munro*)[23] or artificially distinguishing them (as it did in *Farley*[24] and *Trinneer*). It may not often disagree with other judicial authorities in so explicit a fashion. However, the fact that it has done so on occasion means that it is free to do so more often if it chooses. In these areas of law the Supreme Court is rarely constrained by technically binding legal rules. Over any extended period of time, the Court has the authority to make a vital imprint on our law.

This may not seem true if we examine individual cases. Rarely is there a dramatic precedent completely overturning or redirecting an area of law (though *Drybones*, which I shall examine in chapter 7, is an exception to this rule). We must remember that the Court decides a great many cases, over one hundred a year. It is constantly involved in particular areas of the law. Its impact is like the slow dripping of water from a faucet as the judges take over the older doctrines and reshape them to their own inclination. If we look back over a period of twenty years or so, the whole sweep of the law is substantially changed. Up until late 1949, the final court of appeal for Canada was the Privy Council and the Supreme Court felt bound by decisions of the House of Lords. Twenty years later, by the 1970's, the Supreme Court has placed its distinctive, personal stamp on our law. In the next twenty years, a new Court will do the same thing. It is of the very nature of the judicial process to keep the law steadily moving as new cases throw up different issues and cast a novel light on old problems. The law changes incrementally but inescapably.

How should we assess the new legal scene? I think we must be blunt. The law is now made in Canada but this hardly justifies its shoddy quality. My detailed research discloses a general deterioration in craftsmanship in the last ten years. There is an occasional bright spot in the reports—such as *Fleming*[25] or *Beaver*[26] which were decided in the late 1950's—and I deliberately led off these last two chapters with such an example of what the Court could do if it wished. The typical decision is like the others I have discussed and criticized, or is even worse. There are undoubtedly several factors contributing to this malaise. I would identify one critical failing underlying them all. The Court refuses to admit to others (and perhaps even to itself) that it is personally responsible for adopting or retaining in Canadian law the legal rule which it then uses to resolve the case before it. Because it does not admit its immediate influence on the law, the Court does not canvass and appraise (at least on the face of its opinion) the reasons why this rule is preferable to available alternatives. Because these factors are

---

23 [1954] S.C.R. 756, [1955] 1 D.L.R. 465.
24 [1968] S.C.R. 150, 63 W.W.R. 116, 66 D.L.R. (2d) 289.
25 [1959] S.C.R. 513, 18 D.L.R. (2d) 81.
26 Fn. 2, *ante*.

not debated openly, the Supreme Court does not provide leadership in the dialogue which is necessary for any rational evolution in Canadian law. Thus it is deprived of the help that may be obtained in its very laborious task from other judges, from lawyers, from legal scholars, from legislators, and indeed from the public, which the law and the Court are supposed to serve.

What we find instead on the Supreme Court of Canada is the dominance of the formal style of legal reasoning (to use Karl Llewellyn's term). The judges write their opinions as though there is already an established legal rule which binds them. This rule is applied because the law requires it, not because the judges believe it is a desirable rule. We can sympathize with the concerns which are at the root of the formal style. Earlier, I discussed in detail the various legal values which are served by judicial fidelity to the law. They can be summarized as the ideal of predictable and impersonal adjudication in our courts. Though never perfectly achievable, this is an objective worth striving for. But, as I have tried to show, the stance of the Supreme Court is counter-productive of this ideal. If the law does not really bind the Court in the way it assumes, then acting as though it does produces an erratic and subjective process of adjudication. In every one of the cases I have discussed, the Supreme Court of Canada was not formally bound by a legal rule—whether established by statute, its own precedents, or some other judicial decision—to reach the result it did. The results it did reach were not predictable and the distinctions that were drawn often seemed arbitrary. The Court gained nothing by averting its gaze from the irrational and unfair results it seemed constrained to produce. The irony of this complete focus on "the law" is that one can still miss having any law at all.

The alternative which I propose is not a completely policy-oriented court which some political scientists seem to favour. Even in its own terms, this ideal is also self-defeating. A final court of appeal hears only a hundred or so cases a year out of the thousands of decisions which are made by the judicial process in Canada and these in turn are only a small fraction of the many millions of situations to which a legal policy may be relevant. A court which wants to have a real influence on Canadian society must articulate general, legal doctrines which other actors can understand and follow. It must then adhere to these doctrines itself in later cases in a manner which satisfies the expectations of those who have tried to comply with them. However, I believe a court can only achieve this "legal" influence if the rules it uses make sense. This is especially the case in the common law based on precedent, where we have an "unwritten law" emerging from fact-situations that are always distinguishable. Here especially the court can establish as law only a law that embodies some reasonable policy.

Why is this so? The judges of the Supreme Court are sitting in their chambers in Ottawa writing opinions that are supposed to guide the behaviour of many other people (including, I might add, their successors on later panels in this same Court). These other people must be able to understand the guidelines they are supposed to follow. To this end, they do not have to agree, on balance, that the rule laid down is the right one. However, they do have to appreciate the reasons behind the rule, to fathom what the Court is driving at. Only if they can see the point of the doctrine can they make intelligent efforts to comply with it in the many new situations they face in the real world. I suggest that this is not feasible with such a doctrine as the Supreme Court's version of "unusual danger" which produced such divergent conclusions as in *Campbell*[27] and *Farley*.[28]

We come back again to the point I have made several times before. In order to do its job as a final court of appeal, the Supreme Court must always be trying to articulate a principle on the basis of which it justifies the adoption of a legal rule in the case before it. Throughout a series of cases, the Court must formulate a theory which shows why the law is developing as it is, what are the basic values which are being implemented, and then how the law can be sensibly applied in different situations. The Court was groping towards this objective in *Beaver*[29] and *Pierce Fisheries*.[30] The distinction it drew in these cases may not be acceptable to everyone, but it was reasonable. The many participants in the Canadian legal system can start to work out the implications of these doctrines. As the principle is formulated over a period of time, and reflected in many legal rules and decisions, it produces a body of law that is sufficiently "reckonable" to serve the legal values which a court is supposed to respect. Can one really say the same about the doctrine defining police use of firearms in making an arrest, as reflected in a pair of decisions like *Smythson*[31] and *Beim?*[32]

This is not the only reason for requiring continual judicial appeals to principle. Fidelity to law is an important value but it is not absolute. Judges who have made and are continuing to make our law must be equally concerned with the fairness and wisdom of the legal doctrines they are using. A legal principle such as *mens rea* in criminal law, or negligence in tort law, is the vehicle through which the resources of the judicial process can be brought to bear for the incremental refinement of the whole area of law. As stated earlier, there are limitations on the wisdom, legitimacy, and effectiveness of judicial law reform. If a court justifies its innovations by reference to established principles, it will respect these limits. However, there are institutional reasons why

---

27 [1964] S.C.R. 85, 46 W.W.R. 79, 43 D.L.R. (2d) 341.

28 Fn. 24, *ante*.

29 Fn. 2, *ante*.

30 Fn. 6, *ante*.

31 [1959] S.C.R. 615, 30 C.R. 209, 124 C.C.C. 1, 19 D.L.R. (2d) 1.

32 [1965] S.C.R. 638.

the courts are often the only, and sometimes even the best, source of necessary legal reforms from within our governmental structure. Only a court that is ready to overturn outmoded legal rules which can now be seen to be irrational anomalies in the general thrust of the law (and the case of *Fleming v. Atkinson*[33] is a beautiful example), will fulfill this indispensable role in securing a just and coherent legal system.

---

[33] Fn. 25, *ante.*

The Supervisor of the Administrative Process

5

THE SUPREME COURT AND CANADIAN LABOUR LAW[1]

"Certainly it is easier to criticize the work of the Court than to perform it. It behooves any critic of the Court's performance to close on a note reminiscent of the wall plaque of frontier times: 'Don't shoot the piano player, he's doing his best.' It is still possible, however, to wish that he would stick to his piano and not try to be a one-man band."

(Philip Kurland, writing of the U.S. Supreme Court)

We turn now to the Supreme Court's work in a very different legal environment. The previous two chapters have examined the Court's performance in the development of traditional legal concepts in spheres where judges operate essentially by themselves. Labour relations presents much more controversial problems to a judge and one reason is that here the courts are in constant contact with other law-making institutions. The legislature has established a comprehensive regulatory framework for collective bargaining which radically diverges from the common law structure formulated in earlier judicial decisions. Immediate responsibility for administering the statute has been given to a specialized tribunal, a labour relations board. What is the proper stance of the Supreme Court of Canada in such a public law area, as it interacts with legislatures and boards? We had a preliminary glimpse of the problem in the *Barbara Jarvis* case in chapter 2, but I must now develop

---

1 My detailed examination of the Supreme Court's labour relations decisions is contained in "The 'Slippery Slope' of Judicial Intervention" (1971), 9 O.H.L.J. 1. I have also relied on a very recent study of the Court's administrative law work outside the labour law field, published by my colleague Peter Hogg as "The Supreme Court of Canada and Administrative Law, 1949-71" in (1973), 11 O.H.L.J. 187.

the theme in greater detail. Though I will do so primarily with reference to the labour law work of the Supreme Court, I shall refer to a pair of interesting decisions under different statutes which furnish apt illustrations of my general hypothesis.

THE LEGALITY OF THE COMPULSORY CHECK-OFF

Again, I will begin with a good decision—*Le Syndicat Catholique v. La Compagnie Paquet*[2]—an example of what the Court is capable of achieving, although a standard it does not always meet. The Syndicat was a union certified under the Labour Relations Act, R.S.Q. 1941, c. 162A, and after a strike, it signed a collective agreement with Paquet, the employer. This agreement provided for a "check-off" clause whereby all the members of the bargaining unit were compelled to have union dues deducted from their pay cheques. The non-union employees (some 254 of the 607 members of the unit) objected, and the company decided to deposit the money from their wages in a special bank account. The union sued the company for the money under its collective agreement.

The Quebec Court of Appeal (and a minority on the Supreme Court) rejected the claim on the ground that the compulsory check-off was null and void. It was not a "condition de travail" under the labour legislation and thus was outside the contracting power of the union and the company to impose on non-consenting members of the bargaining unit. Mr. Justice Taschereau said that it was not a condition of employment because it was concerned simply with the financial administration of the union. Only traditional objects of collective agreements—such as wages, hours of work or vacations—were contemplated by the legislation, not recent innovations such as this one which stemmed from the famous Rand formula of 1946.[3] As a result, the union was limited by the law of mandate, or agency, which required the actual consent of each of the employees who were its principals.

Mr. Justice Judson wrote the opinion of the majority of the Supreme Court which countered this argument and upheld the union's claim. Just as in *Fleming v. Atkinson*[4] (decided about the same time), Judson J. displayed a feeling for the practical realities of the situation and was sensitive to the underlying direction in which the law was moving. Consider his characterization of the check-off clause:

---

2 *Syndicat Catholique des Employées de Magasins v. Paquet Ltée*, [1959] S.C.R. 206, 18 D.L.R. (2d) 346.

3 This was formulated in the *Ford Motor Co.* arbitration award of Mr. Justice Rand, reported in Canadian Labour Law Reporter, Vol. 1, para. 18,001.

4 [1959] S.C.R. 513, 18 D.L.R. (2d) 81.

The object of the clause is well-known and obvious. It is to throw upon all employees, whether members of the union or not, equal responsibility for the financial upkeep of the union on the theory that the gains achieved by the union on behalf of all employees must, at least to the extent of financial support, be paid for by all. For the union, the advantages and convenience of a compulsory check-off are equally obvious.[5]

This is a very different view of the union's objective than that of Taschereau J., who analogized the clause to one which discriminated against racial or religious groups. Nor was Judson J. prepared to confine the statutory phrase "condition de travail" to the traditional terms of collective agreements which were common when the statute was enacted:

> How can one validly infer that a compulsory check-off clause is not a necessary incident of employer-employee relations or is not the proper concern of those who are negotiating about these relations? It is not an assumption that would be made by one of the parties. The other party that now attacks the clause signed the agreement. The clause is one that has been used in collective agreements for some considerable time. This, in itself, is some indication that it has been found useful to and is accepted as desirable by those who are the interested parties in these agreements.[6]

In the same way Judson J. refused to cabin the statutory character of the collective agreement within the straitjacket of traditional legal concepts:

> The collective agreement is a recent development in our law and has a character all of its own. To attempt to engraft upon it the concepts embodied in the law of mandate would, in my opinion, effectively frustrate the whole operation of the Act.[7]

These comments are reflections of a basic attitude which permeates Mr. Justice Judson's opinion and one which I think is the precisely appropriate stance for the Court to take in the development of labour relations law. This is the posture of judicial restraint. The same framework of legal, institutional, and policy criteria which leads me to advocate judicial innovation in the areas of tort law and criminal law takes me in the opposite direction in labour law. If we take a realistic view of the dimensions of the legal and social problems of collective bargaining, the attitude of the Court should be one of extreme caution. As Judson J. held in *Paquet*, this means "don't put artificial roadblocks in the way of the agreement of the parties and don't try to justify them in terms of transplanted legal concepts!"

---

5 [1959] S.C.R. at 208.

6 *Ibid.*, at 212.

7 *Ibid.*, at 215.

The stance adopted by the majority in *Paquet* is right because it reflects an established legal principle, but one of a very different kind. Unlike the principle of *mens rea*, it did not develop out of centuries of common law precedents. Rather it was imposed by the legislature as the basis for a substantial departure from the traditional law. Labour relations are now primarily regulated by a comprehensive statutory scheme. At its heart is the policy that *free collective* bargaining is the preferred method of settling terms of employment (or "conditions de travail"). The statute provides a legal facility for employees who want to utilize their collective strength as a countervailing force to that of the employer. The employees are free to accept or reject the union as their bargaining agent and they can register their views through a secret ballot. Once a majority of the employees decides in favour of the union, then the union has a statutory authority to negotiate on behalf of all, and to bind the dissenting minority. Collective bargaining is free in a second sense. The government does not set or control the terms of the bargain. It assumes that there is a relative equality of strength between the parties and that each side is best aware of its own needs and interests. The policy of the law is to let them trade and compromise until they reach agreement. The incentive for each is that failure to agree means a strike or a lockout, with consequent losses to both sides.

Anyone acquainted with the evolution and present structure of modern labour legislation must recognize that this is the theory which underlies its many detailed provisions. It is also clear that the value of free collective bargaining is not a self-evident truth. The policy was born in controversy and so lives on. Some people argue that unions are too strong and must be restricted. Others contend that unions are too weak and must be artificially aided. Many observers have recently become disenchanted with both sides and believe that industrial strife is bad, agreements are inflationary, and the system should be replaced by something like compulsory arbitration. No doubt there are situations in which any one of these views is reinforced. Yet all of this is basically irrelevant. The point is that free collective bargaining is the rationale of the existing legal structure. There is no natural necessity about the policy, and judges can reasonably dispute its value (just as they might disagree with a fault-based system of tort liability or lack of *mens rea* as excusing criminal behaviour). However, as long as this policy is at the basis of our laws as established by the legislature, judges must comply with it and try to follow its implications for the new problems thrown up in litigation.

Why does this principle suggest that judicial restraint is the proper stance of the courts in a case like *Paquet*? The reason is that the position of the minority would require the courts to be constantly involved in deciding what are the proper terms to be included in a collective agreement. Judges would have to make these decisions without any meaningful statutory guidance and without even a hint in the legislation that there should be limits. Judges would inevitably make these decisions in the light of their own partial and often stereotyped view of what they are used to seeing in a collective agreement. The result might well be legalistic barriers in the way of creative negotiations about new problems in labour relations (as in the area of management's rights, for example).

There are even more harmful implications of the Taschereau opinion. The essence of collective bargaining is a struggle between countervailing powers. Remember, then, that the attack on the check-off clause stemmed from a combination of the company and the dissenting non-union minority. If the Court sustained this challenge, it would create a legal rule that would aid the company in its struggle with the union. This is the real impact of just about any doctrine in collective bargaining, but the thrust of this particular rule would be especially baneful because it would seriously splinter the bargaining power of the employees.

Those aware of the course of labour history will appreciate the lack of legitimacy in any such judge-made rule. For over 100 years, the judiciary developed a common law framework, founded on the precepts of economic individualism, which strongly favoured employers in their bid to stem the growth of union power. Grudgingly the courts retreated to a stance of non-intervention when unions rode other social forces to a position of strength. Union security clauses are still productive of distaste on the part of judges whose perceptions are formed by such common law values as the individual's "right to work." (Mr. Justice Taschereau, for example, compared the compulsory check-off to a provision limiting employment to members of a particular race or religion.) However, now that the legislatures have intervened in a comprehensive fashion to recognize and domesticate collective bargaining, our judges are obligated to resist the temptation and to stay out.

Unlike the areas of tort law and criminal law which I have analyzed, it is politically realistic to rely on the legislature for the necessary innovations and reforms in labour law. An issue such as the "Rand formula" involves visible controversies over socio-economic principles. Labour law policies form part of a party programme, figure in election campaigns, and receive ample legislative attention and debate. Industrial relations are polarized between important interest groups who throw their support to different sides in the political process. Any change in the law has at least an indirect effect on the balance of power between labour and management and reform usually involves a comprehensive look at many such issues. If changes or additions are to be made to the law, each side should be required to appeal to the representative institution of government. Legislators will be attuned to the different views of an electorate which is aware of the problems and implications of union security, including the check-off clause. Both sides are capable of gaining the ear of the government and making their wishes known. The result will likely be a process of political bargaining and compromise which produces statutory changes that will help both unions and employers to some extent and will carry a degree of authority which is necessary for the long-run success of any law. If the compulsory check-off was to be effectively prohibited, this should have been done by the legislature, not by the Supreme Court of Canada in *Paquet*. A realistic view of the judicial role tells us why and also explains why a different conclusion can be justified for the judicial elimination of the cattle-trespass immunity in *Fleming v. Atkinson*.

We can summarize the argument I have made in these terms. The stance of judicial restraint in labour relations law is needed in order to preserve the neutrality of judge-made law in the area. This neutrality is required both by the substance of our labour relations policy (which favours free collective bargaining) and the unrepresentative character of the judicial process. Judicial restraint is not the same as judicial inaction. A court is not given the luxury of doing nothing. It has to decide each case and in doing so it necessarily settles the law where previously it was ambiguous (as was true in *Paquet*, for example). What the courts must be careful to avoid is the imposition of new restrictions on one side which necessarily strengthen the bargaining position of the other and artificially distort the outcome of free negotiations.

Paquet is a fairly straightforward example of this thesis. The important problem area where courts must constantly remind themselves of it is on the question of picketing. Canadian legislation deals comprehensively with the legality of strikes; with rare exceptions it speaks only tangentially to picketing. Hence, the Canadian law of picketing is largely judge-made. The Supreme Court of Canada has made an important contribution to the evolution of that law. I have analyzed these cases elsewhere and concluded that the problems are too complex to be usefully reviewed here.[8] The one key situation which the Supreme Court has not directly addressed is the legality of consumer-directed secondary picketing. The Ontario Court of Appeal, in *Hersees of Woodstock v. Goldstein*,[9] laid down a blanket rule that this union tactic is illegal, even though it is completely outside the scope of the statute. This is precisely the kind of legal innovation which, in my view, a court is not entitled to make.[10] If and when this issue is raised on a further appeal to the Supreme Court of Canada, one can only hope it will adopt the same position of judicial neutrality which was so well defended in *Paquet*.

---

[8] See my article, "The 'Slippery Slope'", cited in fn. 1, *ante*, at 34 to 50 inclusive.

[9] [1963] 2 O.R. 81, 38 D.L.R. (2d) 449 (C.A.), criticized in Arthurs, "Comment" (1963), 41 Can. Bar Rev. 573.

[10] For reasons which I have outlined in detail, in connection with this very case, in Weiler, "Legal Values and Judicial Decision-making" (1970), 48 Can. Bar Rev. 1 at 42-46.

JUDICIAL REVIEW OF LABOUR RELATIONS BOARDS: THE LEGAL ASSUMPTIONS

Rather than following the tortuous path of our common law of picketing, we must turn to a different area of our law of industrial relations—the one in which the *Barbara Jarvis* case arose. The reader will remember my analysis of that case as an illustration of the problem of interpretation of an existing legal rule. We focused then on the question of which conclusion was the correct one and what was the kind of reasoning which could justify the answer. I deliberately left out of that discussion the underlying institutional dimension. The body which originally made the determination in favour of Barbara Jarvis was the Ontario Labour Relations Board, an administrative agency. The body which ultimately reversed this decision was the Supreme Court of Canada, a court. Labour relations is typical of modern regulation, not only in that a comprehensive, statutory scheme has superseded the traditional common law, but also in that a separate agency was established to administer this statute. In this chapter, we shall consider this pervasive theme of our law, the proper relationship between the courts and the boards.

The legal problem in the *Barbara Jarvis* case was whether the complainant was a "person" within the contemplation of the unfair labour practice sections of the Labour Relations Act, R.S.O. 1960, c. 202 [now c. 232]. After some reflection on the underlying social problems and objectives of the legislation, we saw that the answer is not as obvious as it might appear at first blush. Personally, I think the Labour Board was correct in upholding the claim under the Act but the different conclusion of the Supreme Court majority is not an unreasonable interpretation. But let us look at another provision of that same Act:

> Section 80 [now section 97]: No decision, order, direction, declaration or ruling of the Board shall be questioned or reviewed in any court, and no order shall be made or process entered, or proceedings taken in any court, whether by way of . . . certiorari . . . or otherwise, to question, review, prohibit or restrain the Board or any of its proceedings.

Can it be denied that a decision of the Board was being questioned and reviewed in a court, and that these proceedings were taken by way of *certiorari* (which was the procedure used by A.M.S.) to review the Board? How can the lawyers find any ambiguities in this prohibition? In fact, the Supreme Court majority felt this was no problem at all, and worthy of only a passing comment:

> The effect of the section [80], if it receives the construction most favourable to the appellant [Barbara Jarvis], is to oust the jurisdiction of the

superior Courts to interfere with any decision of the Board which is made in exercise of the powers conferred upon it by the Legislature; within the ambit of these powers it may err in fact or in law; but I cannot take the section to mean that if the Board purports to make an order which, on the true construction of the Act, it has no *jurisdiction* to make, the person affected thereby is left without a remedy. . . . The extent of the Board's *jurisdiction* is fixed by the statute which creates it and cannot be enlarged by a mistaken view entertained by the Board as to the meaning of that statute.[11]

At least one member of the Court was not persuaded by this legal mystification. Mr. Justice Abbott upheld the appeal on this very short ground:

The primary purpose of the Labour Relations Act is to provide harmonious industrial relations within the province. A board such as the Labour Relations Board, experienced in the field of management relations, representing both organized employers, organized labour, and the public, and presided over by a legally trained chairman, ought to be at least as competent and as well suited to determine questions arising in the course of the administration of the Act as a Superior Court judge.

In enacting s. 80, the Legislature has recognized that fact and has indicated in the clearest possible language that the workings of the Board are not to be unnecessarily impeded by legal technicalities. The duty of the Courts is to apply that section, not to attempt to circumvent it.[12]

Notwithstanding the appeal in Abbott J.'s quick, pragmatic disposal of the issue, it cannot be dismissed that easily. There is a long standing tradition that "privative clauses" such as s. 80 do not suffice to exclude review of administrative decisions infected by "jurisdictional" errors. The reason is that a decision taken by a Board when it has no jurisdiction is not really a "decision" at all, at least as far as the protection of s. 80 is concerned. What is the rationale for this? The statute gives the Board jurisdiction to deal only with "persons" who can be "employees", not with persons who are in a managerial capacity. When the Board purports to make an order about a person such as Barbara Jarvis, what it does is a complete nullity and the Court retains the power to so declare in a *certiorari* proceeding. This is the rationale behind another basic principle of Canadian law, firmly established in cases like *Barbara Jarvis*, to the effect that judicial review is always available in the "superior courts" to correct the jurisdictional errors of "inferior tribunals" such as administrative boards. This principle embodies the policy that judicial supervision of such decisions is a good thing; indeed, it is even more, it is an essential ingredient of the Rule of Law. Legislative supervision of such tribunals is inadequate because "legislative correction, no matter

---

11 [1964] S.C.R. at 502, emphasis added.

12 *Ibid.*, at 506.

how efficient its operation in the future, will not restore to the particular litigant his right taken from him by the unauthorized and illegal action of the inferior tribunal".[13] With a few brave exceptions, this has become a dogma within the ideology of Canadian lawyers. That should not deter us from asking a few questions about it.

The first question, and the one asked by Mr. Justice Judson, in *Barbara Jarvis,* is what is meant by a jurisdictional error. The idea is easy to grasp in the abstract. The legislature has carved out a defined sphere of authority in which the Board is entitled to operate. "Within the ambit of these powers", the Board has exclusive authority and "it may err in fact or in law". However, there must be some limits on what it can do. One commentator suggested a "wild example":[14] suppose that "a labour relations board certified a union as bargaining agent of the members of the provincial legislature and named the Lieutenant Governor as the employer". He asks rhetorically, "should the courts simply throw up their hands . . . and say that the only redress lies in the legislature?" and replies confidently "they would be abandoning their constitutional duty to do so". The difficulty with this rationale is that jurisdiction is a "verbal coat of too many colours". No one has ever proposed a satisfactory criterion for labelling one kind of issue "jurisdictional" and the other a matter within the Board's exclusive powers.

After all, what the legislature has done is to lay down a comprehensive legal framework for regulating labour relations. It wants all of these standards adhered to and obviously hopes the Board will make no errors in interpreting any of its wishes. It has not said that some standards are especially vital, and need judicial review, and called them matters of "jurisdiction" (while leaving the remainder within the ambit of the Board's exclusive powers). Instead, it has laid down a blanket prohibition on any review at all. It is the Court which has read in the limitation about jurisdictional errors to preserve the principle of judicial review. The Court used this concept to quash the *Barbara Jarvis* decision but there is not one word in its opinion which tells us why the legal definition of "person" is a condition of the Board's jurisdiction. Perhaps the comment made by an American judge about hard core pornography is *à propos* here: "I may not be able to define it, but I know it when I see it." A sceptic might suggest that if a court sees an interpretation of the statute that it disagrees with as a matter of law, it calls it a jurisdictional error so it can review it. Only if it doesn't find an error will it characterize a matter as within the Board's exclusive authority "to err in fact or in law".

If one considers the total pattern of judicial decisions reviewing Canadian labour boards, this appears to be the only rationale (and at the moment I am not questioning its desirability). Some confirmation

---

13 Or so said Mr. Justice Spence in the *Barbara Jarvis* case, *ibid.,* at 524-25.
14 Lyon, "Comment" (1971), 49 Can. Bar Rev. 365 at 375.

of this thesis may be found in another instance of Supreme Court intervention in Ontario Labour Relations—the *Metropolitan Life Insurance* case.[15] In this case the Ontario Board had certified without a vote the Operating Engineers Union to represent the insurance company's maintenance and cleaning personnel. Under the statute, certification without a vote was allowed only when "the Board was satisfied" that at least 55% of the employees in the unit were "members of the trade union". Under the union constitution, however, only qualified engineers could become members and none of these employees had this qualification. The board decision was based on its policy of not considering itself bound by the terms of the union's constitution in determining who was a "member" under that section of the Act. This policy had originated in 1951 and out of it had evolved four distinct standards which set a uniform pattern for all trade unions seeking certification. To become a member every employee had to make a written application to the union and personally pay a $1.00 initiation fee as a sign that he knew of the commitment he was making in membership. There could be no discrimination in membership against occupational groups the union was seeking to represent because of the danger of a union shop clause which would deprive the employees of their jobs. However, the board looked at the actual treatment of the employees, whether they were allowed *de facto* full participation in the workings and benefits of the union, as the criterion for membership for this purpose. The board did not want to fall into the problems of proving compliance with the internal union membership procedures and it was concerned about the difficulty of changing out-of-date craft requirements in constitutions of international unions which might not be cognizant of the niceties of the Ontario statute.

In sum, the board took a very pragmatic, industrial relations view of the nature and function of union membership under section 7 of the Labour Relations Act, R.S.O. 1960, c. 202. Its justification for this view was carefully spelled out in a detailed board opinion in the *Metropolitan Life* case itself. As stated earlier, the policy originated over twenty years before and had been elaborated since then, during a time when the legislation underwent extensive revision without touching this issue. However the board's treatment of the problem deviated from the view taken in the courts, in a different context, about the legal basis for union membership. In current judicial analysis, rights of membership depended on a contractual relationship which was founded on the union constitution; in this case, the employees could not and did not fulfill one of the essential conditions for this contract. Undoubtedly, there was

---

15 *Metro. Life Ins. Co. v. Internat. Union of Operating Engineers*, [1970] S.C.R. 425, 11 D.L.R. (3d) 336. The background and legislative consequences of this decision are usefully recounted in a Student "Comment" (1970), 28 Faculty of Law Rev. 109.

a possibility of conflict between these two alternative interpretations of the meaning of "member" in section 7 of the Labour Relations Act.

Yet underlying this substantive issue is the pervasive institutional problem. Whose view is to be determinative, the board's or the court's? To put this latter question in the conventional legal jargon, is the meaning of "member" a jurisdictional matter or one within the powers of the board? We have already seen that section 7(3) required that "the *Board* be satisfied" about employee membership in the union. Then section 79(1) was also relevant to this problem:

> The Board has exclusive jurisdiction to exercise the power conferred upon it by or under this Act and to determine all questions of fact or law that arise in any matter before it, and the action or decision of the Board thereon is final and conclusive for all purposes.

If there was ever an issue of statutory interpretation which on the face of it appeared to be within the jurisdiction of the board, this was it. In *Barbara Jarvis*, the board was extending its reach into a new area of human relationships and thus lessening the significance of one of the key boundaries drawn by the legislature (in terms of managerial personnel). *Metropolitan Life* arose at the heart of the board's work, the certification process. It involved the interpretation of only one of dozens of statutory terms channelling that process. If the board is given the power to err in law within the ambit of its powers (as Cartwright C.J. said it was in *Barbara Jarvis*), then this is clearly a decision within its proper sphere of authority. The lower court judge thought so and the unanimous Ontario Court of Appeal agreed, both after an extensive review of the authorities.

Yet, perhaps predictably, the Supreme Court of Canada reversed the Ontario Board, again in an opinion written by Chief Justice Cartwright. What was its reason?

> the Board has failed to deal with the question remitted to it (*i.e.* whether the employees in question were members of the Union at the relevant date) and instead has decided a question which was not remitted to it (*i.e.* whether in regard to those employees there has been fulfilment of the conditions stated above).

> I regard the law as well settled that in so proceeding the Board, by asking itself the wrong question, has stepped outside its jurisdiction and that ss. 79 and 80 of the Act cannot avail to protect its certificate.[16]

This level of analysis is simply not good enough for a nation's highest court. It is very clear, not only on the face of the board's award but even in the summary of its argument in the Court's opinion, that the board did address itself to the meaning of the term "member" in section 7 of the Act. It concluded that this meant a person who satisfied the

---

16 [1970] S.C.R. at 435.

board's own announced standards, rather than the terms of the union's constitution. This policy was visible. I have tried to indicate why it was at least reasonable and the legislature had not thought it desirable to change it. The Court clearly disagreed with the board's view of the law and substituted the criterion of the union's constitution, although there was not one word of explanation for this judgment. Was it really fair, though, to say that the board failed to ask the right *question*, simply because the Court disagreed with the board's *answer*? The adoption of this approach indicates that the Court is extending its powers of review even beyond the limits of *Barbara Jarvis*. Whenever the board makes a decision which is based on *any* error of law, it can be said to have asked the wrong question; when it does so, it "has stepped outside its jurisdiction" and the Court can ignore privative clauses even as strongly worded as sections 79 and 80. *Metropolitan Life* is a key example of several recent Supreme Court decisions extending the scope of judicial review of administrative action.

IS JUDICIAL SUPERVISION JUSTIFIED?

This brings us to the question which is at the heart of this chapter. Is judicial review of administrative action a good thing or not? There are few questions about the judicial role in Canada which are of more importance right now. Within the Canadian legal establishment there appears to be no doubt. Judicial review is intrinsically good, and the more of it the better. The lawyers have captured the ears of our governments and we see a rash of legislation extending and facilitating judicial control. I must be frank and say that this is a tide which is impossible to stem at this point. However, this makes analysis of the basic question more, not less, important. Every day our judges must decide about the spirit with which they will carry on this function. That judgment can only be made with an appreciation of the arguments directed to the fundamental issue, why do we want judicial review, if we do?

If we look at the question realistically, I think we should start with the position that review is presumptively undesirable. No doubt this will offend the ideologues who believe there is something almost sacred about this judicial role. To use Holmes' phrase, I want to wash these legal assumptions in some cynical acid. Why does a legislature create an administrative agency in the first place? One primary objective is an efficient resolution of problems under the statute. There are at least three facets to this objective; the administrative process is quicker than the courts, it is cheaper, and it is much more informal. Introduce judicial review and what do we have? Time-consuming litigation, expensive lawyers, and the rigid formality and mysteries of the courts. Surely it is agreed that these consequences are undesirable. They may be necessary costs to the achievement of a greater good, but the point is that we must establish that there is such an attainable objective. The costs are real and occur every time that judicial review takes place. I suggest that this throws the onus on those who want it to show that there is a realistic justification for its existence.

The defenders of judicial review are ready to meet the challenge. They believe that the process of review will enhance the quality of decisions we will receive under the statute. Indeed, they have a definite view about what this quality consists of. What do we find in the McRuer Report (in which the legal ideology comes to full bloom?)

> The most secure safeguard for the civil right of the individual to have his rights determined according to the Rule of Law lies in the independence of review by the courts.[17]

Given this objective, who is going to worry about a little time and money? So firmly convinced are the courts of the desirability of their supervision that they treat it as a judge-made, constitutional convention. As *Barbara Jarvis* and *Metropolitan Life* show, it is well-nigh impossible for a legislature to eliminate judicial review, no matter how extensive the terms of a privative clause.

What is the rationale of this position? The legislature created the agency or board with specific powers to perform a limited mission. The tribunal is clearly not intended to be a general cure-all for any problem its members may see in society. The statute defines this mission by means of the legal standards laid down in its many provisions. If the agency does not comply with these standards, then the wishes of the elected representatives in the legislature will not be carried out. Moreover, private citizens who are aware of and rely on these legal rules in the statute should have the right to expect that government boards will also respect them in dealing with individual cases. If these agencies do not obey the law, affected citizens must be able to go to court to get the decision quashed. The point of judicial review, then, is to ensure that government officials respect the law as laid down by the legislature when they make decisions affecting the interests of the individuals.

I suggest that the argument is vitiated by a common logical fallacy. It assumes precisely the issue which it must prove. The flavour of this assumption can be gathered from these quotations from a rather sophisticated recent defence of judicial review.[18] Arguing against privative clauses, the writer says that they could give tribunals "a carte blanche, enabling the board to ignore the words of the Act and to substitute policies it deems desirable for those prescribed in the Act", to let them "with impunity, decide questions of law in any way they see fit without regard to law". His tacit assumption is especially clear in this passage:

---

17 "Royal Commission Inquiry into Civil Rights in Ontario" (1968), Vol. 1, at 279.
18 Lyon, "Comment", cited in fn. 14, *ante*, at 366, 371 and 373.

> To put this proposition in the form of a rhetorical question, how can a question be one of law when the person who decides it can, with impunity, decide it according to whatever criteria he chooses, and even contrary to law? This would be the effect of applying the blanket immunity from [judicial] review.[19]

The prevailing rationale of judicial review hinges on precisely this proposition—that the law of the statute is what the courts say it is. Because *Barbara Jarvis* was not a "person" under the Labour Relations Act and the employees of *Metropolitan Life* were not "members" of their union, then it is true that the Ontario Labour Board did not respect the law laid down by the legislature and thus interfered with the legal rights of the employer. But how do we know what is the legal meaning of the terms "person" or "member" in this statute? Because the Supreme Court of Canada has told us so. But then why is its opinion decisive? Because we have a system of judicial review of labour board interpretations of the statute. But why do we have this system? Because this is necessary to protect the legal rights of the individual under the "law" laid down by the legislature.

The circularity of the argument can be seen in another way. Suppose the broader meaning of these two legal terms was the proper one. Then Barbara Jarvis was illegally deprived of her right to reinstatement in her job and the employees at Metropolitan Life of their bargaining rights with the union of their choice. If there were no judicial review, and the Board's interpretation of the legislation was final, this would be the law. The point is that the law does not come "ready-made" on the face of the statute. As I have tried to show in my analysis of legal rules, the decision in difficult cases requires reflection, sound reasoning, and then a sensitive judgment from the interpreter. Once we have an interpretation, the law will be clarified, but we know this is the law only *ex post facto*. The crux of the issue in judicial review is who should have the final "say" in settling the law, court or board. Right now the courts have the last word, but this is merely a fact, not a justification. As Mr. Justice Jackson once said of his own U.S. Supreme Court, "we are not final because we are infallible; we are infallible only because we are final".

The nerve of the problem of judicial review is who is likely to exercise better judgment in unravelling the mysteries of the Labour Relations Act—the Supreme Court of Canada or the Ontario Labour Relations Board. In considering this issue free of the traditional identification of the law with the judges' opinion about the law, we must return to the deliberate legislative decision to leave the administration of the statute to a board, rather than the ordinary courts. There is another reason for this besides efficiency; it is also assumed that the agency will display

---

19 *Ibid.*, at 373.

greater expertise. This should be a critical factor in deciding who is to have final authority.

The notion of administrative competence also has three ingredients. The first stems from the major reason for the adoption of new statutory programmes—the belief that the traditional common law approach is inadequate to deal with the social problems presented by the area (and labour relations is a classic instance). However, there is a natural tendency for the judges who helped develop the older approach to remain wedded to its assumptions, even in interpreting the new legislation. A successful implementation of a different policy, especially in the earlier years, will require the appointment of individuals with a fresh and more receptive outlook. Secondly, when the government makes this appointment, it will realize that it is choosing someone for an agency which will be operating in only one area of law. Usually this selection will be a person with a background of training and experience in the area, who may well have done distinguished work in some other capacity. By contrast, it is only by accident that a judge, selected for a court which general jurisdiction, will ever have had prior experience in the particular area of administrative law in which he is now asked to intervene.

Finally, and most important, the members of an administrative board receive an extensive on-the-job training. Every day they hear and decide new cases and soon gain experience in just about every problem the statute can present. This constant exposure contributes two key elements to the administrator's judgment about the law. He soon obtains an understanding of the underlying socio-economic problems which the legal rules are supposed to solve and he sees how the various elements of labour relations law and policy fit together in a systematic way. Courts, by comparison, present all of the risks of "absentee management". They see the area only sporadically, and those few cases that do reach the court tend to reflect the pathology of the system. Not only will judges have very little personal background in the area, but the adversary process and the procedure for administrative review is not really designed to educate them. Judges have very little sensitivity to the complexity of the situations into which they intrude with their doctrines. There is nothing invidious about this comparison of judges and administrators. The point is that the latter is a specialist and he would have to try hard not to become more competent in his own area than a judge. But we must recognize this as a fact which is critical to the justification of judicial review. Not only is it inefficient to try for a second opinion, but there is a real danger that this second conclusion will be unwise.

Can this two-fold presumption against judicial review be overcome? I think it can, in certain areas and for specific reasons. Let's consider some, with a few Supreme Court cases as examples. In the first place, labour boards, like all specialized tribunals, do present some dangers of government by experts. Specialists tend to be entranced by their own limited objectives and may not always appreciate the claims of other values in our society. There is a role for courts, who do have a general picture of the legal order, to protect these external and enduring principles against erosion for what the expert believes is the immediate need. Two such cases came to the Supreme Court of Canada at the same time in 1953.

In *Alliance des Professeurs*,[20] the teachers in the French Catholic schools of Montreal went out on an illegal strike after a long and acrimonious dispute with the Montreal Catholic School Commission. As a result, the Quebec Labour Relations Board cancelled the union's bargaining certificate, without notice to the union or any hearing. In fact, the board seems to have relied simply on the public outcry to initiate its action, because it was proved that it prepared the order of cancellation before the employer had even applied for it. The Supreme Court of Canada unanimously held that this was a breach of the principles of "natural justice" which were interpreted as being a necessary condition to the legality of any such order. The maxim *audi alteram partem* required the board to wait and hear the union position about whether it had done anything which could justify cancelling its certificate under the statute.

This is exactly the kind of case in which judicial review is appropriate. The situation demands no judicial deference to administrative expertise in the specialized area of labour law. It is an ancient and well founded tradition of our legal system that important decisions of this kind should only be taken after each party affected has had a full opportunity to present his side of the case. This is not peculiar to labour law: it is a general standard of due process and fairness to the individual which should be adhered to by any such body. Officials have an all-too-human tendency to become so caught up in their substantive objectives that they forget for the moment the importance of the means through which they are carried out. With their centuries of experience in procedural issues, the courts are the appropriate institutions to enforce these more fundamental principles. The Supreme Court has performed this task without placing excessive constraints on efficient and flexible administration; if anything, there are cases where it may have been too deferential. Still, in sum, judicial review of administrative procedure is defensible.

To some extent, the same analysis is applicable to judicial review of the substantive administrative decision. A very good example is the case of *Smith and Rhuland*.[21] Here the Nova Scotia Labour Board was given power to certify unions which satisfied the usual statutory conditions. An otherwise qualified union was refused a certificate because of the alleged "Communist domination" of its executive. The rationale for the board policy may have been the supposed dangers to labour peace

---

20 *Alliance des Professeurs Catholique de Montréal v. Lab. Rel. Bd. (Que.)*, [1953] 2 S.C.R. 120.
21 *Smith & Rhuland v. R.*, [1953] 2 S.C.R. 95, 107 C.C.C. 43, [1953] 3 D.L.R. 690.

from political strikes aimed at the country's social structure (and there was some apparent basis to this expectation from experience with Communist-led unions elsewhere).

Again, the Supreme Court of Canada was not prepared to allow these concerns of the specialist to override the more fundamental values of the Canadian legal order. There was no law in Canada against belonging to the Communist party. Party members ran for, and held, legislative office. There was no principle of guilt by association which allowed the board to impute destructive intentions to one Communist because of the actions of another. The Canadian government relied on the enlightened opinion of its citizens against "the dangers from the propagation of the Communist dogma" and the Labour Board must also show "faith in the intelligence and loyalty of the (union) membership". As Mr. Justice Rand put it: "These are the assumptions that have shaped the legislative policy of the country to the present time and they underlie the statute before us".[22]

Smith and Rhuland is an appropriate case for judicial review for much the same reason as *Alliance*. The Labour Relations Act is not the only legal policy of importance in our law. "An agency is not an island entire of itself. It is one of the many rooms in the magnificent mansion of the law."[23] Any one labour case may be the point of intersection with other statutes, basic doctrines of the common law, constitutional limitations, etc. A specialized administrative tribunal will likely be neither that knowledgeable nor that concerned about the claims of external legal principles which place limits on the pursuit of its own objectives. We are right to rely on the courts, with their view of the legal order as a whole, to be the architects responsible for securing the necessary harmony among these conflicting legal doctrines.

What about a case where an administrator's decision is based on a *bona fide* interpretation of the statute he is to apply and there are no external legal principles which are relevant to the case? Can judicial review be justified in such a case? Let us look at a third Supreme Court decision where I think review was appropriate. In *Beatty v. Kozak*,[24] the Court was concerned with a Saskatchewan statute which gave the police power to arrest a person "apparently mentally ill . . . and conducting himself in a manner which in a normal person would be disorderly". Beatty, the deputy police chief, acting on the complaints of Mrs. Kozak's sister, authorized the arrest of the plaintiff when she was working peacefully in her own office (and she was detained as a result for 44 days). The statute was primarily administered by the police. They interpreted its language as empowering them to arrest persons who had persistently displayed disorderly conduct in the immediate past

---

[22] [1953] 2 S.C.R. 95 at 99-100.

[23] Jaffe, "Judicial Control of Administrative Action" (1965), at 327

[24] [1958] S.C.R. 177, 120 C.C.C. 1, 13 D.L.R. (2d) 1.

(and there was substantial evidence of this in the case of Mrs. Kozak). It may be conceded that the language of the statute is reasonably capable of this reading (and in fact Beatty had consulted with a magistrate). However, the Supreme Court majority held that the correct meaning was that this was an emergency power of arrest which was justified only if *at that time* the plaintiff was conducting himself in an apparently disorderly manner (and thus the ordinary procedure of judicial commitment was inadequate).

Surely it is clear that this is the kind of situation in which the court is the institution which should have the final say in interpreting the statute. We cannot let police, inspectors, licensing clerks, and other such lower echelon bureaucrats interpret the scope of their own legal powers free of any external review of the validity of what they are doing. It is a basic assumption of the rule of law that the private citizen should be able to hale such an official into court and make him justify the decision he has made, or pay damages for the harm he has caused. No doubt, as in the case of *Beatty v. Kozak*, the administrator will have made a *bona fide* effort to understand and respect the limits of his statutory powers and his interpretation of their scope may be quite reasonable. However, we give the courts the decisive voice about which legal interpretation is the correct one, and we do so because we rely on the judges being right more often than the police.

If judicial review of the police decision is justified in *Beatty v. Kozak*, is not the same true of judicial review of the labour board in *Barbara Jarvis* and *Metropolitan Life*? I think not. Indeed, the second basic fallacy in the lawyer's approach to administrative law has been the notion that there must be a single stance about judicial review. The natural corollary is that the general principles of review will assume that all administrative action is like that of Beatty, the police officer. I think that review in this latter case is justified. However, when we reflect on the reasons why, they suggest quite a different judgment about labour board decisions.

In *Beatty v. Kozak*, the administrative decision was made by one of many police officers in Saskatchewan. He was not legally trained and had minimal acquaintance with the techniques of analysis of statutory language. Police must make immediate decisions in the heat of their job of maintaining law and order and they have a very partial view of the problems with which the statute deals. Contrast them with the courts. Judges are independent, impartial, and legally trained. They make decisions in the unhurried, rational atmosphere of the courtroom and they do so only after hearing full argument from each side to the dispute. Their legal experience and the forum in which they operate permits them some emotional distance from the concrete situation, which is conducive to the kind of clear judgment we want about matters of general legal principle. No doubt this is a picture of the ideal situation of a court, and one which is always imperfectly realized. However, it is

137

an ideal which almost invariably will be better attained in the court-room than the police station.

I would sum up the case for judicial review as follows: the important characteristics of adjudication are conducive to a judicial cast of mind; we want legal questions, arising out of concrete disputes, to be finally resolved within such an institution. However, I agree with Mr. Justice Abbott in *Barbara Jarvis* that the Ontario Labour Relations Board satisfies these conditions equally as well as the courts. It is presided over by legally trained chairmen who are independent of the govern-ment and impartial as between the parties. Each side to a dispute has the chance to make his argument in a setting which is conducive to dispassionate judgment. The board formulates its legal decisions in written opinions spelling out its reasons, and these opinions are published to form the basis for legal argument in later cases. In fact, anyone who reads the opinions of the labour board and the courts about the same issues of labour law will have no doubt as to which are the more illuminating of the legal issues.

I agree that there is an intimate relation between law and adjudica-tion. Contrary to what the defenders of judicial review assume, this does not mean that law and courts are inseparable. Adjudication is a basic institution of government but, as we saw in Chapter 1, it can be satisfied in different ways and degrees even among final appellate courts. It can also be satisfied equally as well in a specialized administrative tribunal. A legal question can be treated "judicially" even by a person who is not called a judge and does not wear judicial robes. I am not persuaded from the evidence of comparative decisions that we will likely get better interpretations of the Labour Relations Act from the Supreme Court of Canada than from the Ontario Labour Relations Board. The presumption against judicial review (which, need I add, is buttressed by the privative clause which is also part of the Act) has not yet been overcome.

At this point, let me return to what I said at the opening of this section. Judicial review is an integral part of our existing law and is gaining added weight from several recent developments (including the efforts of the Supreme Court in *Barbara Jarvis* and *Metropolitan Life*). I do not expect my arguments to persuade the powers that be that final judicial control should be removed. What I might hope for, though, is some change in the attitude with which our courts approach the task of reviewing independent tribunals such as a labour board. Reflection on these arguments might induce some feeling of judicial modesty and willingness to learn from administrative decisions.

There is language in some Supreme Court decisions which nicely captures this attitude. In the key early decision of *Globe Printing*, Mr. Justice Rand said that the test for the validity of such administrative action should be: "is the decision within any rational compass that can be attributed to the statutory language?"[25] In *Barbara Jarvis*, Mr. Justice Judson adopted a similar test, to the effect that a decision should not be invalidated provided that it "is a *bona fide* attempt to exercise its power, that it relates to the subject matter of the legislaion, and that it is reasonably capable of reference to the power given to the body".[26] This is a judicial review which is appropriate to review of these kinds of administrative tribunals, whatever be their area of jurisdiction. In the area of labour relations, the need for judicial restraint is doubly reinforced by the analysis advanced earlier of the nature of labour relations issues themselves. On whatever dimension one chooses to look at it, the Supreme Court's intervention in *Metropolitan Life* is disheartening.

THE PERILS OF ABSENTEE MANAGEMENT

Let's look at another concrete example of the real nature of judicial review in the Supreme Court of Canada, *Bell v. Ontario Human Rights Commn.*[27] This time I have chosen a case occurring outside the labour relations area but requiring a judgment very similar to *Barbara Jarvis* and *Metropolitan Life* about the statutory limits to administrative power. The decision became something of a *cause célèbre* in Ontario but is of more general interest because it reflects so many of the deficiencies in the public law performance of our courts.

On December 10th, 1968, a Jamaican, Carl McKay, answered an advertisement placed by Kenneth Bell in the Toronto Star of a flat for rent. After phoning to find that the flat was still available, McKay went out to look at it. When he arrived, Bell said that the premises had been rented. Suspicious, McKay had his girl friend phone that same afternoon and she was told the flat was still available. On December 12th, McKay filed a complaint with the Commission charging a breach of the Ontario Human Rights Code because he had been denied accommodation in a "self-contained dwelling unit" because of his race. Bell's eventual explanation was that he did not want to rent his flat to young men who may have been students, and he had lied about the place already being taken "because this is the simplest method and avoids discussion and argument".

---

25 *Toronto Newspaper Guild v. Globe Printing*, [1953] 2 S.C.R. 18 at 30, 106 C.C.C. 225, [1953] 3 D.L.R. 561.

26 *Barbara Jarvis*, cited in fn. 11, *ante.*, at 506, quoting from Mr. Justice Dixon of the High Court of Australia.

27 [1971] S.C.R. 756, 18 D.L.R. (3d) 1. I have relied heavily on "Comments" on this decision by Peter Hogg in (1971), 9 O.H.L.J. 203 and by Hunter in (1972), 7 U.B.C.L.R. 17.

The truth of whether there was actual discrimination or not was never adjudicated by an impartial tribunal because of the procedures adopted in the case. The Act provides for convening an *ad hoc* board of inquiry to hear the complaint laid by the Commission against a landlord such as Bell. Though Dean Walter Tarnopolsky of the University of Windsor Law School was appointed, his inquiry was derailed at the start by an application for "prohibition". This procedure is the equivalent of *"certiorari"*, but brought before the decision in order to prevent a tribunal making a judgment when it has no "jurisdiction". The case raised important questions of the timing of judicial review. The unanimous Ontario Court of Appeal and the dissenters on the Supreme Court of Canada believed the application was premature for two different reasons. Mr. Justice Laskin said review must at least await a decision from the Board of Inquiry, while Mr. Justice Abbott would have the courts stay their hand until the Minister acted on the recommendations of the Board. There was substantial legal authority to support either of these views and of course restraint now might avoid the need for any review later. The Supreme Court disagreed, apparently believing the case raised a "perfectly simple, short and neat question of law", which was ripe for a judicial answer. The Court's decision came down on February 1, 1971, more than two years after McKay's encounter with Bell.

The issue of jurisdiction raised by the case concerned the meaning and application of the term "self-contained dwelling unit". It was illegal to discriminate only in respect of this kind of living accommodation. The Court had to rely on very skimpy evidence, the written affidavit of Bell who was not subjected to cross-examination or contradicted by McKay. This is not at all unusual, given the procedure and timing of a motion for prohibition. From the affidavit, it appeared that Bell was renting the two top floors of his house, which included two bedrooms, a sitting room, kitchen and bathroom. Bell and his wife lived in a suite on the ground floor. The upper flat was reached through the front door and common hallway leading to a staircase. Bell's living room and kitchen opened off this hall. These rooms had glass doors with a lock operated by a skeleton key. Bell's affidavit said that "I have never used locks on my doors since 1965".

Let us recount all of the reasoning of Mr. Justice Martland on this absolutely vital issue in the administration of the Human Rights Code. Martland J. first recited the statutory history of the section. Originally the Code prohibited discrimination in "any apartment in any building that contains more than six self-contained dwelling units". In 1965, this was changed to include buildings with more than three such units. In 1967, it was further amended to prohibit denial of occupancy of "any self-contained dwelling unit" because of race. Here is the sum total of Martland J.'s analysis of the problem:

It seems clear that the words "self-contained dwelling units", as used in the two earlier statutes, referred to dwelling units in the form of apartments in an apartment building. The present s. 3 applies to any "self-contained dwelling unit", but in the light of the past history of the legislation, it would appear to me that it includes now either a self-contained house or self-contained premises similar to an apartment in an apartment house.

In my opinion, the premises leased by the appellant, located in his upstairs floors, may well be "dwelling units" but they were not "self-contained" dwelling units.[28]

It is no accident that the Supreme Court's typical style of legal reasoning produces the kind of *non-sequiturs* we find in this passage. What are the real complexities in the issue which a more adequate conception of a legal rule will disclose? First, it is clear, I hope, that the phrase "self-contained dwelling unit" does not contain the answer on its surface. The ordinary meaning of these terms may suggest some clear examples on either side (e.g., a complete house as contrasted with a bedroom for a boarder), but *Bell* presents the ambiguous penumbral case which goes to court. Martland J. was correct in looking at previous legislation to see what help could be gained from the historical context. The conclusions he draws may appear somewhat mystifying. The legislature has deliberately dropped all references to apartment buildings but they are still taken to have referred to "self-contained premises similar to an apartment in an apartment building". Yet even this step is not disastrous. The Court is not saying the unit must be an apartment in an apartment building, it only has to be similar to one. It is the next, and question-begging assertion that Bell's flat was not similar to such an apartment which baffles me.

Let's try to learn something positive from the case. The surface language and legislative history will not give us the answer to issues like the one presented here. These materials will suggest situations that appear to be clearly covered or not. What the interpreter of the language must do is use these instances as his lead into the underlying purpose of the statutory rule. Why did the legislature place this limitation on illegal discrimination? What was its objective in excluding some denials of accommodation on account of race from the scope of the Code? An answer very quickly appears. Prejudice of various kinds is an unpleasant but real human fact. The law can act to prevent much of the harm caused to the victims of such prejudice but it cannot directly eradicate these feelings. As long as they exist, the law would be counter-productive, and perhaps overly intrusive on the landlord's privacy, in forcing him to share accommodation with a person he dislikes, even for such a reason as his colour. Hence, only when the living

---

28 [1971] S.C.R. at 767-768.

accommodation to be rented is self-contained, and thus maintains the necessary social distance between the two parties, does the law make it illegal to act on one's prejudices.

Given this sense of the rationale of the rule, how do the facts of the Bell case look? McKay will cook and eat in his own kitchen, sleep in his own bedroom, bathe in his own bathroom, and watch television in his own living room. In what sense is his flat not self-contained for purposes of his dwelling in it? Perhaps it is the fact of a common doorway and front hall? Yet this can't be decisive because an apartment building has exactly the same common entrance. Is it the fact that Bell would be living in the same house as his tenant? Again, this is not unusual for the owner of a small apartment building who often acts as his own superintendent. Yet Bell's quarters are closed off only by glass doors and a skeleton key not ordinarily used. What if the black man invades his living room? I would think there are other ways of preventing such an unlikely trespass by one's tenant, short of denying accommodation by reason of his colour.

If one analyzes the facts of the case and what the Court did to them, can it be true that a self-contained dwelling unit need only be similar to an apartment in an apartment building? The Court's decision implies that it must be exactly the same. Such a holding collides with the socio-economic framework of the legislation. Perhaps the Supreme Court could not be expected to divine this context on its own; but then it was this Court which blithely intervened without the aid of an experienced administrator's opinion about a "perfectly simple, short and neat question of law". The people who really need the Code's protection are lower income blacks or other immigrant groups. They naturally prefer the kind of low-cost accommodation offered by Bell, a flat in a converted private home. Yet the Court is saying the protection of the Code does not extend to such accommodation and is basically confined to apartments. Most of these are in large, luxury apartment buildings where there is rarely discrimination, but whose rents are beyond the means of most minority group members. As one commentator on the *Bell* case put it: "pernicious results find roots in muddled logic".[29]

Some time after the *Bell* decision, after experience with the difficulties it presented, the Ontario legislature moved to reverse the Supreme Court ruling by statute. This is certainly desirable for the future but small comfort to Carl McKay and others like him who suffered in the interim. The case is only too typical of situations where the courts reverse the interpretation of a statute given by the tribunal charged with its immediate administration. It should be an object lesson to some of the romantic defenders of judicial review as the essential bulwark of the rule of law.

---

[29] Hunter, article cited in fn. 27, *ante*, at 30.

The kind of case that goes to court is one where the statute is unclear. There is law there, but it lurks beneath the surface of the language. The interpreter must delve beneath this surface to understand the underlying legislative objective and follow through its implications for these difficult marginal problems. Our courts in recent years are eager to assert control in this process. *Bell* is typical in its impatience with any administrative law doctrines which might delay or limit judicial intervention. One must assume that the judges are confident of their ability to produce the right legal answers, and without any help from the arguments of the so-called "expert" boards. I leave it to the reader to decide whether, in *Bell* at least, this confidence was misplaced.

WHEN LEGAL WORLDS COLLIDE

The last case I shall consider in this chapter, *Port Arthur Shipbuilding*,[30] involved a clear confrontation between the opposing views of the role of law and judicial review in the administrative process. That case involved grievances brought by the union on behalf of three employees who had been discharged from their jobs. Two of them, Jack Geravelis and Patrick Manduca, left work before the end of their shift one day, saying they were sick. This was not true and the two men drove to an outlying town where they worked for three days for another employer. The third, John Beaucage, left work quite openly and against instructions of management to go to work for another competitor for a week. The collective agreement prohibited leaves of absence for this purpose and the company decide to fire all three employees.

When the case eventually reached arbitration, some extenuating circumstances appeared. Manduca and Geravelis had customarily been laid-off from Port Arthur Shipbuilding during this season of the year. As usual, they had made arrangements to work elsewhere beginning on the Monday in question. However, it turned out that their lay-off would be delayed somewhat this year. Fearful of losing their substitute job for the whole season, they booked off to work for their second employer for a few days. Beaucage had no such motivation. He had 24 years of seniority and was the union president besides, and so would not be laid-off. He wanted the second job for a week because it paid high wages for long hours and he needed some money for improvements to his summer cottage. However, along with his long seniority, it appeared that he had never before given cause to be disciplined by the company. Geravelis and Manduca also had blameless records during some 15 years of seniority for each. Accordingly, the majority of the arbitration

---

[30] *Port Arthur Shipbldg. Co. v. Arthurs*, [1969] S.C.R. 85, 70 D.L.R. (2d) 693.

board found that discharge was too severe a penalty for this offence in all its circumstances and set it aside. Because the employees had been guilty of serious misconduct which required some punishment, the board substituted stiff suspensions for several months.

The company moved to quash the decision on the grounds that the arbitration board had erred in law in reaching its conclusions. The collective agreement stated that management had the power to "suspend and discharge for proper cause" and then provided that disputes about the exercise of this power should eventually find their way to arbitration under the contract. (I should note that labour agreements normally use the terms "just" or "reasonable" cause but the Supreme Court rightly felt that nothing turned on these linguistic variations.) Stated quite simply, the issue before the Court was the extent of an arbitrator's powers under the standard discipline provisions in a collective agreement.[31]

I should say also that there were two distinct facets to this question. Remember that the arbitration board did two things: first, it found that discharge was too serious a penalty to be "just" (or "proper") for this offence and set it aside; second, it substituted the penalty of suspension which it believed was justified. It is clear from the Supreme Court

---

[31] When the case reached the Supreme Court of Canada, another issue was raised about whether there was any power to review the decision of an arbitrator in a *certiorari* proceeding. Traditionally, this remedy was available only against the decisions of *statutory* tribunals and the Court had already held that *certiorari* could not be used against voluntary labour arbitration under the Labour Relations Act, 1954 (B.C.), c. 17 [see *Howe Sound Co. v. Internat. Union of Mine, etc., Wkrs.*, [1962] S.C.R. 318, 37 W.W.R. 646, 33 D.L.R. (2d) 1]. This arbitration board had the same practical characteristics as the one seen in that earlier case. It was appointed by the parties on an *ad hoc* basis, paid by them, and operated at their private behest. In this it differed fundamentally from a permanent, government-established tribunal like the Labour Board. Yet the parties were required under the statute to use a system of arbitration, unlike British Columbia where they were given a choice (at least in theory). The Supreme Court held that this element of statutory compulsion was sufficient to permit *certiorari* to be brought against any one arbitration board.

The conclusion is reasonable, though not inevitable, and is part of the general thrust of Supreme Court decisions to remove any and all obstacles to the availability of judicial review. What is fascinating, though, is that this opinion was written by Mr. Justice Judson for the Court. We have seen that in *Barbara Jarvis* he dissented from this kind of extension of judicial power, and that is merely one of several important decisions where he advocated this position of judicial restraint. In recent years, he appears to have joined the prevailing tide on the Supreme Court (and he concurred in *Bell*). Even more intriguing is the fact that as a trial judge, Judson J. wrote an opinion in *Re Internat. Nickel Co. and Rivando*, [1956] O.R. 379, 2 D.L.R. (2d) 700 (Ont. C.A.), holding that *certiorari* was not available against labour arbitrators, and he was reversed in this view by the Ontario Court of Appeal. Now he follows the Court of Appeal decision in *Rivando* without even mentioning, let alone meeting, the contrary arguments he had himself made some 12 years earlier. In this trend also, Mr. Justice Judson reflects the stance of the Court in the late 1960's.

decision that they did not clearly focus on the distinction between these two steps and this muddied their whole approach to the problem. There was nothing in the agreement which explicitly empowered the arbitrators to substitute a second penalty. It had been justified as a legally implied remedial power on the same footing as the power to order reinstatement and award damages—and neither of these had been explicitly conferred. Now one can debate whether such an addition to the bargain should be implied or not. However, it is critical to see that the answer to this second question has got nothing to do logically with one's answer to the first issue—can an arbitrator find that discharge is an excessively severe penalty for an employee's offence? Indeed, if one answers the first question affirmatively, it is the employer who is benefited most by the implied power. Otherwise, the employee will escape "scot-free" without any discipline, because the employer over-reacted in his choice of penalty. It is understandable, then, that the employer focused his argument on the first issue, although the presence of the second in the arbitrator's opinion served to obscure it.

Without any further ado, we can say that the Supreme Court quashed the arbitration decision on the grounds that the board exceeded its powers. In two or three, short and confusing paragraphs, unadorned by any legal authorities, there does appear one critical passage: "The sole issue in this case was whether the three employees left their jobs to work for someone else and whether this fact was a proper cause for discipline. Once the board has found that there were facts justifying discipline, the particular form chosen was not subject to review on arbitration."[32] If the parties want to confer such a power on an arbitrator, they must use language that is much more explicit than "proper cause". It is very difficult to see the rationale for this view on the face of Mr. Justice Judson's opinion but perhaps we can reconstruct one from the employer's argument as seen in two lower court opinions (with which Judson J. agreed). If there had been no collective agreement and just individual contracts of employment, the employer would have had "cause" to discharge the three employees for their conduct here. The employer could have exercised his discretion to use a suspension instead, but if he decided on discharge, a court would not intervene and accordingly, neither may an arbitrator under a collective agreement.

I said earlier that the case was a classic confrontation between two different views of the nature of the law of the administrative process. Some further details about the case will illustrate the reason. The author of the arbitration decision in *Port Arthur Shipbuilding* was the then Professor of Labour Law at the Osgoode Hall Law School (and now the Dean), Harry Arthurs. In his opinion, in answer to this same employer contention, he had said:

---

32 [1969] S.C.R. at 89.

145

It is common knowledge that over the years a distinctive body of arbitral jurisprudence has developed to give meaning to the concept of just cause for discharge in the context of modern industrial employment. Although the common law may provide guidance, useful analogies, even general principles, the umbilical cord has been severed and the new doctrines of labour arbitrators have begun to lead a life of their own.[33]

One can sense that this last phrase must have been like a red flag to a bull when it was read by our common law judges. Mr. Justice Schroeder, dissenting in the Ontario Court of Appeal, thundered:

> A domestic tribunal of this character created by the terms of a collective agreement is not an autocrat free to act as it pleases, but is bound by the jurisprudence of the country which must continue to govern the multifarious relations between subject and subject.[34]

However, Professor Arthurs' point, as developed in an important article in the Canadian Bar Review, was precisely that the rationale for the existence of new tribunals, such as labour boards, arbitrators and the like, is that

> they are to decide cases not on common law principles but in accordance with industrial jurisprudence—the statutes, customs and contracts which operate exclusively in the world of labour relations.[35]

He went further to say that the courts, when asked to review such administrative decisions, should

> defer to the system of jurisprudence developed within the industrial community and apply the law of that system rather than the conventional legal doctrines administered by the court.

This challenge was taken up by the majority in the Ontario Court of Appeal, especially by Mr. Justice Bora Laskin who was Canada's leading labour law scholar in the 1950's, as Harry Arthurs was in the 1960's. He met the employer's argument that he could have legally discharged these employees at common law by saying that

> collective bargaining has changed this [common law] approach and, as projected in many collective agreements, has changed it drastically. Matters familiar in a master and servant context have taken on different dimensions under collective agreements.[36]

---

33 *Port Arthur Shipbldg.* (1966), 17 L.A.C. 109 (Arthurs) at 112.

34 *R. v. Arthurs; Ex parte Port Arthur Shipbldg. Co.*, [1967] 2 O.R. 49, 62 D.L.R. (2d) 342 at 346 (C.A.).

35 Arthurs, "Developing Industrial Citizenship" (1967), 45 Can. Bar Rev. 786 at 815 and 826. My own views of the jurisprudential nature of labour arbitration itself are worked out in detail in my article "The Role of the Labour Arbitrator" (1969), 19 U.T.L.J. 16.

36 (1967), 62 D.L.R. (2d) at 363 and 364.

As authority for this proposition, he was able to cite Judson's opinion in *Paquet*, which we looked at earlier.

Then Laskin J.A. went on to explain precisely the reason for the difference. At common law, employees had no right to continued employment. They could be discharged without any cause if given notice, and in the case of hourly employees like the grievors, this notice would be very short. If the employer did not even want to keep the man around for that time, he could dismiss him with payment for the notice period. If an employee was discharged without cause or payment, the courts could not reinstate him and were limited to awarding him the damages he suffered by reason of not having notice. In such a legal environment, it is no wonder that the common law courts did not develop any sophisticated doctrines to regulate the employer's decision to fire an employee once he had committed some offence.

Now the environment has completely changed:

> it is sometimes forgotten that collective bargaining and the collective agreement have given the individual worker security of employment . . . seniority and discharge clauses represent the employees' charter of employment security; and it is reinforced by removing from the employer . . . his previously unreviewable right to rid himself of employees, even if it cost money damages to do so.

The response in arbitration, in deciding whether a particular offence was just or proper cause to *discharge* an employee (rather than simply to *suspend* him) was to look at a broad range of relevant factors in the particular offence and in the background of the offender:

> experience has shown that there must be a pragmatic and not a cut and dried, Medes and Persians approach to discipline . . . room . . . for consideration of the worker as an individual, and not as simply part of an indistinguishable mass . . . a sensible individualization in the assessment of punishment for misconduct.

In this way the new principle of security of employment was given definite legal meaning in an evolving arbitration jurisprudence.

When the case reached the Supreme Court of Canada, this whole dimension to the problem was lost. In typical fashion we were given a conclusion without any justifying argument and, not unexpectedly, the conclusion was disastrous. Remember that the arbitrator here was interpreting the language of a collective agreement and was not a tribunal applying the common law directly. Why is it an error of law to hold that, while an employee may have committed a definite offence, mitigating circumstances mean that it is not just, reasonable, or proper to impose the ultimate sanction of discharge for it? (And discharge is far more serious under a collective agreement where there is tenure of employment to which is attached vital incidents such as pension bene-

147

fits.) On the face of the language, I would suppose it clearly erroneous to come to the opposite conclusion, and hold that any offence justifying some discipline, however minor, thereby justifies discharge.

Maybe we can be charitable to the Court and impute to them the view not that it is proper to discharge long-term employees for a relatively minor offence, but that management should have the unreviewable discretion to decide when discharge is proper. Mr. Justice Schroeder, of the Ontario Court of Appeal, speaking of an employee who commits some offence, had said:

> the law recognizes the employer's right summarily to dismiss the delinquent employee. The officers in charge of the operation of the business know better than any other person whether the evil against which measures are to be taken is a prevalent one, or if the orderly conduct of the business and the efficient management of the working force require that an employee's misconduct calls for discharge or merely suspension.[37]

At least this view furnishes some rationale to the bold legal proposition in the Supreme Court, but, on examination, it also lacks persuasiveness.

Let's look at what the doctrine amounts to. In every discharge case, there will be three questions: Did the employee engage in the alleged behaviour? Is the conduct wrong and worthy of some discipline? Is the offence serious enough to warrant discharge? Management must originally investigate a trouble situation and make all three decisions. If the employee and union disagree, the case will go to arbitration. The Judson-Schroeder view, stated quite simply, is that the arbitrator can review only the first two management judgments, and not the third. To the ordinary viewer, this would seem to be an arbitrary dividing line and one which is totally unsupported in the language of the collective agreement. To those experienced in labour relations, this line of authority is completely incongruous. It is the third management decision which is most in need of arbitral review. In a discharge case, management is usually careful to get the facts right and rarely will there be any question that they do amount to misconduct of some sort. Given this kind of situation, the real danger is that management will overreact to the offence (especially at the lower echelons of supervision) and later on find it very difficult to back down. The primary value of arbitration in discharge cases is that it provides a forum for a neutral and dispassionate review of all the circumstances of the offence and the record of the employee to see whether the very serious penalty of discharge is proper. Only a very naive view of industrial relations would cut out arbitral supervision at precisely the point where it is most needed.

It isn't hard to fathom the reason why the Supreme Court erred so badly. Its opinion ignored the fact that it was a collective agreement which was to be interpreted. That document was negotiated in an

---

[37] *Ibid.*, at 348.

environment which is worlds removed from the "master and servant" relationship of the common law contract of employment. The standard discharge clause was inserted within a context of 20 years of reported arbitration decisions in Ontario which had fleshed out its meaning and implications. One should not be surprised that the Supreme Court, faced with its first-ever discharge grievance, should find that new industrial jurisprudence so alien to its own experience. What is disturbing is the Court's blithe willingness to rewrite the law in a manner which so drastically diverges from the expectations of the participants in collective bargaining.

What were the features of that brave new legal world?[38] Several important arbitration precedents had explicitly held that arbitration boards must review the severity of the discipline chosen by management. More important, this view was implicit in a large number of related doctrines and practices. Employers could not discriminate in the amount of discipline meted out; evidence of provocation or duress could lessen the seriousness of an offence; an employer could look at an employee's previous record only if there was an immediate "culminating incident"; both parties could use the employee's record and seniority either as aggravating or mitigating the instant offence; for some first offences, such as theft from the employer, discharge might be appropriate, but for others, such as fighting, it would not. These are only a few of many examples. They substantiate what Professor Arthurs said of the development of a distinctive arbitral jurisprudence to administer the general language of the collective agreement in many new and complicated situations. In this connection, they suggest that the likely expectations of these parties were that the words "proper cause" would be given the broader meaning accepted in the arbitration process, one which their representatives must have been aware of in negotiating the agreement. If any special meaning were to be adopted, requiring explicit language, surely it would be the common law doctrine now advocated by the employer.

As I said, *Port Arthur Shipbuilding* was a clear confrontation between the two views of the role of law in the administrative process. The response of the Supreme Court typifies the Canadian judicial position at its worst. The vices in this position are captured in the phrase "absentee management". The courts are not directly involved in labour relations and most judges are uninformed about its operations and needs. Then one party, dissatisfied with a particular administrative decision, asks the courts to intervene and they do so with all the effect of a bull in a china shop. Especially, when a judge speaks with the authority of a

---

[38] Here I summarize my own opinion as the arbitrator in *SKD Mfg. Ltd.* (1969), 20 L.A.C. 231 (Weiler), where I was directly faced with the question of what to do with this Supreme Court language. Reference to the arbitral jurisprudence can be found in that opinion.

place on the Supreme Court of Canada, what he says has overriding legal significance. A casual phrase uttered in the course of his opinion can wipe out twenty years of carefully worked out administrative doctrine. Then the judicial bull retires to its lair and leaves the lowly board member to pick up the pieces.

One thing about scantily reasoned judicial opinions is that they leave room for later interpreters to confine general language to its particular facts. Several abitrators did this to Mr. Justice Judson's language in *Port Arthur Shipbuilding*. Shortly afterwards, the Ontario Legislature amended the Labour Relations Act to ensure a complete power of arbitral review in discipline cases. Not all judicial interventions have this happy ending, though, and *Port Arthur Shipbuilding* still has force in provinces where the legislature has not yet acted. We should learn from the example while we can, in order to minimize like dangers in the future.

A REVIEW OF
JUDICIAL REVIEW

What are the lessons to be learned from this and the other Supreme Court cases I have considered in this chapter? One thing we see is the pronounced trend towards the extension of judicial review. There have been many technical legal roadblocks in the way of securing a judicial remedy, most of which grew out of the historical origins of administrative law. The Supreme Court has shown itself impatient with any such restraints on its own capacity to "do good." In this it is in conformity with the legislative tide which has also been in the direction of facilitating judicial supervision of administrative action. Whether this is desirable depends of course on whether there will be an improvement in the quality of legal decisions in the area. This must be tested in those cases where the courts disagree with the agency's conclusions. There is no reason to add an extra layer of litigation if the courts are simply going to ratify the original decision. The critical question is whether we should allow a court to substitute its opinion as to the meaning of a statute for that of the specialized, adjudicative tribunal which is charged with the primary responsibility for administering the legislation.

The last three cases I have discussed in detail—*Metropolitan Life, Bell,* and *Port Arthur Shipbuilding*—all involved precisely this situation. I believe they are a fair sample of the quality of law we receive from the Supreme Court, and indeed from the Canadian judiciary as a whole, when it substitutes its opinion for that of the specialized tribunal. That conclusion could not be demonstrated from this small sample and the reader would have to analyze many other decisions to see whether I am right. However, it is possible to reach some judgments about the work of the Supreme Court in these three cases, on the basis of the evidence I have presented. Let me state my own conclusions.

All three cases testify to the very narrow and inadequate concept of law which is operative in the Supreme Court of Canada and which also underlies current approval of the trend to greater judicial control. Each case dealt with the interpretation of a bare legislative (or contractual) term—"member of a trade union", "self-contained dwelling unit", and "discharge for proper cause". In each case the Court simply recited this abstract language and then adopted one version as to its meaning. Not one of the three opinions sees any need to provide some *reasons* to show that its reading of the law is correct. If one merely saw these opinions, one would assume that the answer was self-evident, the law was clear, and only a despotic bureaucracy could have decided otherwise.

Many casual observers are prepared to make that judgment. The layman naturally assumes that what the Supreme Court says is the law really was the law all along. If a board has reached a contrary result, then it must not have been following the law. Yet in all three cases the Supreme Court of Canada reversed the Ontario Court of Appeal whose opinions were written by Mr. Justice Laskin (who was subsequently appointed to the Supreme Court). At the least, this should alert us to the fact that the legal conclusions in these situations were not self-evident at all. The language of the statute (or of the collective agreement) did not inexorably dictate the judgments which the Supreme Court reached. Different solutions were adopted within the administrative process and I suggest that these readings were reasonably permitted by the crucial phrases in the legislation. In *Metropolitan Life*, the Ontario Labour Relations Board carefully spelled out its reasons for adopting one conclusion. In *Port Arthur Shipbuilding*, the arbitration board did the same and this argument was nicely elaborated by Mr. Justice Laskin. In *Bell*, the courts intervened before Dean Tarnopolsky had a chance to develop his analysis and conclusions. However, other boards of inquiry had articulated the analysis of the statute on which the Ontario Human Rights Commission relied in the *Bell* case. The Supreme Court of Canada did not offer any one of these tribunals the courtesy of an argument to justify its abrupt reversals of their opinions.

That is a small, though not unimportant point. Members of administrative agencies and lower court judges are paid well enough that they should be able to absorb these slights from on high. It is the public, the consumers of our law, who are the real victims. It is bad enough that the Supreme Court adopted one of two possible legal conclusions and quashed administrative and lower court decisions to the contrary without ever trying to justify its conclusion. It is far worse that the alternative it decided to impose on Canadian law was the wrong one. I am not simply indulging in academic, aesthetic criticism of the opinions written by the judges. Inadequate legal reasoning is inherently likely to produce unfortunate results. That was the result in all three of these cases.

This brings us face to face with the critical truth in an adequate theory of administrative law. The virtues of the "rule of law" do not necessarily entail a system of judicial review. The decision to adopt (or extend) such a system should only be made after a realistic comparison of the quality of legal analysis we will receive within the relevant areas of the administrative and judicial processes. The task for each is the same, the interpretation of a statute, and this requires much more than a mechanical application of an abstract legal rule to the immediate factual situation. The typical problem for judicial review is one in which the bare language of the statute permits of at least two readings. When the Supreme Court did not focus on this fact in the three cases, it necessarily ignored the next and vital question: which of these two meanings should be held to be part of our law because it makes the most sense? What is the criterion for answering this second query? As we saw first in *Barbara Jarvis*, it is the underlying purpose, rationale, or principle of the law in the area. Why would we want a dwelling unit to be self-contained before including it under anti-discrimination legislation? What does a legislature have in mind when it permits evidence of membership in a trade union to be sufficient for certification of the union? What kind of review of management's discretion is envisaged by the parties to a collective agreement when they say there must be just or proper cause for discharge? I am not simply suggesting that it would be nice if interpreters of statutory language asked these questions; I think they are legally obligated to ask them. This is the logical implication of a realistic conception of the law that is binding on both administrators and judges.

It is true that the legislature intends to impose legal limits administrative agencies; it is fallacious to infer that there must be external, judicial supervision to ensure compliance with these limits. But suppose that the agency makes a mistake; will there be no forum in which the injured party can secure redress? The answer is that in any system of adjudication someone must have the final say with no possibility of further review. Right now the Supreme Court of Canada is our final judicial authority. Goodness knows, I think they have made a lot of legal errors but I certainly do not advocate adding another layer of review above them (e.g., a return to the Privy Council). We have to accept the risk of human error whatever institutional arrangements are made while trying to locate the final authority in the place where this risk is minimized.

The conventional legal wisdom in Canada is that this objective is best served by extending the authority of the courts. Reflection on these last three cases should give pause to those who hold this view. One need not be terribly enamoured of the performance of Canadian administrative tribunals to be suspicious of judicial reversals of administrative interpretations of their own statutes. The failures of the Supreme Court of

Canada in these cases were not accidental aberrations. Canadian judges, with some few exceptions, take a very narrow view of the considerations that are legally relevant to statutory interpretation. One can understand their reluctance to grapple with the social problems the legislature has faced and the practical designs it has proposed as solutions. It is so easy to go wrong when a judge has so little acquaintance with the area. But then, if these are the vital elements in the decision, why do we take the final say away from the specialized body which understands and can use them?

In *Bell, Metropolitan Life,* and *Port Arthur Shipbuilding,* an appraisal of those underlying factors supports the legal conclusion of the administrative agency rather than that of the Supreme Court of Canada. I have set out my own reasons for this judgment earlier and will not repeat them here. No doubt I may be wrong but there are no arguments in the Supreme Court opinions which might show why. In fact, there is some external corroboration of my view. Following each Supreme Court decision, the Ontario Legislature stepped in, reversed the Court's legal ruling, and restored the administrative tribunal's view of the law. However, if I may paraphrase Mr. Justice Spence's remark from *Barbara Jarvis,* this legislative supervision of the courts came too late to help the unfortunate victims of the original judicial action.[39]

Let me close with one further implication of my analysis. Judicial restraint in reviewing administrative tribunals is desirable whatever be the nature of the statutory area. Judicial caution in industrial relations is desirable whether the particular legal rules are administered by an agency or not. Accordingly, there is a double-barrelled argument against judicial intervention in the area of collective bargaining legislation. It is important to recognize this. A pragmatic and realistic view of the role of law in courts is sometimes associated with the advocacy of judicial innovation in every context. I do not think there is any necessary connection at all. Within the view I am developing in this book, the desir-

---

[39] The prevailing scholarly opinion in the United States holds to quite a different view of the proper relationship of courts and boards than the one developed in this chapter. There the conventional wisdom holds that specialized administrative agencies eventually become captives of the same special interests they are supposed to regulate and, as a result, produce an unsatisfactory elaboration of the basic statute. Independent courts, acting at the behest of such defenders of the public interest as civil rights organizations, conservation groups, and the like, will supposedly be sympathetic to the true legislative purpose and so will require vigorous enforcement of expansive controls on private action. The prescription, then, is an extension of judicial review, not its retrenchment. Now, that diagnosis may or may not be reflective of the American scene; I would not presume to say. However, I do find it totally irrelevant to the Canadian situation, whether in the past, the present, or the foreseeable future. Nor should we be surprised at this. Realistic conclusions from a philosophy of administrative law, as of any area of our legal institutions, have to be sensitive to the capacities and attitudes of the different branches of government. We should not wonder that their interaction will vary so widely in different legal environments.

ability of judicial activism in any particular area of law depends on the nature of the social problem raised and the relative resources of the courts to make a wise contribution. Within the two families of problems I analyzed in torts and criminal law, this approach does support judicial creativity. Within collective bargaining law the same approach suggests judicial restraint.

CHAPTER 6

The Umpire of Canadian Federalism[1]

THE SUPREME COURT AND THE B.N.A. ACT

"We are under a constitution, but the Constitution is what the judges say it is."[2]

We are told by our Mr. Justice Hall that this truism of American constitutional law also describes the situation in Canada.[3] Almost any student of the evolution of our federal system would agree with him and it is good to see such frank recognition by judges of their personal responsibility for the decisions they reach. We can readily appreciate, then, why "both in the popular imagination and in the view of most Canadian statesmen, the primary role of the national Supreme Court is to act as the final arbiter of the Constitution or the 'umpire of the federal system.'"[4] Indeed, this role was the primary reason for the Supreme Court becoming the final court of appeal for Canada and is the source of most proposals for reform of the institution. In this chapter, I want to take a critical look at the implications of Hughes' remark. What does it mean and why is it so? What is there about constitutional cases which produces rule by judges? Is it a good thing and should it lead to redesign of the Supreme Court in ways which will make it a more effective "constitutional court"? Most fundamentally, do we really want, or do we really need, this kind of constitutional umpiring of our federal system?

---

1 An earlier version of this chapter was delivered in the Osgoode Hall Law School Lecture Series and published as Chapter 3 (The Supreme Court of Canada and Canadian Federalism) of the book *Law and Social Change*, Ziegel (ed.) (1973). A review of the Supreme Court's federalism decisions since 1949 can be found in my article "The Supreme Court and the Law of Canadian Federalism" (1973), 23 U.T.L.J. 307.

2 Quoted in Pusey, *Charles Evan Hughes* (1951), at 204.

3 Mr. Justice Hall, "Law Reform and the Judiciary's Role" (1972), 10 O.H.L.J. 399 at 408.

4 Russell, "Constitutional Reform of the Canadian Judiciary" (1969), 7 A.L.R. 103 at 123.

THE CHICKEN AND EGG WAR

I shall begin my analysis by a sketch of a case study—our recent constitutional cause célèbre arising out of the "chicken and egg war".[5] This was primarily an engagement fought by the bordering provinces of Ontario and Quebec. Ontario farmers produced an abundance of cheap eggs and Quebec farmers an abundance of cheap chickens. The surplus producers were naturally interested in the market of the consumers in the neighbouring jurisdiction. Equally naturally, the somewhat less efficient producers of each product were not so enamoured of competition within their own bailiwick. When they went to their own government for protection, the response was legislation facilitating the creation of marketing schemes. These provided for the controlled marketing, at fixed prices, of all the chickens sold in Ontario and all the eggs in Quebec, whatever the source. Unfortunately, it appears that the marketing boards became a little greedy and went even further, giving undue preference in marketing to those products coming from within the province. This had particularly adverse effects on farmers in other provinces such as Manitoba, which, as a consistent producer of agricultural surpluses, was the classic innocent and injured bystander in the "chicken and egg war".

On the surface, I find it rather hard to see what the courts have to contribute to the resolution of this essentially political and economic conflict. There certainly was ample scope for bargaining and negotiating terms of settlement which might offer at least something to everyone. One could understand that the federal government, which represented producers and consumers from all affected jurisdictions, might have been an appropriate arbiter. Unfortunately, earlier judicial decisions of the twenties and the thirties had themselves created the very institutional gaps which fostered such interprovincial marketing conflicts. At this very time, the federal government was attempting to shepherd through Parliament a new Farm Products Marketing Act which would endeavour to solve these problems through a complicated process of inter-administrative delegation. Though there appeared to be substantial consensus in favour of the general scheme of the Bill by both federal and provincial ministers of agriculture, it was being delayed by opposition members who largely represented western farming interests. In the interim, the federal government had carefully resisted many calls to refer the "political" dispute to the Supreme Court of Canada for immediate "legal" resolution.

Unfortunately, Manitoba, which was understandably loath to wait for a political decision on the larger questions, devised a scheme for

---

5 This was the name given by the newspapers to the situation eventually triggering the Supreme Court decision in *A.G. Man. v. Man. Egg & Poultry Assn.*, [1971] S.C.R. 689, [1971] 4 W.W.R. 705, 19 D.L.R. (3d) 169. For the political background to the Court's decision, I relied essentially on newspaper accounts, the most useful of which was in the Financial Post on May 29, 1971, at 1 and 6.

circumventing the reluctance of the federal Justice Minister. This provincial government manufactured a controversy by initiating a carbon copy of the Quebec scheme, a proposed Order-in-Council which provided for Manitoba control of the marketing of extraprovincial eggs in Manitoba. It then referred these regulations to the Manitoba Court of Appeal for a decision about their constitutionality, under its own provincial reference legislation. When the Manitoba Court of Appeal decided against the constitutional validity of the scheme, the Manitoba government was entitled as of right to appeal this "loss" to the Supreme Court of Canada. In this way, it could achieve a binding decision as to all such schemes which would be authoritative in all the provinces.

Some may be troubled by this apparent subversion of the adversary process. Manitoba purported to argue for, and then appeal on behalf of, laws which it was proposing to enact for the sole purpose of having the Supreme Court declare them unconstitutional. I am more concerned by the general deficiencies of the "reference" procedure which made this ploy possible. A direct reference of a legal question to the courts is a means of overcoming the limitations of adjudication in having constitutional policy settled quickly. For that reason, it enjoys some favour among lawyers. Unfortunately, while we may get the law established quickly, we may also get it wrong. Many of our worst constitutional decisions have come from references and this case did not prove an exception to that rule.

The point of a reference is to bring a legal problem before the courts without having to wait for litigation about a situation in which the legal issue is important. This changes only one factor in a complex institutional equation without considering the unhappy effect on the other elements. We are still relying on the courts for the right answer to the constitutional question. What mainly qualifies a judge to reach an intelligent conclusion is that he acts as an impartial arbiter of a dispute arising in a concrete setting. Because a specific fact situation triggers the litigation which requires a constitutional ruling, the judge has the benefit of seeing the real-life implications of his decision and he can carefully tailor the reach of his conclusion as he sees fit. His judicial neutrality is preserved by an adversary process which allows the interested parties to bring all the relevant factual background before him, depicted in as favourable a light as possible from each point of view.

In the *Manitoba Egg Reference*, both of these advantages to adjudication were dissipated. There was no concrete focus around which the reasoning of the Supreme Court could be organized nor was the factual economic background to the statute presented. The Manitoba government conspicuously omitted to set out in the Reference the relevant economic evidence which might well have supported the reasonability of provincial action in the area. Ontario and Quebec, both of which were vitally interested in sustaining this kind of legislation, did not have an opportunity to present this factual support. Indeed, the questions which the Manitoba government posed to the Court did not focus on what appears to have been the real character of the dispute—the discriminatory application of provincial marketing quotas against out-of-province producers—and instead required the Court to make a blanket decision about the legality of any such marketing scheme, no matter how favourably it might be applied to extraprovincial products. In my opinion, the most sensible response would have been a forthright refusal to answer the question on the grounds that the dispute was not appropriate for judicial resolution. One senses that Mr. Justice Laskin, who was especially critical of the abstract character of the Reference, was drawn in this direction, but eventually the legal mystique surrounding issues of federalism overcame his reluctance. The majority opinion proceeded blithely ahead, without any apparent concern for the complex and inter-related political or economic interests involved in the dispute, and the Court gave Manitoba the broad legal weapon it wanted.

Are there any inadequacies in the substantive reasoning and results of the Court which may have reflected some of these procedural deficiencies? A casual reading of the opinion certainly indicates the truth of Hughes' dictum that "the Constitution is what the judges say it is". In the first place, the Supreme Court is attempting to work out a distinction between regulation of interprovincial and intraprovincial trade. However, this is a purely judicial gloss on the text of the B.N.A. Act, which has become constitutional dogma with little real assessment of the reasons for it. It began with *Citizens Ins. Co. of Can. v. Parsons*,[6] a Privy Council decision which upheld the validity of fairly innocuous provincial legislation regulating the terms of insurance contracts. In order to do so, the Court excluded provincial intervention from the economy only when it amounted to "regulation of trade in matters of interprovincial concern". Soon this formula became constitutional doctrine for the converse problem—determining the ambit of valid dominion legislation. Because there has never been any real assessment of the reasons why we should have such a judge-made allocation of legislative authority, it is not surprising that the courts have never discovered how to apply it in anything but a wooden and legalistic way.

The underlying functional problem is that consumers of farm products, who are making purchases through a national currency and credit system, cannot effectively be regulated by a legislative body which has jurisdiction over a portion only of the undifferentiated products which are being marketed to them. If the federal government alone can control the marketing of extraprovincial products or trade, and the provincial government alone can control intraprovincial products or transactions, then there will have to be substantial identity in the content of co-ordinated legislation if the regulatory goals of either are to be achieved. Otherwise, the supply of unregulated goods will frustrate the

---

6 (1881), 7 App. Cas. 96 esp. at 113.

orderly marketing and price supports which are the major thrust of current farm policy. Yet, the attainment of co-operation always faces the obstacle of possible federal disinterest in a relatively localized problem or a parochial local veto of legislation desired by the federal government and a majority of the provinces. Hence, the requirement of co-operative action is always risky, time consuming and in the interests of those who do not want to be regulated (and who win from a governmental decision not to intervene whether it comes on the merits or not).

This is the economic background to the various statutory schemes which came up for constitutional review by reference to this concept of "interprovincial trade". A lengthy series of precedents had sustained the constitutionality of non-discriminatory, provincial schemes for the orderly marketing of products within their borders, whatever the source or destination. In *Shannon*,[7] the Privy Council upheld compulsory marketing through provincial boards of all milk sold in the province and their Lordships considered it quite unimportant that some of this milk was produced outside the province. Shortly afterwards, in *Home Oil Distributors*,[8] the Supreme Court upheld provincial fixing of minimum and maximum prices of gasoline and fuel oil in reliance on *Shannon*. It was clear from extrinsic evidence that this legislation was aimed at extra-provincial (in fact foreign) producers who were dumping surplus fuel oil in B.C. at such low prices that it was destructive of the B.C. coal industry, and were then recovering their losses from exorbitant prices charged for gasoline for which there was no local alternative. The Court simply relied on the formula that the regulation applied only to producers once they were inside the province and said that if the plaintiffs "desire to carry on their business in the Province of British Columbia, they must comply with provincial laws in common with all provincial and independent dealers in the same commodities". In the face of these two precedents, it would seem difficult indeed for the Supreme Court to have held the Manitoba scheme invalid under existing law.

However, some retreat from the very wide compass given to provincial powers might have been seen in the *Ontario Farm Products Reference*[9] which dealt with the opposite side of the marketing coin—provincial competence over locally produced products destined for outside the province. The Court for the first time appeared to recognize that there are few, if any, marketing transactions which cannot be described, at least abstractly, as taking place within one province, and that there are few intraprovincial transactions which do not have ramifications outside the province. Accordingly, some of the judges tried to articulate criteria as to when transactions could be said to be in interpro-

---

7 *Shannon v. Lower Mainland Dairy Products Bd.*, [1938] A.C. 708 esp. at 717, [1938] 2 W.W.R. 604, [1938] 4 D.L.R. 81.

8 *Home Oil Distributors Ltd. v. A.G. B.C.*, [1940] S.C.R. 444, [1940] 2 D.L.R. 609.

9 [1957] S.C.R. 198, 7 D.L.R. (2d) 257

vincial trade and thus outside provincial control. The important factor appeared to be whether the products were intended to be sold directly or indirectly (i.e., after processing) to consumers within that province. Unfortunately, the very abstract character of this Reference deprived these efforts of any real significance. This was indicated by the next case, *Carnation Company*,[10] involving real facts and a concrete dispute.

In the *Carnation* case, a Canadian incorporated company with its head office in Toronto operated both a receiving station for milk and a processing plant in Quebec. It bought raw milk from about 2,000 farmers in the relevant area, sent most of it to the plant to be processed into evaporated milk, and skimmed some of the milk and sent it to be processed in an Ontario plant. The major consumer market for the evaporated milk was outside Quebec. Under provincial marketing legislation, a majority of area milk producers organized a marketing plan which regulated all sales of raw milk to Carnation and provided for government arbitration of price in case of non-agreement. It appears as a result that Carnation had to pay a significantly greater price for raw milk than other purchasers from the same area, and eventually Carnation objected to the constitutionality of an arbitration award. However, the Supreme Court, in an opinion written by Martland J., upheld the provincial scheme on the theory that each transaction and each regulation must be examined in relation to its own facts:

> In the present case, the orders under question were not, in my opinion, directed at the regulation of interprovincial trade. They did not purport directly to control or to restrict such trade. There was no evidence that, in fact, they did control or restrict it. The most that can be said of them is that they had some effect upon the cost of losing business in Quebec of a company engaged in interprovincial trade, and that, by itself, is not sufficient to make them invalid.[11]

In the face of this course of decision, it would seem very difficult to legally invalidate the proposed Manitoba Egg scheme. In order to do so, the Court would have to make and justify a very substantial change in the direction of Canadian constitutional law. Of course, the two older cases—*Shannon* and *Home Oil*—were directly on point and firmly in favour of provincial jurisdiction. Whatever hints to the contrary we might have seen in the 1957 *Reference*, dealing with an analogous situation, seemed put to rest by the *Carnation* case. Yet the Court, without a suggestion that it was doing any more than follow a long, unbroken line of decisions, turned around and held the Manitoba scheme invalid. The opinion for the Court majority was again written by Mr. Justice Martland. The sum total of his reasoning to this conclusion is contained in the following passage:

---

10 *Carnation Co. v. Que. Agricultural Marketing Bd.*, [1968] S.C.R. 238 esp. at 253.
11 [1968] S.C.R. at 254.

It is my opinion that the plan now in issue not only affects interprovincial trade in eggs, but that it aims at the regulation of such trade. It is an essential part of this scheme, the purpose of which is to obtain for Manitoba producers the most advantageous marketing conditions for eggs, specifically to control and regulate the sale in Manitoba of imported eggs. It is designed to restrict or limit the free flow of trade between provinces as such. Because of that, it constitutes an invasion of the exclusive legislative authority of the Parliament of Canada over the matter of the regulation of trade and commerce.[12]

I suggest that this argument is question-begging as a response to the legal authority of the *Carnation* case decided less than three years before (let alone the older but more direct precedents of *Shannon* and *Home Oil*). No doubt there are factual distinctions between the two marketing schemes, but I do not believe that there are meaningful economic differences relevant to the central legal issue—should one province have the power to control agricultural marketing inside its boundaries when this necessarily affects or "concerns" the interests of citizens in other provinces? I will indicate my reasons for this judgment, but I should first point out that even if I am wrong there is not one sentence in the majority opinion which purports to show why one scheme is valid, but the other is not. Instead, we are given only labels—*affects* interprovincial trade or *aims at the regulation* of such a trade. We have met other instances of the same tendency in earlier chapters; the reader may remember the notion of "unusual danger". Constitutional law is shot through with such verbal formulae masquerading as legal guidelines. These the individual judges apply in some mysterious fashion to produce a result which they tell us is the law, or at least the law for the time being.

What is the functional economic significance of the scheme in the *Manitoba Egg Reference* and how does it compare with that in *Carnation?* Manitoba producers were authorized to create marketing boards composed of people elected by them and charged with achieving the most advantageous marketing for their product. To this end the boards were given powers to market all eggs sold in the province and to require the grading, packing and marketing of all such eggs at a station, the operation of which was under the control of the board. All eggs coming from outside the province were subject to the scheme, and the place of origin of such eggs was to be marked on the container. No doubt, the major problem in this legislation was that it could be administered in a discriminatory fashion (and, as I have said, apparently was so operated in other provinces). If extraprovincial eggs were not given a fair share of marketing quotas and were kept out of provincial markets until provincial eggs were sold, this would be an obvious reason for invalidating the legislation in operation. However, actual discrimina-

---

12 [1971] S.C.R. at 703.

tion was not the assumption on which the Reference was made, argued and decided.[13] Thus the danger in the decision is that it seems to bar subjection of extraprovincial products even to a fairly administered, provincial regulatory scheme.

The economic purpose of this kind of marketing legislation is protection of the markets and prices of Manitoba producers at the expense of Manitoba consumers. In order to achieve this result through price supports and orderly marketing in an undifferentiated market for eggs, it is necessary to subject producers from other provinces to the same limitations in dealing with Manitoba distributors. By contrast, the purpose of the legislation in *Carnation* is to protect Quebec producers, at the expense of mainly non-Quebec consumers, without any limitation on non-Quebec producers. In the final analysis, the only difference is that in *Carnation* the wholesale marketing and pricing of all Quebec milk is controlled by Quebec law whether it is destined for inside or outside Quebec, while in the *Manitoba Egg Reference* case, all eggs sold in Manitoba are to be marketed and priced under Manitoba controls, whether they come from within or without Manitoba. Yet Martland J. decided that "on its own facts", the Manitoba legislation is *in relation to* trade and commerce (rather than simply affecting it), and thus is unconstitutional. As to the *Carnation* scheme, again "on its own facts", he said that the law merely had some effect on interprovincial trade, and was valid. If there is a difference which is relevant to the federal division of legislative power, it is not apparent to me, and certainly it is not adverted to on the face of the opinion.

Mr. Justice Laskin's opinion is much more sophisticated, especially in recognizing the difficulties faced in trying to answer such a question of constitutionality on a Reference with no supporting factual or economic data. However, he does not appear to consider the possibility that, in such a situation, discretion may be the better part of valour. He says that the "proposed scheme has as a direct object the regulation of the importation of eggs, and it is not saved by the fact that the local market is under the same regime". His only practical reason for holding this to be invalid is that it denies "one of the objects of Confederation . . . namely to form an economic unit of the whole of Canada". Unfortunately, he does not tell us why this is the case for this kind of legislation and not so for the legislation in *Carnation*. Nor does he detail the evils in a non-discriminatory provincial scheme for controlled marketing and price supports for all eggs sold in the province, whatever their source.

---

13 I should note that Mr. Justice Pigeon, in a cryptic concurring opinion, agreed with the majority conclusion only for the reason that the scheme enabled the marketing board to give a preference to the sale of local eggs, even if this might mean a total prohibition on the sale of out-of-province eggs.

The functional problem which the Court is required to face in this case is the degree of latitude which a province should be allowed in subjecting the business sector of our society to regulation within its borders. As a matter of plain economic fact, the interdependent nature of business activity in this country is such that almost all provincial regulations will have ramifications on citizens and enterprises outside the province, whether or not the legal rule technically applies only to a purely intraprovincial trade or transaction. Moreover, the citizens of these provinces, who are so affected by these regulatory decisions, have no real say in the election of the representative governments which make them. Hence the arguments which can be made for judicial *laissez-faire* with respect to democratically elected parliaments do not have the same weight as in many of the other constitutional areas decided by the Court.

Although our Court has never looked for illumination in American cases since 1949, there has been a very sophisticated debate in the U.S. Supreme Court about the proper judicial role in controlling state-enacted "burdens" on interstate commerce.[14] There are three logical alternatives. One position holds that if a state enacts a law which imposes a significant burden on commerce within the national free trade economic unit, the Court should strike it down. At the opposite pole, it is argued that if the state has a reasonable interest of its own in the object of the regulation, and the law does not attempt to discriminate against out-of-state business as such, it should be upheld. An interim position—formulated by Chief Justice Stone and probably reflective of the majority view on the Court and among academic commentators—requires that the Court balance the legitimate benefits achieved by the states from the regulations against the burdens inflicted on inter-state commerce and only invalidate the law if the latter exceeds the former.

This brief statement of the opposing positions does not, of course, convey a sense of the detailed and sophisticated examination undertaken by the U.S. Supreme Court in making these enquiries. It is clear, though, from a comparison of the reasoning and results in *Carnation* and *Manitoba Egg Reference*, that our Court is either incapable of performing or unwilling to undertake the same function. If the Court had taken the first approach, I believe both schemes would be held invalid (at least on their face); while if the Court had taken the second approach, both laws would have been sustained. If the intermediate view was adopted, the Court would have had to weigh the competing interests of the legislating province in the respective schemes and those of the nation in the free flow of a national market. What we received, though,

---

14 A recent book by Benson, *The Supreme Court and the Commerce Clause* (1970), has an excellent discussion of these different positions in its Chapter 7. Perhaps the leading case illustrating the alternative views in operation is *Southern Pac. v. Arizona* (1945), 325 U.S. 761.

was only a judicial *ipse dixit* which may have authoritatively resolved the dispute—in the way Manitoba wanted—but did so with no supporting reasoning.

There are some observers who will not be troubled by this, and will believe that what the Court says is law, and must be followed, and that is the end of that. Unfortunately, others, especially those adversely affected by this "law", will ask why they should accept the intuitive judgments of the Court as final. Ontario and Quebec may simply say that they believe their legislation is somewhat different from that involved in the *Manitoba Egg Reference* and one can find no principle or reasoning in the latter case which would indicate whether or not the distinction is specious. In any event, it seems that shortly afterwards the affected governments met and engaged in some serious bargaining which was directed towards the real conflicts and problems in the area. This was to be expected because it is hard to see how the "winner take all" kind of judicial decision could be an acceptable basis for resolving a very complex problem involving not only a conflict between different groups of producers, but an equally vital conflict between producers and consumers who vote in the same province. The most intriguing comment made just before the meeting of the ministers of agriculture was that they were all agreed then on just one thing—that the Supreme Court decision would *not* be the basis of their final settlement.

CHANGING CONCEPTIONS OF JUDICIAL REVIEW WITHIN CANADIAN FEDERALISM

(a) The Original Rationale

What is the significance of the *Manitoba Egg Reference?* I believe the case to be typical of the very complicated political and economic conflicts which are the "stuff" of constitutional adjudication. Further, it suggests the paradoxical character of "government by lawsuit" as the preferred technique for resolving these conflicts. Why do we have the institution of judicial review within Canadian federalism? It is not provided for in the text of the B.N.A. Act, and the Confederation Debates do not reveal an explicit agreement that it should be adopted. In fact, the preamble to the B.N.A. Act indicates an intention to establish a constitution similar in principle to that of the United Kingdom. As Dicey was to record shortly thereafter, the basic principle of the British constitution is parliamentary sovereignty, which means that British courts do not have the power to review and invalidate legislation. Perhaps this aspect of the British model was inapplicable to a federal system of divided legislative authority. However, there is no record of an explicit consensus among the Fathers of Confederation that Canadian federalism did require judicial review, and there is some indication that they believed conflicts of jurisdiction would rarely arise.

Yet judicial review did come to be exercised in Canada immediately after Confederation and encountered so little inquiry or debate that it must have been tacitly assumed by everyone to be proper. An understanding of its legal basis at that time is important for anyone who is assessing the continued viability of the institution one hundred years later. By virtue of the Colonial Laws Validity Act, which clarified earlier judicial practice, colonial statutes would be void for repugnancy if they conflicted with Imperial laws extending to the colony. Colonial courts, as well as the Privy Council, had customarily reviewed subordinate governmental legislation in the colony and assessed its legal validity in this way. The B.N.A. Act was an Imperial statute extending to the colony of Canada, and it explicitly authorized legislative jurisdiction only when it fell within certain "exclusive" areas allocated to either the Dominion or the provinces. When either of these "subordinate" bodies purported to act beyond the powers created by the British statute, its legislation would conflict with an Imperial law, thus triggering the Colonial Laws Validity Act. Hence, a private citizen affected by any Canadian law could always impugn the validity of such legislation by persuading a court that it was inconsistent with the superior Imperial law, which the court was duty-bound to consider in deciding the instant case.

It is because of this legal background that Canadian constitutional theory has never enjoyed a debate similar to that in the United States since *Marbury v. Madison* about the propriety of judicial review of legislative action. There is no logical necessity for judicial review in a federal system, even though federalism by its very nature involves the creation of *limited* legislative powers. A further inference is still necessary to show that the ordinary courts have the final say in determining whether legislation duly enacted by a representative body is *ultra vires* and thus null and void. Indeed, there was explicit provision in the B.N.A. Act for a political forum as a possible vehicle for enforcing the federal limitations. This was the provision for dominion disallowance of provincial legislation and Imperial disallowance of dominion statutes. However, the constitutional conventions of the British Empire in 1867 prevented the question even arising in the Canadian legal environment as to whether the existence of an explicit, political avenue for review excluded the implicit, judicial alternative.

Given this fundamental assumption about the legal rationale of judicial review, certain further implications seem natural. The first corollary is that any ordinary citizen who is affected by the operation of allegedly invalid statutes should have standing to require that the Court adjudicate upon his claim to unconstitutionality. If a statute is sought to be applied to him, he should be able to impugn the validity of the statute by appealing to the more fundamental law defining the competence of the enacting body. A second corollary deals with the question of whether constitutional powers are *exclusive* or *concurrent*. The notion that there is a basic law setting out spheres of legislative jurisdiction suggests strongly that the courts may hold legislation invalid because it encroaches on the constitutional authority of another jurisdiction, even where the latter has not passed inconsistent legislation, or perhaps has not occupied any part of the field at all. What if the competent legislatures have not only refrained from exercising their exclusive powers but have also granted permission to the other legislatures to act as they did? A third logical corollary of the institution of judicial review in classical federalism is that such delegation is impossible. It offends against the principle that the basic constitutional law is the source of a limited and subordinate authority in the legislatures, and they are not entitled even by mutual agreement to amend the original legal scheme which belongs to the people (or at least their surrogate, the courts).

This view of the source of judicial review within our federal constitution and the legal corollaries of review is internally coherent and was originally plausible. I suggest that later developments have lessened considerably the case which can be made in defence of judicial review at the very same time that the institution has become even more solidly entrenched. In fact, the course of events in Canada may be symptomatic of logical tendencies in any federal system.

Why are federal unions created in the first place? The reason is that the constituent units face the need for merger—usually because of an external threat—but cannot accept total legislative unity. Political, economic, social and cultural concerns are simply too divisive. Hence the constitution makers strike a political compromise and divide up the various governmental functions in a way which best serves these opposing interests in unity and diversity. At that time there is great appeal in the view that the written bargain is really a fundamental law, and that it has a sufficient core of legal meaning to be left to the administration of the ordinary courts, even at the behest of the private individual. Why is this so? First, the negotiators of the federal union have been able to canvass the governmental functions which are important at that time, and to reach a decision about the body to which they are to be allocated. The language which is used to describe these functions is likely to be fairly accurate, and, in any event, there is a sufficient substratum of common understanding and practice to admit coherent and objective interpretation even in the difficult marginal cases. Second, the very reasons why a federal (and only a federal) union was created in the first place in turn require an impartial arbiter to administer these controls. The original federal bargain reflected important and divisive interests in allocating some functions to the central government while protecting local autonomy with respect to other legislative activities. These needs continue to be deeply felt during the time that the institutions of the new federal union develop authority and support, and an impartial arbiter is a necessary source of assurance that the original bargain is being adhered to.

(b) Judicial Responsibility for Constitutional Change

Each of these conditions for the "law-like" character of a federal constitution gradually erodes as the document ages. There are two related reasons for this tendency: first, social change eventually renders most of the original federal bargain outmoded; second, a constitution by its very nature is difficult to amend. There are several kinds of changes which are relevant to a federal constitution. The original law-making functions which were explicitly allocated by the constitution substantially alter their character in ways which are significant to their proper distribution (e.g. the emergence of the rehabilitative ideal in the criminal law). New social problems arise and demand legislative responses which were not foreseen by the draftsman, and thus must be dealt with in terms of the residuary clauses in the constitution (e.g., orderly farm marketing). The governmental units themselves change their character and capacities for legislative action (e.g. Canada's international status). New fundamental values evolve within the nation, and so alter the principles which shaped the original federal bargain (e.g. the claim to equalization of basic social security protections in different regions). The cumulative result of these several tendencies is that, over the largest area of constitutional decision-making, the original written understanding becomes simply irrelevant to the real human and social issues which governments must deal with.

On the other hand, as I have said, amendment of a federal constitution is necessarily difficult, and the Canadian experience certainly verifies this. There are a number of parties to the bargain, they have important conflicts of interest, and, conventionally, they must be agreed unanimously on any explicit change. Not only is it politically difficult to secure constitutional amendments, but the perception of this difficulty exacerbates the problem even further. If everyone knows that an amendment is, practically speaking, almost irrevocable, it becomes much more difficult to persuade a jurisdiction to concede certain constitutional powers for immediate reasons, when the long-term significance of the change is necessarily unforeseeable. Finally, the longer the document remains unchanged, the easier it is for those who are opposed to specific amendments to appeal to the constitution's symbolic and tradition-laden character.

In such a legal situation, it is not defensible for a court to say that its only function is to apply the "law" as it is written and, if the proper authorities do not amend the constitution to keep it in tune with changes in society, the resultant misfit is not the responsibility of the judges. This attitude is founded on the legalist assumption I criticized earlier, the notion that the "law" inheres in the ordinary meaning of the surface language of a document like the B.N.A. Act. These rules are believed to remain there, pure and unaltered, waiting to be applied by a later judge whatever be the changes in the social context into which he will insert them. This conception of law is much too limited. It is impossible to separate the meaning of a legal proposition from the context of the procedure by which it was originally enacted, the demands of the situation within which it was created and the purposes or intentions of those who drafted it. There is an inescapable act of judgment in applying such general standards to concrete cases. A judge who is required to administer the rules must appeal to these elements in the background to preserve the integrity of the system he is administering. Gradually the significance of the original scheme recedes as the gap widens between the frozen constitutional language and the rapidly changing society. As this happens, the courts inevitably begin to elaborate a new federal scheme in the course of adjudicating many novel and unforeseen problems. As we look back, we can see that this is the objective impact of the work of the courts even though judges may have disguised their personal responsibility for the results—from themselves as well as from others—by adoption of a very formal style of legal reasoning.

The major thrust of constitutional literature in Canada in the last thirty years or so has been built on this insight into judicial responsibility for constitutional innovation. Writers have not only described the nature and extent of judicial alterations to our federal structure but have also tried to articulate the factors which ought to influence the courts in their allocation of legislative power to one jurisdiction or another. This whole effort is directed at one basic constitutional question: "which is the better physician for a social malady, the dominion or provincial government?" This scholarly effort to understand and improve the constitutional product of our courts was given extra impetus by a further fact. A series of unfortunate judicial decisions in the interwar period, more than a half century after the birth of the Canadian constitution, threatened the capacity of our political structure to respond to Canadian political needs.

This series of cases dealt with challenges to some very different legislative schemes which were not within the experience of those who negotiated and drafted the specific categories of the B.N.A. Act. Hence, each had to be classified by the Privy Council and Canadian courts within the general or residual powers the document conferred on the two levels of government. These clauses did not have the kind of internal content which could be discerned by a process of legal interpretation and then used to solve the novel problem. Genuine creativity was required from the courts in distilling the essence of the new statute and deciding whether it was properly enacted by the jurisdiction in question. With their somewhat insulated perspective on social problems, the judges

168

were naturally unfamiliar with the objective of such legislation and could easily be unsympathetic to such "new-fangled" schemes. The tendency in the cases was to find the statutes invalid from their immediate source, without much concern for the adequacy of the alternative. The total impact was a constitutional straitjacket on Canadian government.

There was a strong consensus among constitutional scholars that these cases had to be overruled or ignored. Yet this would mean that in the very area where judges were faced with controversial issues to which the B.N.A. Act did not speak, they would receive no aid from stable judicial authorities and principles. However, the recognition of judicial responsibility for constitutional choices, and the hope for new directions in constitutional policy, did lead to one significant change. The Supreme Court of Canada replaced the Privy Council as our final court of appeal. The expectation was that a Canadian court, composed of Canadian judges, might produce a higher quality of judicial adaptation to social change—especially since these judges would have to live in the society which was governed by the political institutions they were helping to mould.

(c) The Call for a Constitutional Court

Out of this structural reform, founded as it was on the frank recognition of judicial responsibility for constitutional evolution, a second theme in our constitutional literature emerged. It was natural to ask whether even a Canadian body such as our Supreme Court was institutionally equipped to exercise the judgments needed for rational policy-making. It is easy to see why lawyers are attracted to the notion of constitutional reform through the judiciary. It is legally possible to assert that the judges are merely engaged in adjudication of new situations, the decisions are available as of right and are authoritative and changes can be spaced out in an orderly and incremental way. The real difficulties develop when the courts try to perform this task, and then especially as we realize they are performing it. Recognition of these difficulties has led to a series of proposals for the redesign of the Supreme Court to improve its constitutional performance.

A major concern is with the quality of judge-made constitutional policy. Very intricate analysis is needed to answer the basic federalism question, what level of government should be in charge of this kind of law-making? A judge should understand the nature of the social problem (e.g., the economics of farming reflected in the *Manitoba Egg Reference*), appreciate the rationale of the regulatory scheme a government believes is needed (controlled marketing) and assess the relative capacities of different jurisdictions to implement the scheme. Intelligent policy-making has two requirements at each of these stages: the decision-maker must be apprised of the relevant information and he must have the kind of background and expertise which enables him to assess the data

169

intelligently. The judicial process as we know it in Canada places road-blocks in the way of both of these.

The adversary process of adjudication has been designed to present a true picture of a specific event. It is hardly an apt instrument for portraying the complex and ambiguous character of a changing Canadian society in a manner relevant to the demands of federalism. The narrow and distorted forms of concrete litigation may be avoided by referring the statute as such to the courts: the result is that the judges are lost in an abstract legal world. Nor can we remedy this deficiency through judicial notice of the relevant facts by wise and statesman-like members of the court. As we have seen, Supreme Court judges are recruited from a very narrow stratum of society—middle-aged and respectable lawyers— a practice which is justified by the need for adjudication of specific disputes within a framework of law. It is only by accident that men picked for this purpose will be able to perform the special and esoteric function of administering our federal system (which, after all, is only a small percentage of the Court's work). Nor will they be educated in the realities and needs of government in Canada by the haphazard character of the litigation which does happen to move them to action.

Various structural changes in the Supreme Court have been suggested as a result. Some merely tinker with the existing institution, as, for example, the favourite proposal of deleting the private law function of the Court. Supposedly this would free the judges for greater exposure to the policy-laden questions of public law and perhaps justify the appointment of people without such an emphasis on narrow legal expertise. Others propose the use of extrinsic aids (such as Brandeis briefs) to facilitate the process of finding and understanding constitutional facts. These measures might achieve marginal improvements but the nature of the problem calls for a more fundamental revision. The real alternative is the removal of constitutional decision-making from the ordinary courts of law and the creation of a specialized tribunal for this purpose. This new body would be composed not only of lawyers but of specialists from other disciplines who were appointed because of their understanding of the problems of federalism. It would have its own research arm which could anticipate constitutional conflicts and make independent investigations of what the situation demanded. When the matter was brought before the tribunal, its members would be capable of a much more informed evaluation of the arguments from each side about how Canadian federalism should be adjusted to meet the problem.

There is another line of criticism of the present structure of the Supreme Court which also leads to this proposal of a new constitutional court. Federalism issues are not just technically intricate. They involve irreducible conflicts among deeply felt values held by different groups and regions in Canada. The most obvious of these is the French Canadian language and culture but this is only the tip of the iceberg. Any adequate resolution of these conflicts does require an awareness of their complexities and well researched and reasoned analysis of the alternative ways out. Something more is needed though, something which is not provided by rule by our constitutional experts. The surface acceptability of our law relies on a broad based consensus about the authority of the bodies which make these decisions. Remove such a consensus, and it will not be long before the losers will be loath to accept the decisions that go against them. This is the hidden weakness in the judicial edifice.

There is a paradoxical character at the roots of judicial review. The Supreme Court strikes down a decision made by a democratically elected legislature. The paradox is hidden at the beginning because judicial decisions can be justified by reference to a supreme law, agreed to at the founding of the nation. The court can appeal to the superior authority of such a standard to measure the legality of decisions made by subordinate (and merely colonial) legislatures. Now this original document has faded into the misty past and judicial review reflects quite a different reality. The Supreme Court is, of necessity, engaged in a continuous process of devising new constitutional standards to evaluate, and sometimes to strike down, laws enacted by a government responsive to a popular majority.

The uneasy legitimacy of constitutional law can be shortly explained in this way. The reason why continual innovation is necessary is that constitutional amendment is so difficult to achieve. The reason why constitutional amendment is so difficult is that any revision of legislative authority involves vital, unforeseeable and almost irrevocable alterations of political power. As a result, the interested governments can rarely agree on the explicit changes needed to update the original document. Yet, if this is the nature of constitutional amendment, why should it be any more acceptable when gradually but unilaterally imposed by the courts? Once the political institutions absorb the lessons of constitutional scholarship and see that this is what is really happening, they can only live with the process if they have some control over the court which is making these decisions.

Within this perspective, the Supreme Court of Canada exhibits a basic flaw. The source of an umpire's authority is his impartiality, a quality which assumes his lack of special dependence on any one side. Right now the members of the present Court are all picked by the federal government which has an unfettered discretion in evaluating their competence and attitudes and need not defend its choices in an open forum. Yet the federal government is one of the parties at interest in every dispute where the Court must allocate legislative authority. Even worse, there are no constitutional guarantees of the status of either the Court or its members after they are selected. The judges are all paid and protected in their tenure only under a statute which is within the sole legislative authority of Parliament. Legally speaking, the impartiality of the umpire of our federalism may be said to exist only at the sufferance of one side.

171

It does not matter that the federal government would be unlikely ever to exercise these legal powers out of displeasure at a course of constitutional decisions, or that our judges would not be influenced in their work by their present legal status. It is important not only that justice be done but also that it seem to be done. Ever since the Tremblay Report, French Canadian legal opinion has focused attention on this issue and called for the necessary changes. Some deference was paid to this view in the abortive Victoria Charter of 1971 which would have required consultation with the provinces about appointments to the Supreme Court. This is merely a step towards the ideal of those who favour a new constitutional court. Such a body must have a status and tenure which is constitutionally defined and its members must be selected proportionately by both the federal and provincial governments. Only in this way can every side be sure that its own values and positions are shared by at least some of the experts on the body making these absolutely vital decisions.

Let me summarize this simplified sketch of the intellectual history of judicial review in Canada. Judicial review was originally justified in terms of the duty of the ordinary courts to apply the relevant law in the adjudication of concrete disputes in Canada. In particular the courts were to measure the subordinate Canadian statutes against the terms of the more basic Imperial law which legally created and defined these colonial law-making powers in the first place. After a period of time, fifty years or so, social and political change rendered the specific sections of the frozen constitution outmoded, and the courts were required to found their decisions on the vague residual categories. Criticism of the inflexible federal structure produced by these decisions led to a call for a much less legalistic and more policy oriented view of the judicial function in Canadian federalism. An immediate result was replacement of the Privy Council by the Supreme Court of Canada as the final authority in administering the B.N.A. Act and all other areas of Canadian law. It was not long though before it was recognized that the Supreme Court, designed as it was for the job of adjudication, was not up to the rigorous demands of constitutional policy-making. A series of proposals have come forward for the redesign of the Court for the better performance of its constitutional function. Yet as we reflect on the cumulative impact of these proposals, the ideal institution which emerges is not really a court at all.

DO WE STILL NEED A JUDICIAL UMPIRE?

In the course of this sustained intellectual critique of judicial review—of the way it is and should be carried on—the one question which is never asked is the most fundamental of all. Should we continue to have any judicial review at all in Canadian federalism? As I have said, the original rationale for review was in terms of the ordinary courts applying a law. However, the contemporary reality, as reflected in the *Manitoba Egg Reference*, is that there is no longer a meaningful law to apply and the precent function of federal umpiring appears unsuited for the adversary process of the ordinary courts. If I may put the matter a little more bluntly than did Mr. Justice Hughes, current judicial review in the Supreme Court of Canada means that the Court is holding legislation valid or invalid on the basis of standards which it is making up as it goes along. If this is indeed true, we must seriously question whether our constitutional structure has outgrown the role of judicial umpire.

Obviously I cannot demonstrate my thesis about the lack of law in Canadian federalism decisions from one case, and I do not propose in this book to document my view that the *Manitoba Egg Reference* is a typical example. I have reviewed all the constitutional cases in the Supreme Court of Canada since 1949 and have published the results elsewhere.[15] Two pronounced trends are visible in the decisions. First, the substantive direction of the Court's constitutional policy is in favour of a gradual and sensible widening of the ambit for legislative action. This is particularly the case for the federal Parliament which the Court— in deed though not in word—no longer attempts to restrict in any significant way. As regards the provincial legislatures, while the trend has been less marked, there has been a relaxation of judicial control in the sixties. The Court still intervenes occasionally if only to remind everyone that it does have the final say.

The cases in which the Court does intervene and tries to draw a negative constitutional line exhibit the second pronounced trend. This is the Court's inability to articulate any legal principles which show why some provincial statutes are valid and others are not. For example, the Supreme Court simply did not apply to the facts of the *Manitoba Egg Reference* any legal standard which could fairly be said to have controlled the decision in *Carnation*, though the legal and functional problems presented by the cases are very similar. This objection is by no means unique to constitutional law. We have seen many other examples of the Supreme Court "flip-flopping" back and forth on an issue. However, I think there is something about this subject-matter which aggravates these deficiencies in our constitutional opinions. Some confirmation of this view can be found in the experience of the United States Supreme Court. However activist that body is elsewhere, in the area of federalism it also has given up trying to restrain the national government. In the few cases where it still tries to control the states, even its admirers are unimpressed by the reasons advanced.

The explanation is that federalism questions are not amenable to stable legal principles. Our judges are working with a century old docu-

---

15 In my article "The Supreme Court and the Law of Canadian Federalism", cited in fn. 1, *ante*.

ment whose basic objectives are largely irrelevant to modern legislative problems. The courts are left to fill such empty verbal categories as "peace, order and good government", "property and civil rights", etc. It is always easy to support a conclusion in favour of the validity of the legislation in question. Invariably the jurisdiction which has acted will have some legitimate claims in the area which the court can rely on. The critical cases, the areas where judicial review must justify its existence, occur when a court decides to invalidate challenged legislation on the ground that another jurisdiction has a compelling claim to exclusive control. This is essentially a political controversy, complicated by different capacities and attitudes in the several legislatures and variations in the objectives and structures of statutory schemes. All the court can really do is act on some intuitive sense that the immediate legislation just goes too far (and this is the probable explanation of the decision in the *Manitoba Egg Reference*). Unfortunately, no one can propose any legal standards to tell us how far is too far. In this, constitutional adjudication resembles nothing so much as compulsory, interest dispute, labour arbitration.

The analogy with compulsory arbitration is instructive. Ordinarily, if an issue is politically charged and there are no established legal standards which are applicable to it, we do not believe that it can be satisfactorily resolved by an adjudicative body such as a court (or an arbitration board). Yet sometimes the political (or bargaining) process is not a viable alternative, and judicial intervention is better than nothing. I do believe that federalism cases (such as the *Manitoba Egg Reference*) involve essentially non-legal conflicts which will not be dealt with very successfully in the judicial process, and that courts should avoid the area unless their intervention is absolutely vital. I must still address myself to the question whether a federal system—in particular, Canadian federalism —really does need a judicial umpire to survive in an acceptable way.

The lawyer's natural response is, "of course, we need a federal umpire because how else will we resolve conflicts between different governments, when each believes it has a distinctive legislative claim in a particular area?" One of the most basic tenets of the lawyer's ideology is that where there is conflict, there must also be a neutral and authoritative body, preferably a court, which can render a decision to resolve the conflict. If there is no procedure for making binding decisions about disputed issues and thus enforcing the rules against those who are tempted to non-compliance, one may wonder how the legal system or any part of it could long survive. Yet further reflection should suggest that law without judges—in particular, federalism without an umpire—is at least possible, if not probable and desirable. Who has not played in a game which has successfully been carried on within the rules but in the absence of an umpire? Further, the plausibility of the role of the court as an umpire of our federal rules must be substantially lessened when we fully appreciate the fact that the court is developing the rules of the

174

game as it goes along. Constitutional conflict is not always so bad and, even when it is, I doubt that judicial review can make a durable contribution to its resolution.

Instead, it seems to me that a federal system is precisely the kind of relationship for which an external umpire may not be necessary and in which the better technique for managing conflict is continual negotiation and political compromise. In fact, Canadian federalism exhibits many of the conditions which are highly conducive to bargaining. There is a small number of governments, they are constantly talking to each other, they are dependent on each other's co-operation in many different areas, there is always room for trading in new or recurring problem areas, and they are quite capable of spending the time and energy to formulate a compromise. Occasionally, perhaps, an issue may arise in which compromise appears impossible because neither side can make any concession from its vital interests. However, this is precisely the area where unilateral imposition of a settlement by an unresponsive body such as the Supreme Court will be equally unacceptable. It will still require the further techniques of political bargaining to secure the effective implementation of the judicial decision.

It is sometimes suggested that, in the more typical and less critical issues which might be resolved by compromise, the process of bargaining will be enhanced by the presence in the background of a neutral umpire who could provide an authoritative ruling in the case of disagreement. If the experience in the labour area is any indication, the contrary is true. There is a real possibility that the availability of the judicial alternative may actually hinder the achievement of more functional solutions through compromise. The aura which surrounds courts tends to convert real but limited conflicts of interest into an artificial controversy over basic principles. Adjudicative responses to a dispute ordinarily speak of absolute legal rights—enjoyed by one party and not the other— rather than recognizing that each side has a political claim of varying weight. Negotiations are usually more productive in an atmosphere in which ambiguous claims may be gracefully conceded, one in return for another, rather than one side having to give up its rights which are guaranteed to it by a court.

Hence I suggest that as lawyers we must take a new view of the process of constitutional policy-making, a view which emphasizes the political character of these issues and their awkward fit with adjudication. There is good reason to believe that the original participants of Confederation assumed a high degree of political interdependence which would deal with federal conflicts through these resources, and the tacit assumption of judicial review was merely residual. The legalistic cost to Canadian constitutionalism may have been appropriate in our earlier years as a nation. However, both the federal and provincial governments have matured along with the rest of our society to an extent that makes the categories of exclusive, self-contained, legislative functions no longer tenable. We must now allow either representative government to decide not only whether affirmative legislative action is desirable for a social problem but also whether it is the appropriate body to enact such legislation. The court should not have the job of making this second but equally political decision.

It is no doubt possible, even likely, that both the federal and provincial governments would each like to intervene, and that joint occupancy of the field would be awkward. However, this is a reason why the two competing jurisdictions should negotiate a solution whereby one agrees to retreat and let the other have full sway. Suppose such an agreement does not materialize. Are private citizens to be left subject to two sets of laws with somewhat unco-ordinated policies? What should be the role of our courts in this situation, and how is it relevant to my main proposal? First of all, it is a minimum demand on a legal system— if not of its logic, at least of its "internal morality"—that citizens not be subjected to contradictory laws, and that courts must have the power to refine the administration of the legal order to prevent this situation arising. Even in a unitary legal system, there are potential cases of legal conflict because of the existence of multiple decision-makers in any complex society. The courts in such a society are required to play the narrower (though still vital) judicial role of interpretation of the relevant statutes to avoid legal conflicts and then application of doctrines of paramountcy to resolve the few remaining situations of unavoidably contradictory legal rules. Undoubtedly the courts in a federal system must also perform this function, and it will probably arise even more often because of the nature of modern federalism.

On the other hand, I do realize the possibility that the courts could become almost as involved in the politics of federalism through the apparently more limited vehicle of paramountcy as they would be when assessing the validity of laws enacted under exclusive legislative powers. The corollary of my general thesis about the role of courts in a federal system is that the scope of judicial action in this sphere should be confined to the same range as in a unitary legal system. Where a court sees that there are two statutes apparently relevant to one factual situation, it must first interpret the statutes to see whether each is really applicable. Only if the result of such a process of interpretation is an inescapable contradiction of legal directives, should the court proceed to hold one of these to be inoperative. An appropriately restricted judicial role would not allow for the application of vague doctrines of "occupying the field" or "pre-emption" to find "implied" conflicts when two legislatures have each tried to deal with the same problem. If the solutions adopted by the two legislatures are not legally contradictory, then even though the court believes the legislative policies to be somewhat incompatible, it should leave it to the legislatures to take responsibility for creating an explicit conflict and thus invoking the doctrines of paramountcy (and facing the electorate for the results, whatever they may be). The only possible exception to this logic might be the case of provincial laws burdening interprovincial trade and thus being harmful to the economic interests of the citizens in other provinces to whom the legislating province is not electorally responsible. My own view is that the only limitation on provincial laws in this area should be a prohibition on discrimination against extraprovincial citizens or products. Without a finding of such discrimination, the federal government should have the exclusive jurisdiction to decide that provincial laws are an undue interference with the national market.

The key question remaining concerns the content of the paramountcy doctrines which should be adopted in a federal system where the role of the courts is to be minimized. The natural conclusion is that there should be one easily applicable rule, singling out one jurisdiction's legislation as dominant. There seems also no doubt that, if such is the character of the rule, the dominant jurisdiction must be the Dominion Parliament which is responsive to the whole electorate, including voters in the province whose legislation is being overridden. The argument will be made, of course, that this gives the national government the legal power to erode the federal system through a gradual process of self-aggrandizement. My response is that legal possibility does not equal political feasibility and that we can and must rely on the political constraints of the federal system to ensure that this does not happen.

Since I first proposed this thesis, I have observed a continuous refrain in the reactions of constitutional lawyers. While there is surprising agreement with my diagnosis of the ailments of contemporary judicial review in Canada, there is also great reluctance to face its demise. Lawyers worry about how viable an alternative the process of political negotiations would be. Better the evil they know than a future about which they are insecure. The very fact that the courts do have the final and authoritative say has diverted us from the task of devising informal mechanisms which could do a better job. Yet, as long as we do not see the alternative ready at hand, the preservation of judicial review will appear the safer course.

However, if we were to expand our field of vision for a moment and look at all our federal arrangements, not just those which figure in constitutional litigation, we would see the alternative in operation. There are two important areas of government from which constitutional law is almost totally absent: (1) control of the economy through fiscal and monetary policies; and (2) provision of services, social security, welfare benefits and so on to Canadian citizens. For several technical reasons (especially the limitations on "standing", and Canadian conceptions of the legal discretion of our governments to raise money and spend it as they will), we do not have judicial supervision of these activities. The courts have not tried to carve out a system of abstract, exclusive and enduring jurisdiction, dividing the responsibility among different levels of government. That effort has been just about totally confined to cases where the legislature enacts statutes regulating the behaviour of its citizens, which eventually trigger constitutional challenges to the validity of the law. Yet not only are the federal arrangements viable in the former area without judicial control, but I believe they work much better, precisely because the courts do stay out.

Why is this the case? Mainly because legal discretion just does not spell political freedom. In reality no Canadian government can simply raise taxes and spend money as it sees fit without regard to what the other levels of government are doing. There is an ongoing framework for the division of governmental labour, which has developed for over a century (and to which, I might add, the courts made an important contribution in the early years). It is this *status quo* which sets the present ground rules, not the language of the B.N.A. Act. But each government retains the legal power to take the initiative in new areas of social concern (such as welfare policy) and experiment with a novel solution. This constant process of incremental change and diversity is, after all, one of the primary values of a federal system.

Sometimes such an initiative will be seen to infringe on another's bailiwick. When it does, it triggers a heated reaction, intergovernmental consultation, tough bargaining among those immediately involved, and usually, ultimate agreement. This whole exercise is focused around the particular legislative action in question. The parties do not have to worry about setting a legal precedent, based on some general principle of jurisdiction. If the exercise of governmental power is accepted, with or without modification, it is because the others can live with the immediate policy. This process of informal, flexible, constitutional adjustment is directed at co-ordinating and articulating the policies the governments have in mind now, not the hypothetical actions they might take twenty years hence.

Needless to say, sometimes the different governments may be loath to agree because of their deep attachment to mutually conflicting policies. A virtue of the process is that over a period of time many different issues arise and there is ample room for trading, log-rolling and compromise. It is surprising how often such governmental negotiations are successful. But suppose each side decides to take an unyielding stand on an issue and neither will retreat. Would this not be extremely uncomfortable for Canadian citizens and isn't the court the only vehicle for breaking the log-jam?

I think not. Each of these governments is answerable to the electorate. In the areas of taxation, welfare and so on the problems of federal jurisdiction have a high political saliency in Canada. A party's constitutional views figure prominently in election campaigns. No one government can afford to be too intransigent if it can foresee that this will be harmful to the interests of its citizens. Otherwise it will be thrown out of office. Sometimes, it may be convinced that its constitutional views will be popular with the electorate. Why shouldn't it have the freedom to test this judgment and let the other side take a close look at the results?

178

I know that to the legal mind this kind of decision-making process appears messy and unprincipled. Unfortunately, that is the reality of government in a complex and highly interdependent federal system which is trying to stay abreast of a constantly changing society. The alternative is not, and cannot be, the judicial administration of a set of enduring principles embodied in an ancient constitutional document. The best we can expect from our courts is the occasional *ad hoc* judgment about an immediate problem. I believe that much more flexible, informed and responsive solutions will be produced in the political forum, and that the continued availability of judicial review serves only to hamper that process.

THE FUTURE OF THE SUPREME COURT'S CONSTITUTIONAL ROLE

I must now move a little closer to the practical realities of Canadian law in the seventies. Judicial review within our federal system will not be abolished in the foreseeable future, if ever. Like judicial review of administrative action, we can expect to have it around for a long time. Perhaps its symbolic value may justify its presence, though its functional usefulness is minimal. This does not mean that theoretical analysis of this fundamental issue is irrelevant. The critical questions now are "how much judicial review?", and "in what way will it be carried on?" If our judges are properly oriented at the heart of the problem, then intelligent navigation around these immediate issues is possible. While my ideal is abolition of review, my immediate practical concern is minimizing its incidence and the harm it may cause.

A good example is implicit in an earlier part of this chapter. We see more and more proposals to change the structure of the Supreme Court to facilitate its constitutional role and some of these are beginning to appeal to the politicians. The logic of these proposals leads down the path to a specialized constitutional court, a body which would be quite unsuited to other important judicial functions. From my diagnosis of the significance of judicial review for an established federal system, the prescription is exactly the opposite. Instead of trying to redesign the Supreme Court to make it a better constitutional umpire, let's try to reduce as much as possible the significance of this function in its work.

The primary recipients of this advice should be the Supreme Court judges themselves. They should be fully aware of the political desirability of judicial restraint in the area of federalism. In fact, with only a few exceptions, the results (if not the explicit reasoning) of Supreme Court work in the last twenty years have been in this sensible direction. Judicial control of Parliament is almost non-existent, which is only as it should be for a government that is politically responsive to all regions of the country. The pattern regarding provincial legislation is more erratic, but the same direction can be seen in the last few years. "Functional concurrency" has been adopted in the sphere of economic regulation. A very important gain was judicial ratification of the kinds of consensual change in legislative power which can be produced through "co-operative federalism". There will likely be some critical tests of this new judicial attitude in the next few years, especially in some more adventurous regulatory schemes from Parliament. If, as I hope, these statutory innovations are consistently sustained against constitutional attack, we might approach very closely the functional elimination of judicial review, simply through the low visibility, incremental process of judicial change.

There is one procedural change which would help this judicial retreat and might be politically feasible now. It involves a sharp tightening of the law of standing to challenge the constitutional validity of a statute. The implications of what I suggest are graphically illustrated by the recent Supreme Court of Canada decision in the *Bell Telephone* case[16] (one of the few recent decisions actually holding provincial legislation to be invalid, even in part). Here Bell Telephone resisted a government suit for over $50,000, a levy which was imposed under the Quebec Minimum Wage Act, on the ground that the Act could not constitutionally apply to Bell Telephone and its employees (because they were within the dominion regulatory jurisdiction under s. 92(10) of the B.N.A. Act). It should be noted that the constitutionality of a direct taxing statute as applied to Bell could not have been attacked, but the legality of this administrative levy depended on the constitutional validity of applying the general scheme of the statute to regulate Bell's minimum wages, maximum hours, etc. The Court accepted the company's constitutional argument and thus rejected the provincial government's monetary action.

In my view, there is something wrong with a legal system which allows a private business to impeach in this way the validity of laws enacted by a representative legislature. The Minimum Wage Act had been in existence for a long time and, along with similar employment legislation (such as the child labour legislation, for instance), had been understood to apply to all companies employing people in Quebec. The federal government had not then enacted similar social legislation dealing with industries within its own jurisdiction, and there was no evidence that it had ever objected to provincial laws setting such minimum standards for companies such as Bell. Suddenly, because they are faced with a monetary suit, the company raises a legal defence which is not once but twice removed from the legitimate interests it has in the dispute.

---

16 *Commn. du Salaire Minimum v. Bell Telephone Co.*, [1966] S.C.R. 767, 59 D.L.R. (2d) 106. The decision is sharply and accurately criticized in Gibson, "Interjurisdictional Immunity in Canadian Federalism" (1969), 47 Can. Bar Rev. 40 at 53-56.

As a result, the Supreme Court responded with a ruling which created a shadowy enclave of business immunity from provincial regulation.

Within my conception of the role of judicial review in constitutional law, there is a sensible way of avoiding this kind of result. We should simply not allow private individuals of their own motion to impeach the validity of statutes on the ground that they infringe the "exclusive" jurisdiction of another legislative body. (By analogy, we do not allow taxpayers' suits or defences on the ground of the alleged unconstitutionality of the expenditure of tax revenues.) Not only should we require the private citizen to give notice of a constitutional challenge to the offending jurisdiction (as we do now), but we should also require that he obtain consent for this challenge from the Attorney General of the jurisdiction whose "turf" he is defending. The only time that a private citizen should have a legal claim of his own right to a constitutional decision is when there are two contradictory statutes from contending jurisdictions and he is asking for the minimal judicial decision about paramountcy.

In a situation such as we find in *Bell Telephone,* no one could deny that the province had a legitimate interest in the regulation of the minimum working conditions of its own citizens employed within its own provincial boundaries. It may well be true that for a national industry such as telephone communications, it is preferable that there be uniform regulation imposed by Parliament. However, surely this was a matter for the political judgment of the federal government which had not yet responded with any legislation of its own. The point of a federal system is to allocate governing power to different regions and groups, not to confer immunities from regulation on private citizens (unlike the Canadian Bill of Rights). The best judge of whether legislation enacted by one jurisdiction unduly encroaches on the sphere allocated to another is surely the government elected by the voting majority in the latter jurisdiction. Certainly it is not the courts who are acting at the behest of a private individual whose primary interest is not the integrity of the federal system but rather the avoidance of a law he does not like.[17]

---

[17] I don't want to imply any crude "economic" interpretation of constitutional adjudication. I do believe that business interests have been the prime beneficiaries of that process, but they have not been the only ones. Indeed, in the fifties the Supreme Court of Canada used the doctrines of federalism to protect the civil liberties of minority groups (especially the Jehovah's Witnesses) against oppressive provincial legislation. In these cases also, we can discern the malleability of vague constitutional categories in the hands of judges who are understandably tempted to do something about legislation they believe unwise. (The rise and fall of activist Supreme Court protection of civil liberties through the vehicle of federalism is recounted in section 4 of my article, "The Supreme Court and the Law of Canadian Federalism", cited in fn. 1, *ante.*) Many of those who were most distressed by Privy Council activism against economic regulation between the Wars vigorously applauded this Supreme Court effort in the fifties. While I think that

Nor should we be deterred by the predictable response of lawyers who will protest that we are depriving the private litigant of his right to a judicial examination of the validity of a statute which might affect his position in a legal dispute. It makes sense to talk of legal rights only when there are meaningful legal rules imposing a legal obligation on one actor which we also feel justifies conferring on another the ability to enforce that duty. Even when there are legal rules, there is no need to conclude that courts should have the final say in interpreting them, as was seen in the analysis of administrative law. A *fortiori*, this is true of constitutional decision-making, which has long since outgrown the legal context in which it originated. If the *Manitoba Egg Reference* is a typical example, as I believe it is, the Supreme Court can really do no more than engage in *ad hoc* dispute resolution. If the best we can hope for from our judicial umpire is a Delphic utterance—"valid" or "invalid"—is there really any reason to allow the private litigant to consult the oracle?

Elimination of the power of the private citizen to lodge a unilateral challenge to the validity of a statute on federalism grounds would sharply lessen the incidence of judicial review and resolution of constitutional questions. It would require the creation of much more extensive procedures for intergovernmental consultation in the area of conflicts of regulation. I believe we can assume that the *Coughlin* case[18] has removed almost all of the significant limitations on the power of governments to agree to alterations of legislative power, at least where administrative agencies are involved (which is, in any event, almost invariably the case in the area of legal regulation). If this is true, we can expect much the same *ad hoc* consensual adjustments and arrangements in this area as are found shaping economic policy or social security. This will force the interested governments to face their own responsibilities for the essentially political and technical questions of allocation of government responsibility in such fields as pollution control, wage and price regulation, competitions policy, Canadian economic nationalism, etc. It will enable these decisions to be made in a forum much more conducive to an informed and acceptable resolution of the immediate problem, without undue fear of a legal precedent. If access to judicial review is made more difficult and an alternative political forum is set up to

---

judicial defence of our civil liberties is a worthy objective in our democracy, I do not approve of the use of the Court's federalism role as a means to this end. The more appropriate techniques will be analyzed in the next chapter. For now I would just make it clear that the denial of standing to make a constitutional challenge should apply equally to those whose objective is the preservation of our political and religious freedom as it does to those who seek to defend the freedom of the market.

18 *Coughlin v. Ont. Highway Tpt. Bd.*, [1968] S.C.R. 569, 68 D.L.R. (2d) 384. The significance of this case for my general thesis is developed in detail in section 2 of my article, "The Supreme Court and the Law of Canadian Federalism", cited in fn. 1, *ante*.

canvass the issues at the first stage, then many of the questions posed to the Supreme Court since 1949 would never bother a court again. It is even possible that we could become accustomed to the demise of judicial review, and it might gradually wither away of its own accord.

CONCLUSION

In this chapter I have tried to sketch the logic of the evolution of some fundamental notions of Canadian constitutionalism. At the root of any ongoing intellectual discipline there are certain assumptions which define the direction of enquiry at any one time. Ordinarily, the participants in this intellectual enterprise do not focus on and question these assumptions. This is as it should be because no collaborative progress in understanding could ever be accomplished unless there is tentative agreement about the fundamental concepts. After a period of time, incongruities and discontinuities in these assumptions begin to make themselves felt in specific problems and their cumulative result begins to dissolve the established consensus. When this occurs, we are ready for the articulation of a new framework for inquiry which can redirect the intellectual search along more satisfying avenues. I believe we are at this stage in our current assessment of the judicial umpiring of our federal system.

Judicial review originated with the notion that the Canadian constitution, the British North America Act, was an Imperial statute and thus fit for administration in the ordinary courts of law. The logical corollaries of this view were that private citizens had standing to require the court to invalidate subordinate Canadian laws which were beyond the powers of the enacting legislature because they went beyond the limits laid down by this Imperial statute. Moreover, this finding of invalidity could be made by the courts even though the actual recipient of the legislative power had not yet exercised it, because its legislative jurisdiction in the area was exclusive. In fact, the original donee of this legislative power could not even consent to its exercise by the other jurisdiction through a form of interdelegation because of the binding and authoritative character of the basic law.

This originally coherent rationale began to come unravelled because the demands of social change for a redistribution of political authority could not be reflected in explicit amendments to the constitution. The burden was placed on the courts to make the necessary adjustments and this immediately placed them in a dilemma. Taking one view of the nature of their role, they could adhere to the letter of the original document, a stance which would only have the effect of placing a constitutional straitjacket around our governmental institutions. On a more adequate view of their obligations, they could begin consciously to update the original allocation of legislative authority in the light of current social needs. Unfortunately, this generates severe pressures on the structure of a judicial process which is designed for the adjudication of disputes within a framework of law.

The discontinuity which is thus apparent in Canadian constitutionalism lies in the institutional incapacity of the ordinary court to perform adequately the function of constitutional innovation and adjustment. When we perceive the discontinuity, it is no longer difficult to discover the reasons for its existence. A statutory enactment which has been effectively frozen for more than a century, but which purports to govern so fluid and politically charged an area as the allocation of legislative authority, must inevitably lose its legal integrity, no matter how wide a view we may take of the nature of law. I have suggested that when we perceive the true character of constitutional decision-making in the courts, at least the corollaries of traditional judicial review must be altered. Private citizens should no longer have standing to impeach the validity of legislation on the ground that it encroaches on the exclusive preserve of another jurisdiction. As far as individuals are concerned, this would leave the constitutional regime in a state of functional concurrency. Each government could enact laws in an area and the citizen would have to obey both unless they contradicted each other (in which case the courts would apply a rule of paramountcy to resolve the conflict). That is now the operative rule in the area of penal controls over private behaviour, and there is no reason why it should not spread to the sphere of regulation of economic activities (typified by the *Bell Telephone* case). The device for achieving a more efficient use of legislative power would be some form of delegation. Various governments would agree to enter or withdraw from different fields of legal regulation as their needs and capacities change. Again, the evolving "law in action" is judicial non-interference with such consensual changes in legislative authority.

Each of these doctrinal changes is based on recognition of the fact that we no longer have a system of constitutional law which citizens should have a right to have applied to their disputes in court. Rather, we have a political process of adjustment of our governmental institutions to social change. The primary vehicle for such adjustment must be a continuous process of bargaining and compromise and it is the respective governments which should have the direct interest and responsibility in preserving the integrity of Canadian federalism. Yet, superimposed on this framework is the continuing possibility of judicial review. No one seems to question the basic premise that where the political institutions do not agree, the courts must remain the final and authoritative umpire. For the reasons I have given in this chapter, I think we should draw the further conclusion that federalism disputes are no longer justifiable. In the absence of meaningful legal standards, the Supreme Court of Canada should not be asked to intervene in the kind of political and economic conflict which triggered the *Manitoba Egg Reference*.

I can sum up my analysis of the judicial contribution to the future of Canadian federalism by paraphrasing a famous appraisal of the place of courts in labour relations.

The federal allocation of legislative authority is an integral part of our system of self-government. When it works well, it does not need the sanction of constitutional *law*. It is only when the system breaks down that the Court's aid is invoked. But the Supreme Court cannot, by occasional sporadic decisions, restore the parties' continuing relationship and its intervention in such cases may seriously affect the on-going system of self-government. When their autonomous system breaks down, might not the parties better be left to the usual methods for adjustment of political disputes, rather than to court actions on the constitution? I suggest that the law stay out—but, mind you, not the lawyers.[19]

---

[19] The paraphrase is of the oft-cited passage in Shulman, "Reason, Contract and Law in Labour Relations" (1955), 68 Harv. L.R. 999 at 1024.

CHAPTER 7

The Defender
of our
Civil Liberties

THE SUPREME COURT
AND THE BILL OF RIGHTS

"Ah, but a man's reach should exceed his grasp,
Or what's a heaven for"
(Browning)

When the Supreme Court became Canada's final court of appeal in 1949, it was indisputable that the Court's constitutional role was its most important work. Some two decades later we are well on our way to outgrowing the judicial umpiring of our federal system. While the *Manitoba Egg Reference* discussed in Chapter 6 did stir considerable interest in the media, the ultimate decision was an exceptional exercise of a fading power. But there seems to be a natural rhythm in the evolution of an institution such as the judicial system. As the courts slough off one traditional function they take on other tasks. In late 1969, the Supreme Court of Canada announced its decision in the case of *Regina* v. *Drybones*[1] which carved out a new judicial role in protecting fundamental civil liberties against governmental erosion. Civil libertarians applauded vigorously: John Diefenbaker, understandably, called it a "monumental decision". Some observers felt nagging doubts and worried about the shoals ahead. In this chapter I shall try to analyze in a systematic way the crucial factors which move me to an attitude of, at best, hesitant approval.

---

[1] *R. v. Drybones*, [1970] S.C.R. 282, 10 C.R.N.S. 334, 71 W.W.R. 161, 9 D.L.R. (3d) 473, [1970] 3 C.C.C. 355. The importance of the case is attested to by the extensive comments it generated in the law reviews: Sinclair, "The Queen v. Drybones" (1970), 8 O.H.L.J. 599; Smith, "R. v. Drybones and Equality Before the Law" (1971), 49 Can. Bar. Rev. 163; Cavalluzzo, "Judicial Review and the Bill of Rights" (1971), 9 O.H.L.J. 511; Tarnopolsky, "The Canadian Bill of Rights from Diefenbaker to Drybones" (1971), 17 McG. L.J. 437. I also found very interesting an unpublished paper, Dais, "Judicial Supremacy in Canada in Comparative Perspective" (1971).

PROTECTING THE
JEHOVAH'S WITNESSES

In order to appreciate the dimensions of the problem presented by
Drybones, one must be aware of some of the background of Supreme
Court involvement in civil liberties cases. To this end I shall deal with
one decision in detail, *Boucher*,[2] decided shortly after the Court became
Canada's final appellate tribunal, and then sketch the trends in the intervening twenty years. The issue raised by *Boucher* is a logical beginning
to my argument in this chapter. However, the real reason I will give it
extensive treatment is that it is my favourite case in all of the work
of the Court throughout the whole era.

Aimé Boucher was a farmer in rural Quebec and a member of the
Jehovah's Witnesses. He distributed in his district a short pamphlet
prepared in Toronto and entitled (in English) "Quebec's Burning Hate
for God and Christ and Freedom Is the Shame of all Canada." It was
proved that Boucher did hand out the pamphlet, but there was no
evidence of the situation in his area, or the effects it may have had.
Boucher was charged with sedition simply because of the contents of the
document.

The pamphlet first asked for calmness and reason in appraising the
evidence it would present about the persecution of the Witnesses in
Quebec. It then described a long series of attacks on the sect's practices
of distributing Bibles or tracts, conducting religious services in private
homes, and holding public lectures to teach the Christian truth. In
response to these practices, the Witnesses were assaulted and beaten,
their Bibles and publications were torn up by individuals and mobs, their
homes were invaded and property taken, while hundreds of their members were arrested, charged and held on exorbitant bail. Details were
given in the pamphlet of many such incidents. A key comment referred
to the role of the Quebec courts:

> What of her judges that impose heavy fines and prison sentences against
> them, heap abusive language upon them and deliberately follow a mali-
> cious policy of again and again postponing cases to tie up tens of thou-
> sands of dollars in exorbitant bail and keep hundreds of cases pending?
> Do these legislators, policemen and judges in Quebec show their love for
> liberty? Honestly, do you believe that these fruits are the product of love
> or of hate? "By their fruits you will know them". (Matthew 7:20)[3]

After referring to some examples, the pamphlet said: "All of the French
Canadian courts were so under priestly thumbs that they affirmed the

---

2 *Boucher v. R.*, [1951] S.C.R. 265, 11 C.R. 85, 99 C.C.C. 1, [1951] 2 D.L.R. 369.
3 [1951] S.C.R. 265 at 345 (translation).

infamous sentence." The pamphlet concluded on the note that the "force behind Quebec's suicidal hate is priest domination. Thousands of Quebec Catholics are so blinded by the priests that they think they serve God's cause in mobbing Jehovah's Witnesses."

The procedural history of the case is fascinating. The accused was charged with publishing seditious libel and was conviction by the Quebec jury. This conviction was upheld in the Quebec Court of Appeal with two dissenting votes. On further appeal to the Supreme Court of Canada, the conviction was quashed by a unanimous five man panel because of errors by the trial judge in rejecting evidence and directing the jury. The further question arose as to whether a new trial should be ordered because it was legally possible to find the document seditious. Three judges said "yes," Rinfret C.J., Kerwin J. and Taschereau J., and two said "no," Rand and Estey JJ. The legal issue turned on the definition of "seditious intention". The answers of the judges were so disparate that it would have been almost impossible to direct a new jury as to the standard to be applied in this case, let alone in the future administration of the law. Accordingly, a rehearing was allowed in front of the full court and the happy result was a directed acquittal. Rand and Estey JJ. remained firm, and attracted Locke and Kellock JJ., two of the additions, but the key was that Kerwin J. changed his mind. Rinfret and Taschereau JJ. were adamant in favour of a new trial and the other newcomers, Fauteux and Cartwright JJ. joined them.

Boucher was charged with publishing a seditious libel, an offence which requires a writing that is "expressive of a seditious intention". This phrase was left completely undefined in the Criminal Code and the Court was forced to explore other avenues in elaborating its meaning. The concept of sedition had a lengthy common law background which had been summarized in Stephen's famous Digest at the very time that he drafted the Model Code in the late 19th Century. His version had been accepted as definitive by judges, text writers, digests and other authorities since that time. The Supreme Court of Canada was presented with the clear alternative of ratifying this established doctrine or subjecting the whole area to searching re-examination. The judges took the latter course and carried it off with several opinions of great scholarship and wisdom.

What made this choice so important is that the traditional view summarized by Stephen was potentially very repressive of freedom of speech. Only two elements of Stephen's definition were directly in point in *Boucher*, but the approach adopted by the Court would tell as to the authority of the whole. The phrase primarily relied on by the lower courts proscribed writings "calculated to promote feelings of ill will and hostility between different classes of His Majesty's subjects." It may seem hard in the 70's to believe that Boucher could actually be convicted of a serious crime for what was said in that pamphlet. However, the lower courts in Quebec were prepared to apply this definition literally to do so and Chief Justice Rinfret, also from Quebec, firmly agreed with this conclusion. Nor were they driven to such a legal result against their personal inclinations. This passage from Rinfret's dissent aptly sums up that perspective on freedom of speech:

> I would not like to part this appeal, however, without stating that to interpret freedom as licence is a dangerous fallacy. Obviously pure criticism, or expression of opinion, however severe or extreme is...to be invited. But..."there must be a point where restriction of individual freedom of expression is justified...on the ground of the democratic process and the necessities of the present situation". It should not be understood...that persons..."can insist on their alleged unrestricted right to say what they please and when they please, utterly irrespective of the evil results which are often inevitable". It might well be said in such a case ... "Licence they mean when they cry liberty".[4]

Fortunately, this was a decidedly minority view in the Supreme Court of Canada. The majority recognized that the prosecution of Boucher on such a ground offended against the basic value of freedom of speech which needed judicial nurture to survive. Even more important, it recognized its own independent power to shape the character of our law of sedition to this end. The common law definition of sedition had ancient origins and had undergone major shifts in its evolution. There was no reason to assume that the Code froze this evolution at around the year 1880 and required that such a formula be applied in the Canada of 1950. The occasion demanded that the judges discern the logic of the evolution of this law and draw out its implications for contemporary Canadian life. The Supreme Court rose to the occasion.

Mr. Justice Rand's opinion concentrated on the issue of principle. He found that the law of sedition arose at a time when our governors were believed to be superior beings, ruling by divine mandate. They were to be obeyed, not censured, because criticism implied equality with and accountability to the governed. The legal expression of this fundamental constitutional view was a doctrine which made any language which was contemptuous of the government or its actions seditious. These conceptions of political authority underwent radical changes, especially in the 19th Century. Now we live in a democracy where our governors are looked upon as servants who are supposed to be accountable to us. Vigorous or even harsh criticism is not just a privilege, it is a duty. Stephen's definition, which summed up the earlier developments in the common law, was no longer compatible with this understanding. As Rand J. said:

> The basic nature of the Common Law lies in its flexible process of traditional reasoning upon significant social and political matter; and just

---

4 *Ibid.*, at 277.

as in the 17th Century the crime of seditious libel was a deduction from fundamental conceptions of government, the substitution of new conceptions, under the same principles of reasoning, called for new jural conclusions.[5]

Acting on this view of its own role in the evolution of our law, the Supreme Court articulated a new and much narrower definition of sedition. In Mr. Justice Kellock's words,

incitement to violence toward constituted authority, i.e., government in the broad sense, or resistance having the same object, is, upon the authorities, a necessary ingredient of the intention.[6]

Using this formula, the majority found it legally insufficient that Boucher's pamphlet might excite bad feeling and hostility among Quebec Catholics, because of the chilling effect of such a doctrine on the "clash of critical discussion" and controversy in many areas, including politics and religion. To the suggestion that the pamphlet should be illegal because it might trigger Catholic reprisals against the Witnesses, Mr. Justice Kellock's simple reply was that "any such view would elevate mob violence to a plane of supremacy".

A second issue arose which dominated the discussion at the second hearing and produced a vigorous dissent by Mr. Justice Cartwright (with whom Taschereau and Fauteux JJ. agreed). I quoted earlier some passages from the pamphlet which referred to the courts as implicated along with other governmental authorities in the persecution of the Witnesses. A second element of Stephen's definition referred to "an intention to bring into hatred or contempt, or to excite disaffection against the administration of justice". Cartwright J. had supported the Rand-Kellock position which drastically limited the general scope of Stephen's doctrine. Why did he differ from them here? While believing that there was more legal support for this part of the definition (though it was still rather tenuous), he frankly states his belief that a broad scope for the offence of sedition to protect the courts "was right in principle." The priority of values embodied by such a legal standard is reflected in this passage which Cartwright J. quotes approvingly:

The Constitution has provided very apt and proper remedies for correcting and rectifying the involuntary mistakes of judges, and for punishing and removing them for any voluntary perversion of justice. But if their authority is to be trampled on by pamphleteers and newswriters, and the people are to be told that the power given to Judges for their protection, is prostituted to their destruction, the Court may retain its power for some

---

5 *Ibid.*, at 286.
6 *Ibid.*, at 296.

little time, but I am sure it will instantly lose all its authority, and the power of the Court will not long survive the authority of it.[7]

Again, it is fortunate that a majority on the Supreme Court was not prepared to deny Canadian citizens the right to make even truthful statements imputing deliberate misconduct to a judge in his judicial character. The burden of meeting this position was carried primarily by the opinion of Mr. Justice Locke who also entered the case only on the rehearing. His approach is exactly that of Rand J. on the first issue:

> Assuming Coke's statement accurately declared the common law of England at that time, the reason which formed its basis has disappeared with the changed status of the judges and the manner in which they are chosen and appointed and this is, in my opinion, no longer the law either in England or Canada: cessante ratione legis cessat ipsa lex.[8]

After examining the problems of criticism of judges and the relationship between sedition, defamatory libel, and contempt of court, he concluded that basically the same qualifications must be introduced at this level as before. There must be some intention to create resistance to the law and the courts, not merely a loss of esteem:

> The existence of this right of public discussion is wholly inconsistent with a rule of law that judges or others administering justice or Ministers of the Crown are immune from criticism on the ground that to impugn their honesty or capacity is a reflection upon the government.[9]

Boucher is a text-book example of judicial craftsmanship and demonstrates that Canadian judges are perfectly capable of it. If the Supreme Court of Canada had emulated this model in the next 20 years, this book would have a very different tone. Be that as it may, let me summarize the essential elements we find in work of such high quality. First, the Court is aware of what will be its own decisive influence on the growth of Canadian law, when it either ratifies or modifies Stephen's summary of "seditious intention". Its critical analysis of the legal authorities which disclosed the unsettled character of our law left room for a frank exchange of views about what the law ought to be like. However, these were not simply personal statements to the effect that "I like this policy, or that one". The judges maintained continuity with the flow of the law by trying to fathom the rationale of the offence of sedition, to formulate the principle which reconciles the competing values in the area. Only on the basis of this legal principle does the majority fashion a new formula sensitive to modern needs. The doctrine they arrived at was certainly a libertarian one for that era, if we compare it with work of other English-

---

7 *Ibid.*, at 343, quoting from the judgment of Wilmot J. in *Almon's Case* (1765), Wilm. 243, 97 E.R. 94.

8 [1951] S.C.R. 265 at 329.

9 *Ibid.*, at 330.

speaking courts at that time. As a contemporary commentator said of *Boucher*:[10]

> Finally, it is impossible to leave this case without saying that the judgments inspire pride and confidence in the court that is now in all matters Canada's final court of appeal. The judgments reveal boldness in approach to authority, a scholarship in research and expression ... and a sensitiveness to basic principles of law and democracy that represent the judicial process at its best. They will bear comparison with the products of any courts anywhere.

THE LEGAL INSTRUMENTS OF JUDICIAL INTERVENTION

Boucher is not only noteworthy as a model of judicial craftsmanship. It also exhibits a distinctive judicial technique in the protection of civil liberties. The Supreme Court interpreted the common law and statutory doctrines so as to avoid an excessive interference with freedom of expression. Its tacit assumption was that this freedom was a basic value which was protected by legal principles built into the structure of our legal system. The Court would require a very clear statement from the legislature of its wish to encroach on this established principle before concluding that such was the result demanded by the law in any concrete case. Wherever there are legal ambiguities requiring judicial clarification, judges must approach this task with the view that our civil liberties occupy a preferred position in the scale of competing values.

If one believes that many (perhaps even most) legal infringements of civil liberties come from legislative inadvertence, then this is a vital tool in the judicial kit. Boucher was prosecuted as the result of the initiative of a few local officials (police, prosecutor, etc.), responding to the emotions of an immediate situation, but operating under cover of a vague legal doctrine which would literally cover the marginal situation. Any victim of such an action can appeal to the courts who may protect him from injustice through the device of interpretation and, in effect, pass this question forward to the legislature—"do you really want to write a general definition of sedition which not only would convict Boucher but would also have this effect on a lot of other people in the unknown future?" The assumption is that, put to this test, the legislature would rarely come out into the open and answer "yes".

Boucher inaugurated almost a golden age of Supreme Court protection of Canadian freedom in the 1950's, and in that era the "clear statement" technique figured largely. We have already seen one instance of its use in *Smith v. Rhuland*[11] where the Court refused to interpret a general

---

10 Brewin, "Comment" (1951), 29 Can. Bar Rev. 193 at 202.
11 Discussed in Chapter 5, at pp. 135-136.

administrative discretion of union certification as an authority to limit freedom of political beliefs and associations. One of the most striking examples is *Roncarelli v. Duplessis*[12] which brought the era to a close. Here the Premier of Quebec had instigated a cancellation of Roncarelli's liquor licence because the latter had furnished bail to Jehovah's Witnesses arrested for activities similar to Boucher's distribution of the pamphlet. The Supreme Court was asked to restrict the broad discretion conferred in administering the liquor control legislation by excluding this as a relevant factor and then expansively construe the civil law to provide Roncarelli with a tort remedy for the harm caused by the action of Duplessis, the Premier. In another display of judicial skill, the Supreme Court judges showed they were up to the task.

The technique is by no means foolproof. In that same period, the Court totally submerged the important values of freedom of the press in settling the law of defamation of a public official, though this was even more ambiguous than the law of sedition. There is an ever present danger of such an erratic pattern in decisions based on the apparently narrow function of "interpreting" the wide variety of legal doctrines. More visible is the problem that sometimes the legislature will accept the judicial challenge and respond with repressive legislation that is crystal clear. This was the dénouement to another important Supreme Court effort in the 1950's—the defence of the values of due process in *Alliance*.[13] The Duplessis government promptly reversed this decision by legislation. A committed civil libertarian who wants to exclude this possibility will need a second legal device.

The Supreme Court developed such a tool in several other cases in the fifties. As we saw in the previous chapter, in our federal system a court has the power to declare even unambiguous legislation invalid on the ground that the body which enacted it had no constitutional authority to do so. A basic legal principle which underlies this judicial umpiring of the federal system is that the power of the legislature to enact laws of that general category must not be defined by reference to the particular merits of the statute which is now being challenged. Yet this spirit of detachment may be hard to maintain in the face of a particularly oppressive situation. One can understand why judges would be driven to declare particular laws invalid in the federal system because of their impact on civil liberties. This "jurisdictional" technique received its main impetus in another case which reached the Supreme Court of the 1950's dealing with Quebec's war on the Jehovah's Witnesses. In *Saumur*,[14] the City of Quebec administered its leaflet distribution by-law so as to bar access of the Witnesses to the streets for distribution of their

---

12 [1959] S.C.R. 121.
13 Discussed in Chapter 5, at p. 135.
14 *Saumur v. Quebec (City)*, [1953] 2 S.C.R. 299, 106 C.C.C. 289, [1953] 4 D.L.R. 641.

literature. Four members of the Court (who were joined by Kerwin J., an advocate of the "clear statement" position, to form a majority in the case) held this legislation to be "in relation to" freedom of religion and thus beyond the jurisdiction of the provinces. The approach gained full sway on the Court in two more cases from Quebec, *Birks*[15] (dealing with Montreal by-laws regulating commercial activities on Catholic holy days) and especially *Switzman*[16] (dealing with Quebec's infamous Padlock Law, the *Communist Propaganda Act.*

There is an apparent loophole in the "jurisdictional" technique. What the Court takes away from the one legislature, it must perforce give to the other, and how is the cause of civil liberties advanced? That this is merely a formal objection can be gathered from the fact that it is always provincial legislation which is challenged on this basis. Both historical and functional considerations suggest that the provinces are more likely to enact laws restricting basic freedoms. Their legislatures need not respond to as wide a variety of affected interests and minority groups and are more prone to hasty, prejudiced and emotional actions. If a court consistently denies them the power to enact such laws when they encroach on important liberties, it must logically confer this power on Parliament. It can reasonably anticipate that Parliament will rarely exercise that power.

I find the "jurisdictional" technique objectionable for other reasons.[17] It poses the wrong questions about the statutes in question: "who should be able to enact this unwise law?" rather than "is this law really so unwise that it should be disallowed?" Civil liberty is a very unsatisfactory concept with which to characterize and allocate legislative power. It distorts the process of neutral umpiring of the federal system and creates precedents for judicial activism which are not easily avoided when non-civil libertarian statutes are challenged. Some may be willing to take the risk on the grounds that this very important end justifies these means. The evidence of almost twenty years experience with the technique is that it is at best sporadic in its results. With rare exception, the Supreme Court has shown itself consistently unwilling to use the jurisdictional approach since the late fifties.

Accordingly, one can understand why those who favour aggressive judicial protection of civil liberties advocate the adoption of a third approach, embodied in a Bill of Rights. This technique permits judicial invalidation of laws infringing on our basic freedoms, not because some other jurisdiction should have enacted them, but because the very nature

---

15 *Henry Birks & Sons (Montreal) Ltd. v. Montreal,* [1955] S.C.R. 759, [1955] 5 D.L.R. 321, 113 C.C.C. 135.

16 *Switzman v. Elbling & A.G. of Que.,* [1957] S.C.R. 285, 117 C.C.C. 129, 7 D.L.R. (2d) 337.

17 Which I have developed in much greater detail in my article "The Supreme Court and the Law of Canadian Federalism" (1973), 23 U.T.L.J. 307.

of these values renders them legally immune. At the same time as Supreme Court action had reached its peak with the "clear statement" and "jurisdictional" techniques, Parliament debated and adopted the Canadian Bill of Rights to provide this third instrument. It is true that this Bill was not a perfect response to this demand: it explicitly applied only to federal, not provincial laws; it was not constitutionally entrenched; Parliament could exclude its operation on any one statute by adding a *non obstante* clause to the latter; finally, it was unclear about the precise judicial role envisaged in its administration. Despite these imperfections, there surely could be no doubt it would increase judicial effectiveness in preserving individual freedom.

Yet, amazingly enough, in the sixties the Supreme Court beat a retreat from its interventionist role. As I have already noted, it made much less use of the interpretative and federalist approaches to provide relief to individual victims of heavy-handed governmental action. This might have been justified to some extent on the grounds that the explicit protection afforded by the Bill of Rights should be resorted to instead. Yet throughout the whole of the sixties the Bill remained a "paper tiger" in our courts. A primary reason for this prevalent judicial attitude was the example of the Supreme Court's very timid and passive approach in its first encounter with the Bill in the case of *Robertson & Rosetanni*.[18] One may or may not agree with the decision to uphold Sunday observance legislation in the face of the principle of freedom of religion; one could not deny that the reasoning used by the Court to justify this conclusion deprived the Bill of Rights of almost any significance.

Suddenly everything seemed changed when the Supreme Court decided *Drybones* in late 1969. Here the Court was directly confronted with the issue of the precise legal impact of a Bill of Rights and it abruptly shifted from its path in *Rosetanni*. The judges seized the opportunity to carve out a visible and full fledged judicial role as the protector of our civil liberties against Parliamentary intrusion. Yet one wonders how committed the Supreme Court was to this different stance. These doubts are felt especially by those who are acquainted with two other important cases the Court decided shortly afterwards, but without attracting the popular attention of *Drybones*. In *Wray* and *Osborn*[19] the Court was asked to play a similar role in protecting the values of due process from intrusion by police and prosecutor respectively (though under the immediate authority of the common law rather than the Bill of Rights). Unaccountably, the Court shrank from this task. In the rest of this chapter I am going to examine in detail the situations and reason-

---

18 *Robertson & Rosetanni v. R.*, [1963] S.C.R. 651, 41 C.R. 392, [1964] 1 C.C.C. 1, 41 D.L.R. (2d) 485; see Laskin, "Comment" (1964), 42 Can. Bar Rev. 147.

19 *R. v. Wray*, [1971] S.C.R. 272, 11 C.R.N.S. 235, [1970] 4 C.C.C. 1, 11 D.L.R. (3d) 673; *R. v. Osborn*, [1971] S.C.R. 184, 12 C.R.N.S. 1, 1 C.C.C. (2d) 482, 15 D.L.R. (3d) 85.

ing in all three cases and use them as a vehicle for asking what should be the role of a final appellate court across the whole spectrum of civil liberties cases.

THE CIVIL LIBERTIES TRILOGY

(a) The Queen v. Drybones[20]

Late one Saturday evening, April 8th, 1967, an Indian trapper named Joe Drybones was found dead drunk in the lobby of the Old Stope Hotel in Yellowknife. He was arrested, convicted on Monday morning, fined $10 and costs (or 3 days in jail), and released after he paid the fine. Certainly it is hard to find a less auspicious beginning for a legal decision which will reverberate in Canadian law for decades, perhaps even centuries. The seeds of this result lay in the police decision to charge Drybones under s. 94(b) of the Indian Act, which made it an offence for an Indian to be intoxicated off a reserve. This law contrasted with section 19(1) of the Northwest Territories Liquor Ordinance, which made it an offence for any person to be intoxicated in a public place. The differences in these two offences enabled Drybones to challenge his conviction under the Indian Act on the grounds that this provision denied him his right to "equality before the law" under the Canadian Bill of Rights "without discrimination by reason of race". When the case eventually wound its way up to the Supreme Court of Canada, the judges were required to decide whether there was indeed a denial of equality before the law and, if there was, whether this rendered the legislation inoperative *pro tanto*. In a split decision the Court held that the offence in the Indian Act violated the Bill of Rights, that as a result the provision should not be applied, and so Drybones must be acquitted of the charge.

I should point out some further peculiarities in the factual situation. First of all, while the law prohibited Indian intoxication "off a reserve", there were no reserves in the Northwest Territories. The argument that the absence of this condition made the provision inapplicable in the territories was rejected in the lower courts. As a result, the Indian Act was read as prohibiting intoxication by an Indian anywhere, while a non-Indian committed a crime only if he was drunk in a public place. Yet this distinction appears irrelevant to Drybones' conduct since he was found in the public lobby of the Old Stope Hotel. There was a second difference between the two offences, this one relating to the penalty structure. The Indian Act alone provided for a minimum fine of $10.00 and it had a longer maximum jail sentence, 3 months rather than 30 days. Again one must feel some unease at relying on this factor; Drybones did receive the minimum fine of $10.00 and it is hard to

---

[20] Fn. 1, *ante.*

believe a white man would have received less than that under the Ordinance.

Hence any discriminatory inequality in the two laws produced at best a trivial injustice in Drybones' own situation. The Court was prepared to deal with the two statutory offences on their face and to let the *Drybones* facts be the vehicle for presenting the critical issue of principle. With a very inadequate analysis of the real dimensions of the problem, the majority found a denial of "equality before the laws". Within the confines of this chapter I cannot develop the criticisms that have been made of the Court's reasoning; suffice it to say that the *Lavell* case is now before the Supreme Court with all of the intractable conflicts of which Mr. Justice Pigeon warned us in his dissent in *Drybones*.[21]

The focus of my attention will be the second, more fundamental issue for which *Drybones* will likely prove an enduring authority. Once a conflict appears between a federal statute and the Bill of Rights, what is a court to do about it? The language of the Bill of Rights pointed to two clear alternatives. In technical legal terminology if the immediate legislation cannot be interpreted in a manner consistent with the Bill of Rights, the judges may either apply the law as written or hold it inoperative because of the clear conflict. As I read the Bill of Rights, it does not give unambiguous evidence on its face of what its parliamentary authors wanted the judges to do. Numerous lower court opinions and academic articles had taken different positions throughout the decade. There was no clear precedent in the Supreme Court of Canada one way or the other: a dissenting opinion of Mr. Justice Cartwright in *Robertson & Rosetanni*[22] opted for the overriding effect of the Bill of Rights but the majority judgment written by Mr. Justice Ritchie viewed that case from a rather different perspective. This was a case where conventional legal materials left us uncertain about what the law is and we would expect from the Supreme Court, which now had to decide it, a real dialogue about the direction in which this absolutely vital area of our law ought to move.

Anyone with this expectation would be sorely disappointed when he read the several judicial opinions. To a journalist, "the judgment read like a stock quotation . . . technical, dry and barren of philosophic reasoning".[23] The opinion flitted about the inconclusive surface of the language of the Bill of Rights without ever coming to grips with the fundamental questions. Should the traditional principle of parliamentary

---

21 *Lavell v. A.G. Can.*, [1971] F.C. 347, (*sub nom. Re Lavell and A.G. Can.*) [1972] 1 O.R. 396n, 22 D.L.R. (3d) 188, 14 Cr. L.Q. 236 (C.A.). There is an excellent discussion of the issues raised by this case, following *Drybones*, in Sanders, "The Bill of Rights and Indian Status" (1972), U.B.C.L.R. 81.

22 [1963] S.C.R. 651 at 658.

23 Cameron Smith, "The Highest Court", in *The Globe Magazine*, March 14, 1970.

sovereignty prevail, tempered by the use of the Bill of Rights to facilitate the "clear statement" approach to protecting civil liberties? Should the Court go further and decide that it now has the further technique of invalidating even an unambiguous expression of the legislative will, when the judges believe it encroaches on our fundamental freedoms? Mr. Justice Ritchie, writing for the majority, answered "yes" to the second question and thus radically changed the posture of restraint he adopted in *Rosetanni*.[24] Yet he provided only a fleeting glimpse of his personal feelings which led him on this course. Although he recognizes that "the implementation of the Canadian Bill of Rights by the Courts can give rise to great difficulties",[25] he believes that the alternative "appears . . . to strike at the very foundation of the Bill of Rights and to convert it from its apparent character as a statutory declaration of the fundamental human rights and freedom which it recognizes, into being little more than a rule for the construction of federal statutes".[26]

The several minority judges are much more impressed by the "difficulties". Chief Justice Cartwright went to the extent of explicitly recanting the error into which he thought he fell in *Rosetanni*. He is worried that "the responsibility . . . if imposed at all, is imposed upon every justice of the peace, magistrate and judge of any court in the country who is called upon to apply a Statute of Canada or any order, rule or regulation made thereunder".[27] He is much too modest and delicate to name the august body to whom he may be comparing these lower echelon judges. Mr. Justice Abbott takes the same short and blunt way with the problem of judicial power that he did in *Barbara Jarvis*.[28] The majority view "necessarily implies a wide delegation of the legislative authority of Parliament to the Courts" and he will require very plain language to believe that Parliament really intended "to extend to the Courts such an invitation to engage in judicial legislation."[29] Only Mr. Justice Pigeon frankly reveals his operating assumptions in any detail:

> In the present case the judgments below hold in effect that Parliament in enacting the *Bill* has implicitly repealed not only a large part of the *Indian Act* but also the fundamental principle that the duty of the courts is to apply the law as written and they are in no case authorized to fail to give effect to the clearly expressed will of Parliament. It would be

---

24 I am aware that this comment is not beyond dispute, since Mr. Justice Ritchie himself apparently perceived no change of direction. Its truth, nevertheless, is neatly demonstrated in Lyon, "Drybones and Stare Decisis" (1971), 17 McG.L.J. 594.

25 *R. v. Drybones*, [1970] S.C.R. 282 at 298.

26 *Ibid.*, at 293.

27 *Ibid.*, at 287-288.

28 *Barbara Jarvis v. Associated Medical Services Inc.*, [1964] S.C.R. 497, 44 D.L.R. (2d) 407.

29 [1970] S.C.R. 282 at 299.

a radical departure from this basic British constitutional rule to enact that henceforth the courts are to declare inoperative all enactments that are considered as not in conformity with some legal principles stated in very general language, or rather merely enumerated without any definition.

The meaning of such expressions as "due process of law", "equality before the law", "freedom of religion", "freedom of speech", is in truth largely unlimited and undefined. According to individual views and the evolution of current ideas, the actual content of such legal concepts is apt to expand and to vary as is strikingly apparent in other countries. In the traditional British system that is our own by virtue of the *B.N.A. Act*, the responsibility for updating the statutes in this changing world rests exclusively upon Parliament. If the Parliament of Canada intended to depart from that principle in enacting the *Bill*, one would expect to find clear language expressing that intention. On the contrary, what do we find in s. 1 but an apparent desire to adhere to the traditional principle and to avoid the uncertainties inherent in broadly worded enactments by tying the broad words to the large body of existing law and in effect declaring the recognized human rights and fundamental freedoms to be as existing in the laws of Canada.[30]

One could hardly dignify these sparse comments by describing them as a dialogue about the role of a court in protecting our civil liberties (and I have quoted substantially all the language in the opinions which goes beyond the surface of technical legal analysis). Matters worsened in the other two cases—*Wray* and *Osborn*—which faced the question of judicial intervention to protect standards of due process in the system of criminal justice. More important for our purposes, patent inconsistencies appeared in the attitudes of several of the judges to the scope of the Court's role.

(b)   The Queen v. Wray[31]

John Wray was prosecuted for the murder of a service station operator in an attempted robbery near Peterborough, Ontario. A key element in the prosecution's case against Wray was evidence that he took Ontario Provincial Police officers to a swamp and pointed out a rifle which ballistic tests showed had fired the bullet that killed the operator. This occurred as a result of a confession he made following lengthy questioning in Toronto. Though none of the appeal court opinions described the methods by which this statement was obtained, all agreed they involved "trickery, duress, and improper inducement". However, I think a summary of the transcript might be helpful here. Wray was taken to Toronto by an Inspector from the O.P.P., supposedly

---

30 *Ibid.*, at 305-306.
31 Fn. 19, *ante*.

for a lie detector test to be administered by a Mr. John Jurens, a private investigator. With the police watching through a peep-hole, Jurens went after his real objective, which was to condition young Wray into disclosing where the rifle was. He suggested that the shooting was an accident, that Wray would have to spend no more than seven or eight years in prison and perhaps much less, but that if he did not confess, the victim's family might kill him in revenge. After several hours of these tactics, Jurens broke Wray down and the police got their confession. During all this time, a lawyer engaged by Wray's father was trying to locate the youth to advise him, but O.P.P. officials would not disclose his whereabouts.

In these circumstances, there is no doubt that the confession as a whole was involuntary and thus legally inadmissible. The trial judge went further, and excluded evidence of the discovery of the gun (and also that part of the statement relating to it). The Ontario Court of Appeal agreed that a trial judge has the discretion to reject relevant and otherwise admissible evidence, even of substantial weight, "if he considers that its admission would be unjust or unfair to the accused or calculated to bring the administration of justice into disrepute." Some recent English cases had initiated this exception to the conventional principle that the sole purpose of the rules of evidence is to produce trustworthy, probative evidence at trial. The British Columbia Court of Appeal disapproved of the innovation in *Sigmund*[32] but, as we have seen, the Ontario Court of Appeal adopted and used it in *Wray*. The Supreme Court of Canada was faced with the same kind of crossroads that it encountered in *Drybones*, and again without any binding authority at all. Should the judiciary confine itself to its traditional, restricted role of ensuring a fair trial to the accused or should it use the rules of evidence for the expanded purpose of controlling pre-trial police behaviour and preventing abuses in the administration of criminal justice?

The majority answer was clear in *Wray*, but the Court took a very different direction than it did in *Drybones*. Mr. Justice Martland wrote the Court's opinion which rejected judicial exclusion of cogent evidence for this purpose. The sum and substance of his reasoning is contained in this passage:

> The difficulty of achieving any sort of uniformity in the application of the law if a broad discretion of this kind is recognized is clearly illustrated in the cases which I have considered. What is the standard of "unfairness" which excludes the medical opinions in the cases of *Court* and *Payne* in which the accused had been misled as to the purpose of the medical examinations, and yet permits the admission of evidence obtained by an illegal search of the person in the *Kuruma* case and in the

---

[32] *R. v. Sigmund* (1967), 60 W.W.R. 257 (B.C. C.A.).

King case, and evidence obtained through deception by agents provoca-
teurs in the *Murphy* case?

In my opinion, the recognition of a discretion to exclude admissible
evidence, beyond the limited scope recognized in the *Noor Mohamed*
case, is not warranted by authority, and would be undesirable. The
admission of relevant admissible evidence of probative value should
not be prevented, except within the very limited sphere recognized
in that case. My view is that the trial judge's discretion does not extend
beyond those limits, and, accordingly, I think, with respect, the definition
of that discretion by the Court of Appeal in this case was wrong in law.[33]

Similar sentiments are elaborated in the concurring opinion of Mr.
Justice Judson.

In this appeal we are clearly faced with the question whether we should
make new law and give a trial judge a discretion to exclude relevant and
admissible evidence if he thinks that it will operate unfairly against
the accused or, according to his opinion, bring the administration of
justice into disrepute. The reason given for the unfairness here is that
the weapon was discovered partly as a result of an inadmissible confession and partly as a result of the accused going with the police officers
and pointing out the place where the weapon was concealed. In my
opinion, there is no justification for recognizing the existence of this
discretion in these circumstances. This type of evidence has been admissible for almost 200 years. There is no judicial discretion permitting
the exclusion of relevant evidence, on the ground of unfairness to the
accused.

If this law is to be changed, a simple amendment to the Canada
Evidence Act would be sufficient an amendment to the effect that
no fact discovered as a result of an inadmissible confession shall be
provable in evidence against an accused person. Such a change should
not be effected by turning to a theory of judicial discretion to admit
or reject relevant evidence based upon the unsubstantial *dicta* to
which I have referred in these reasons. Judicial discretion in this field
is a concept which involves great uncertainty of application. The task
of a judge in the conduct of a trial is to apply the law and to admit all
the evidence that is logically probative unless it is ruled out by some
exclusionary rule. If this course is followed, an accused person has had
a fair trial. The exclusionary rule applied in this case is one that should
not be accepted.[34]

I find the distaste of Pigeon and Abbott JJ. for this novel judicial
discretion to be consistent with their views in *Drybones*, but how are
we to reconcile the attitudes of the other members of the majority?

---

33 [1971] S.C.R. 272 at 295-296.
34 *Ibid.*, at 299-300.

Of the minority in *Wray*, Hall and Spence JJ. are consistently in favour of the expanded judicial role to protect civil liberties which they defended in *Drybones*. Mr. Justice Spence was very firm in his views, although not terribly elaborate in his reasons:

> I am most strongly of the opinion that it is the duty of every judge to guard against bringing the administration of justice into disrepute. This is a duty which lies upon him constantly and that is a duty which he must always keep firmly in mind. The proper discharge of this duty is one which, in the present day of almost riotous disregard for the administration of justice, is of paramount importance to the continued life of the state.[35]

However Chief Justice Cartwright, who is again in the minority in this case, seems to be as inconsistent with his stance in *Drybones* as is Martland J. He does recognize the "difficulty and importance of the question", as is indicated by his quotation of this passage from the Scottish judgment in *Lawrie* v. *Muir*:[36]

> The law must strive to reconcile two highly important interests which are liable to come into conflict: (a) the interest of the citizen to be protected from illegal or irregular invasions of his liberties by the authorities, and (b) the interest of the state to secure that evidence bearing upon the commission of a crime and necessary to enable justice to be done shall not be withheld from courts of law on any mere formal or technical ground. Neither of these objects can be insisted upon to the uttermost. The protection for the citizen is primarily protection for the innocent citizen against unwarranted, wrongful and perhaps high-handed interference, and the common sanction is an action for damages. The protection is not intended as a protection for the guilty citizen against the efforts of the public prosecutor to vindicate the law. On the other hand, the interest of the state can not be magnified to the point of causing all the safeguards for the protection of the citizen to vanish, and of offering a positive inducement to the authorities to proceed by irregular methods.[37]

Although he recognized that there was no binding authority, that the situations for the exercise of discretion could not be defined without reference to all the material facts in a case, and that "the choice is a difficult one", he held "not without hesitation" that the trial judge could reject evidence on the grounds "it was obtained or extorted by such means that to admit it would bring the administration of justice into disrepute in the minds of right-thinking men". He does not advert to his qualms in *Drybones* about "the responsibility being imposed upon

---

35 *Ibid.*, at 304.
36 [1950] S.C. (J.) 19 at 26.
37 [1971] S.C.R. 272 at 284-285.

every justice of the peace, magistrate and judge of any court in the country."

(c) The Queen v. Osborn[38]

The third critical case in this period was *Osborn*. It raised the same fundamental issues as the other two about the role of the judiciary, but the Supreme Court's answer was much more ambiguous. Osborn was discovered by the police to have seven signed and uncashed cheques in his possession in incriminating circumstances. He was prosecuted originally for possession of cheques "adapted and intended to be used to commit forgery". Unfortunately for the prosecutor, the trial judge dismissed the charge on the grounds that the cheques had already been forged, and the Ontario Court of Appeal upheld this conclusion on the Crown's appeal. Not satisfied to let the matter rest there, the prosecutor lodged another charge against Osborne on the same facts, but under the different offence of "conspiracy to utter" the already forged cheques. Clearly this second prosecution offended the principle of double jeopardy, but because of earlier, restrictive Supreme Court decisions, the technical pleas of *autrefois acquit* or *res judicata* were not available as defences to the conspiracy charge. The Ontario Court of Appeal, again relying on an English innovation (the House of Lords decision in *Connolly*),[39] held that there was a discretion to stay criminal prosecutions which are oppressive and vexatious in order to prevent abuses in the criminal law process.

As in *Wray*, the Supreme Court of Canada reversed the Ontario Court of Appeal and unanimously permitted the second prosecution of Osborn, but on much hazier grounds. Mr. Justice Pigeon (writing for Martland and Judson JJ.) refused to say whether judges had some over-riding discretion to stay criminal trials to prevent an abuse of process. However, Pigeon J. clearly held that there was no discretion to control successive prosecutions by the Crown (outside of the strict rules of *autrefois acquit* and *res judicata*). He maintained the limited role in protecting civil liberties that he stated in *Drybones*.

> It is basic in our jurisprudence that the duty of the courts is to apply the law as it exists, not to enforce it or not in their discretion. As a general rule, legal remedies are available in an absolute way *ex debito justitiae*. Some are discretionary but this does not destroy the general rule. I can see no legal basis for holding that criminal remedies are subject to the rule that they are to be refused whenever in its discretion a court considers the prosecution oppressive.

> In our legal system, it is not considered unfair or oppressive to have an accused undergo several trials on the same charge when his conviction is

---

38 Fn. 19, *ante*.
39 *Connolly v. D.P.P.*, [1964] A.C. 1254, [1964] 2 All E.R. 401.

quashed even if this happens repeatedly. In other words, it is not considered desirable that a criminal should escape punishment for a misdeed because an error was committed in his trial that requires his conviction to be quashed. I fail to see why a totally different view should be taken if the error consists in not laying the correct charge so that instead of being irregularly convicted and then ordered to stand a new trial, he is acquitted of the incorrect charge and then brought to second trial on a fresh indictment for the correct charge.[40]

Strangely, Mr. Justice Hall (with whom Spence J. and Ritchie J. concurred) appeared to retreat from his activist stance in *Drybones* and *Wray*, but he eventually confined his decision to the conclusion that there was no particular oppression on these facts warranting the exercise of a judicial discretion. The seventh judge, Mr. Justice Fauteux, refused to commit himself any further than to say that "the appeal should be allowed". Hence it is possible to argue that the ratio of this case can be confined within a narrow compass and is no authority against a judicial discretion to control the prosecution in appropriate cases. Yet when we read this case along with *Wray*, and reflect on the kind of prosecutorial conduct which was sustained in *Osborn*, one must be very sanguine to expect any such ruling from the Supreme Court in the near future.

Let us step back now from the details of these three decisions and look at the picture they present together. In all three cases the Supreme Court of Canada had to decide whether the Canadian judiciary should undertake a new job of protecting individual freedoms. Undoubtedly this function would place our judges in an unaccustomed and perhaps uncomfortable position and the Supreme Court had to make a delicate judgment about whether the task was worth it. No binding authorities stood in the way of the new position and, in fact, there were significant legal developments which favoured it. What was needed was a sustained analysis of the demands of this new civil libertarian role and a reasoned judgment about whether our judges could perform it. We did not receive it.

Further comment from me about the quality of argument in these several opinions would be superfluous. I want to concentrate my attention on the pattern of conclusions which emerged and evaluate them on their merits. We can take *Wray* and *Osborn* as a unit, dealing with different facets of the same basic problem, and then three vital differences emerge in comparison with *Drybones*. In *Drybones*, the Supreme Court was asked to review the decision of the elected Parliament expressed in a public statute; in *Wray-Osborn* it was asked to review the decisions of appointed officials exercising individual discretion at a low level of visibility. In *Drybones*, the Court would have to judge the substantive

---

[40] [1971] S.C.R. 184 at 190-191.

reasonability of the different legislative classification of Indians; in *Wray-Osborn*, it was required to judge the procedural fairness of decisions made within the criminal justice system of which the judiciary also is a part. In *Drybones*, the source of the Court's legal authority to make these judgments was a Bill of Rights which would render its conclusions largely irreversible; in *Wray-Osborn*, the Court could appeal to the developing principles of the common law which would admit of further appeals to the legislature.

This way of stating the contrast does not disguise my view that the problem in *Wray-Osborne* invited judicial activism while that in *Drybones* suggested judicial restraint. I do not mean to suggest that a judgment in favour of restraint or activism in both situations would be logically untenable. Mr. Justice Pigeon took such a consistent position. The point is that if the Supreme Court was going to reach divergent conclusions, then *Wray-Osborn* was the place in which the judicial intervention should begin, not *Drybones* (as Chief Justice Cartwright concluded). Unfortunately, of the four possible pairs of legal results, the majority on the Supreme Court of Canada eventually arrived at the pair which makes the least sense of all.

TWO FALLACIES ABOUT THE JUDICIAL ROLE

In order to appreciate fully the grounds for this judgment, the reader must understand the complexity of the judicial role in civil liberties. To convey this sense I will have to draw together the various strands in my argument about the proper functions of an appellate court. At the outset I want to pinpoint two common fallacies often encountered in analyses of issues such as the ones arising in *Drybones*. Because each of these views is exactly the opposite of the basic assumptions of my theory of the law in courts, they may serve to introduce the analysis of the role courts can play in defending our fundamental freedoms.

The first such position, though rarely expressed so bluntly, amounts basically to this: Joe Drybones was saved from an injustice by the decision of the Supreme Court. Civil liberties are an important enough value in our society that we should applaud any such decision that is right in result, no matter where it comes from. The task should not be delayed, Hamlet-like, by agonizing over whether the courts are the proper vehicle to produce such good results. This stance stems from the fallacy of "institutional fungibility"—the notion that if there are certain moral principles which define the legitimate exercise of state power, then every decision maker in its government (in particular a judge) is entitled to apply them where he thinks proper.

This is a fallacy to which courts are particularly prone. They get drawn into an area by a *cause célèbre*, in order to right what is commonly agreed to be a blatant injustice, but then remain to do a lot of damage in the long run in the exercise of their new jurisdiction. The field of administrative law which we encountered in Chapter 5 is particularly prone to such evils. The only way to minimize this risk is by adding a second dimension to the enquiry, concerned with "institutional policy"—which is the right body to provide the just result in a particular case? This question is the focus of this book, in which I have tried to develop a view of the different capacities of our several institutions which are implied by their differences in design. Only on the basis of such an understanding can we make intelligent decisions about what parts should be played by each in order to secure the optimum flow of decisions for our society as a whole.

There is another, contrasting fallacy, though, to which adherents of this second view are themselves often prone. This amounts to the notion that "the good is the enemy of the best". If one reflects on the global problem of the unequal condition of the Indian in Canada, of which the situation in *Drybones* is just a minor symptom, most people would agree that only the legislature can provide the best solution. Because the legislature can hypothetically perform this role better than the court, then the court should not actually perform it. The conclusion simply does not follow from the premise. Only if judicial intervention on behalf of the Indian will be worse than judicial non-intervention is judicial restraint warranted. Perhaps the implicit logic of this fallacy is that if the court does its limited best, the more competent legislature will do nothing. No doubt this is a logical possibility, but it is one which is produced in the real world only in complicated ways which we should not lightly assume are operative. The more realistic assumption is that legislative and judicial efforts can be complementary, and we should not deny ourselves this cumulative protection simply because one institution may be more qualified than another.

CIVIL LIBERTIES IN COURTS: TOWARDS A GENERAL THEORY

The Foundations of Judicial Authority

There is a vast literature on the pros and cons of judicial administration of a Bill of Rights, most of which is the work of American scholars concerned with their own Supreme Court. Three critical dimensions have emerged in the debate about the judicial competence to perform this role: the authority, wisdom, and influence of courts. Perhaps the most important focus of this debate is the first, the legitimacy of judge-imposed restraints on official invasions of individual freedom. By what authority does a court presume to define and defend our fundamental liberties in the face of encroachment from legislator, administrator or policeman? The most immediate source of this judicial title is the notion that the courts are simply applying the standards of the law. The Canadian Bill of Rights looks like a law and was made like a law. It's a judge's duty to apply *all* the law, even that part which limits the authority of the legislature *et al.* to pass specific legal rules. Hence a court is simply following its normal course when it measures the validity of the challenged rule against the more basic legal standards embodied in the Bill of Rights. This is the classic rationale for judicial review under the American Constitution and under our B.N.A. Act and one senses it beneath the surface of the majority opinion in *Drybones*. Its reasoning is essentially spurious, nonetheless.

One can admit that the Bill of Rights has the formal attributes of a law. It does not follow that it possesses the same substantive characteristics as the ordinary laws which courts normally and legitimately apply. The whole point of a Bill of Rights is to express in enduring and symbolic terms the fundamental principles and values through which government is to function. It is almost imperative that the document be drafted in vague and largely question-begging terms. For some time at least, judicial interpretation can tie these terms to the prevailing pattern of the law (as the Supreme Court of Canada did in its first encounter with the Bill of Rights, in *Robertson & Rosetanni*). Eventually, a court will want to break loose and give these fundamental standards some real bite in forcing the revision of specific rules which are seen to be inconsistent with basic libertarian values (and this new judicial desire is apparent in *Drybones*). When the court does, it must recognize the truth of Mr. Justice Pigeon's observation that phrases such as "due process", "equality before the law", and so on are simply grants of an open-ended discretion to the judges to develop their conceptions of the principles of just governance.

The view that constitutional guarantees are somewhat lacking in true legal character will sound strange to those who cannot see that "law" is always a matter of degree. To one who appreciates Lon Fuller's analysis of law as an "enterprise of subjecting human conduct to the governance of rules", this conclusion should be no surprise at all. For some time a Bill of Rights can achieve a fair degree of "legality", because the terms it uses retain some customary focus and specific meaning. Gradually these existing patterns of legal rules (for example, those defining the scope of freedom of speech) will lose their familiarity and favour. As this takes place, the basic document will also lose its legal character. It will no longer communicate standards which channel the conduct of judges and the courts will have to develop these rules themselves as they go along. We must return to our first question, then, where do they get the authority to do so?

If judicial administration of a Bill of Rights is not really the inter-pretation and application of the "law", then how is judicial review com-patible with a democratic form of government? We should all be accustomed to the notion that courts do make a great deal of interstitial law. However, here we have the very different situation of a court making choices about vital public policies and often overriding the earlier legislative judgment in the process. The proper answer to these questions is often in grave doubt. This is because in the typical civil liberties case to come before a court, there will be a conflict between legitimate com-peting interests, some of which will have to give way. The formula "equality before the law" does not have an easily decipherable meaning to be literally applied to the problem in *Drybones*. The desirability of a bar to prosecution in *Osborn*, or an illegally obtained evidence rule in *Wray*, is not at all self-evident. We may all subscribe to the very abstract value of "due process" but someone has to work out its implications for concrete situations. Why should the views of the Supreme Court judges, "nine Platonic Guardians", in Learned Hand's phrase, prevail?

Now the institutional character of the Court becomes significant. Judges are appointed to a position in which they hold tenure. They are removable only for cause, and even then with great difficulty. In Canada, certainly, neither the prospective nor the past course of his decisions is considered a legitimate factor in the appointment or removal of a judge. We consider it a positive value that a judge is free from public account-ability for what he decides. This makes perfectly good sense when we conceive of the judge's task as adjudication of a concrete dispute within an established framework of law. We want to foster the ideal of judicial impartiality which can block out the influence of the personal attributes of the parties or the passions created by the setting. With this set of mind, the judge will be able to develop his conclusions from the imper-sonal norms of the law that are supposed to bind him as well as the private parties. Yet this institutional trait of non-accountability does not look so desirable when we focus on the different judicial role of develop-ing the basic legal policies of the Bill of Rights. Here the judge must commit himself to those values to which he is partial and make authori-tative choices in areas of great popular concern. Why should this role be performed by someone who is insulated from the ballot, our normal mechanism for holding an official accountable to the public for his pro-gramme or his performance?

The problem is complex precisely because the nature of modern government is so complicated. We do not and cannot live in the Rousseauan ideal of democracy. A modern, industrialized society cannot conduct a constant town hall meeting in which everyone participates and eventually most concur in the making of political decisions. Differences in citizen interest, expertise, and available time have led to a division of labour among a large set of governmental institutions. Some of these are elected and representative, but most are manned by professional appointees. Right here appears the first complication in our analysis of judicial review.

The officials whose behaviour was to be supervised in *Wray* and in *Osborn*, the police and the prosecutor respectively, are no more personally responsible to the electorate than is the judiciary. Hence one cannot really object to judicial control here on the basis of democratic values. In fact, for several important reasons, judges have a better title to resolve the issues of "due process" than do these appointed officials. Policemen and prosecutors make their decisions through the exercise of low visibility, *ad hoc* discretion. By contrast, a judge makes an adjudicative decision only after hearing detailed representations from each side, he commits himself openly and for the record, and then must justify his conclusions by appealing to principles he finds in public sources of law. We saw earlier how firmly the Supreme Court has cemented into Canadian law the principle of judicial review of administrative tribunals. It is strange, indeed, that it felt such qualms about subjecting the administration of pre-trial criminal justice to effective judicial supervision.

These observations do not apply, of course, to the legislature which enacted the law in *Drybones* and then expressed it in public and observable form. When the Court struck the provision down, it overrode the wishes of an elected body. Many advocates of judicial review have pointed out how even elected legislatures inevitably deviate from the ideals of representative government and have shown that there are ways by which courts are made responsive to the popular will. These qualifications indicate that there is no total dichotomy between court and legislature but cannot obscure the real institutional differences which remain. In the flow of decisions over the long run, an elected legislature is much more likely to be responsive to the majority than a tenured judiciary. To allow a court the power to override a legislative judgment about fundamental issues of civil libertarian policy is, *prima facie*, a deviation from democratic values. Even while recognizing this, can we still defend the stance of judicial activism adopted by the majority in *Drybones*?[41]

Another critical distinction points to a plausible defence of the judicial role in a second important area. The majority in a legislature is not a democratic talisman. Rather, majority rule is a procedural device for achieving more fundamental democratic values, which have been called self-government, popular consent to the laws, etc. Simply because a decision has been agreed to by a majority at one point of time does not always confer on it this "democratic" character. A clear example

---

41 I should note here that the vast majority of unjustified invasions of individual rights are made by appointed officials exercising an authority conferred by vague common law or statutory standards. Judicial intervention does not often require the overruling of a clear legislative mandate. *Wray* and *Osborn* are the typical cases and *Drybones* is the exception. However, to establish the legitimacy of the result in the latter case will provide even stronger support for judicial authority in the former.

would be where the majority votes to end the system of majority rule, or, more likely, to dilute the integrity of the vote by apportionment or gerry-mander. Moreover, some of the most important civil liberties—the political liberties of belief, speech, press, and association—are constituent elements in this process of self-government. When the majority in a legislature votes to encroach on these liberties, we must not assume that it is "undemocratic" to invalidate such a measure. To be meaningful, democratic government must have an enduring form, an institutional core within which the process of popular discussion and debate plays a critical role. If a court requires a society to adhere to the principles of the democratic process, even against the wishes of immediate majorities who want to ignore them, this can often be the course which is conducive to the long run success of the risky enterprise of self-government.[42]

The same answer is not available for the kinds of substantive issues presented in either *Drybones* or *Wray* and *Osborn*. Neither egalitarian nor due process values are part of the internal logic of democracy itself. If we choose judicial supervision of legislation which may run afoul of these values, we must do so with full recognition of the infringement on democratic principles. This decision can be justified only if we accept that certain moral limits must be placed on the pursuit of governmental policies, even when these policies are endorsed by strong majorities. These moral limits are ultimately reducible to the principles of fairness, which forbid our sacrificing vital individual interests even if this is conducive to the achievement of the goals of the majority. Judicial review at this point is founded on the view that the claims of democracy are not absolute and may have to give way on occasion to fundamental legal and egalitarian preserves.

This conflict is easier to accept in the area of due process which was considered in *Wray* and *Osborn*. Libertarian standards here are designed to provide procedures which protect individuals against erroneous judgments and excessive interferences in the administration of pro-grammes for the general welfare. The court is not placing a roadblock in the way of the substance of the government's policy; it simply makes the government "turn square corners" by complying with basic procedural proprieties. The infringement of democratic values is much sharper when we consider the concept of "equality before the law" to which the Court began to give some content in *Drybones*. The whole point of laws is to treat defined categories of people differently than others. Complaints of

---

[42] *Boucher v. R.*, see fn. 2, *ante*, is a good example of a case demanding such judicial intervention to permit vigorous discussion of the governmental and clerical policies towards the Jehovah's Witnesses. As we saw, there was no clear decision from a legislative majority in favour of a repressive law of sedition and the Supreme Court was able to reach the proper result through the avenue of legal interpreta-tion. One would hope that it would reach the same conclusion under the Bill of Rights, in the unlikely event that the legislature tried to enact a sweeping exten-sion of the definition of sedition.

inequality emerge when the differences in treatment appear unreasonable. Yet the loser in any hotly disputed legislative battle usually believes that the majority was unreasonable in its conclusions. The anguished cries from both sides in the recent battle over tax reform is as good an example as any. Full fledged review by an elderly, sheltered court of the reasonableness of all governmental measures would be intolerable in a democracy. Yet it is clear that a majority can go too far. The values of self-government do not give it the moral authority to impose excessive burdens on permanent minorities.

In a case such as *Drybones*, the majority was imposing a sacrifice on members of the Indian race, an enduring and visible group which has great difficulty in securing redress through the political process, and is vitally different from such groups as the rich, the entrepreneur, etc., who may feel excessively burdened by tax laws, anti-trust regulations, and the like which are enacted by the majority. Yet, visible in that same Indian Act is the problem of other laws that confer a benefit on the category of Indians, perhaps at the expense of other groups (such as the woman in *Lavell*).[43] Hence *Drybones* embodies the intractable problem at the core of a Bill of Rights. The majority in a democracy must enjoy substantial freedom but it must not go too far. Assuming that there should be moral limitations on the authority of the representatives of the majority, why should we leave it to the consciences of our judges to express these limitations through legal restraints? When we reflect again on the structure and responsibility of these different institutions, an answer can be seen.

It is logically possible for the immediate decision maker, be he legislator, administrator or policeman to take account of these moral limitations in his original decisions. Indeed, there are good practical reasons to believe this will be the best protection for fundamental freedoms. However, a proponent of judicial review believes there are better psychological reasons for not relying exclusively on this expectation. The point of civil liberties doctrines is to restrain an official from infringing unduly on certain individual interests. Yet the primary function of this official is the furtherance of governmental policies which involve some infringement on these kinds of interests. Police and prosecutors focus their attention on the job of crime control which must have some impact on individual freedom. Legislators are concerned to adopt the policies responsive to the objectives of the majority with the necessary impact this will have on certain minority claims. How can we rely on these same officials to strike a nice balance at the point where this invasion becomes unfair and unjustified? It is simply because we cannot expect, from the very persons we are trying to restrain, an impartial decision about when they have become too zealous that we are uneasy about relying solely on official self-control.

---

43 Fn. 21, *ante.*

At this very point many of the institutional characteristics of courts which were the source of concern earlier now appear in a different light. The structure of adjudication is designed to preserve as high a level of impartiality as is possible. Because judges are tenured, they are not beholden to the majority for re-election. Because judges are generalists, they are not committed to any one administrative goal, such as crime control. They operate within the framework of the adversary process which provides access to the "one man lobby" to complain about political injustice done to a minority. Within this forum, each side, government and individual, is represented only by counsel whose function is to provide arguments for the resolution of the dispute on the merits. The criterion for decision is not the number of voters represented by each party, a standard under which the individual would almost invariably be the loser.

One need not hold the naïve belief that the ideal of judicial impartiality is ever fully attained. It is sufficient to expect, realistically, a more dispassionate concern for libertarian values in courts than will be obtained from officials who perceive them as roadblocks in their way. Similarly, one must recognize that a court cannot hold out against the deeply felt and enduring demands of the majority. In the long run, the elected branches of government wield ultimate power. However, in a democracy most threats to civil liberties are transitory, either fed by sudden popular passions or protected by their low visibility. The virtue of judicial review is that it provides a forum where these can be brought out into the open, deflected and delayed, or channelled into less harmful paths. The technique of judicial restraint of the majority is to require a clear and unambiguous legislative statement, sometimes in fact a restatement, of its wish to offend against a fundamental principle of fairness within the society. It is easy to envisage cases where this technique is not effective, but experience suggests that it usually is. When it does succeed, a democracy is richer, not poorer, for it.

THE WISDOM OF JUDGE-MADE LAW

The most common argument against judicial enforcement of a Bill of Rights is the fact that it is "counter-majoritarian" in its operation. The unrepresentative character of courts can help establish a solid case against judicial intervention in some fields (such as industrial relations and federalism which I have reviewed earlier). However, when we reflect on the purpose and justification of civil liberties, the anti-democratic character of judicial protection is not a compelling objection. It should make courts hesitant but not compliant. The thesis to this stage has developed a case only for external review of governmental action by a body which displays some of the characteristics of an appellate court. There are other key dimensions along which the institutional competence of our judiciary must be measured, such as its wisdom and its influence. The authority of our courts is fragile and can be endangered by confrontation with the popular will. We must be confident that judicial protection of civil liberties will be both intelligent and successful before risking the court's standing in an essentially symbolic quest.

To my mind, the most problematic is the likely rationality of judge-made libertarian policies. This generates concern about judicial involvement in any area of law but there are distinctive features of a Bill of Rights which aggravate the problem. Ordinarily courts interpret and apply legal standards which are made elsewhere, whether by statute or judicial precedent. There is always room for marginal growth and refinement of these standards in individual judicial decisions. As I have tried to show in earlier chapters, the cumulative impact of judicial work over a period of time is likely to be substantial. Yet in each individual case the court is normally limited to interstitial additions to the law. Even better, in areas of social complexity and controversy, the legislature continues to furnish new standards by which the judges can orient themselves in their marginal improvements. Neither of these resources is available in the administration of a Bill of Rights. Here the judges are faced with essentially open-ended moral categories into which they must pour precise meaning and content. In this task they cannot rely extensively on legislative or administrative definitions because these are precisely the bodies from which originate the definitions that are under examination.

This concern hinges on my conception of the nature of the question involved in a typical civil liberties case. In recent years one often hears the more liberal voices proclaiming about any alleged infringement on individual freedoms that it is the first step in the way to disaster. If one assumes that a Bill of Rights should be read as a form of absolute "higher law" whose demands are clear to every enlightened persons, then such fears might be justified. But then, if a majority and its government are going to engage in blatant and sustained invasions of minority rights, will they likely suffer judicial controls? A fair analysis of the flow of civil liberties cases coming before a court will show that most of them involve conflicts between legitimate interests on either side, and require a delicate adjustment for a satisfactory resolution by the law.[44]

---

[44] There is one important exception to this proposition which I believe only goes to show the rule. In a federal system, a national court may have to review decisions made by a local government. Here we can find cases of gross infringements on individual rights for which the national court must give redress. Examples are the actions of the Duplessis government towards the Jehovah's Witnesses in Quebec and of the American southern states towards the blacks. Yet it is largely because there was a national majority in favour of the protection of the minority group

If we look at the substantive questions in the three cases under examination, we can perceive important interests on either side whose ultimate balance is not crystal clear. *Wray* and *Osborn* involved basically the same issue. In *Wray*, a police officer had used improper techniques in interrogating a suspect but this had led to the discovery of trustworthy physical evidence as to who committed a murder. In *Osborn*, a prosecutor had not laid all the reasonably available charges against a defendant at once, and had picked the one which turned out to be legally mistaken. The defendant in each case asked that the court hold that the conduct of the official be a bar to government action against the defendant, whether in a new prosecution or in the use of the illegally obtained evidence. Persuasive arguments have been made in favour of such a rule; this may be the only way to enforce limitations for our protection on the behaviour of police and prosecutors. Yet the ambiguity in this position is also clear; the immediate beneficiary of such a rule is a criminal defendant who would otherwise be convicted of a crime and who is now allowed to go free at a risk to the rest of us.

The same kind of uncertainty lurks in the background to the *Drybones* case. The defendant is charged under a law which imposes somewhat more restrictive controls on the drinking habits of Indians, stemming from a traditional belief that this racial group encounters greater problems and exploitation from the use of alcohol. This regulation is part of a systematic pattern of governmental policies towards Indians; some are restrictive and others more beneficial, but all are founded on a paternalistic attitude towards this minority. In recent years, serious attacks have been levelled at both the underlying spirit of this legislation and at specific elements within it. On the other hand, a great many of these regulations were originally initiated by Indian leaders themselves and many Indian spokesmen still favour special legislative treatment, at least during an extended period of adjustment to the white man's world. In such a setting, the conclusion that the Indian Act denied Joe Drybones "equality before the law" is not a self-evident one.

A cool-headed appraisal of the kinds of civil liberties problems which can be successfully handled in litigation should produce a tentative and experimental attitude. We need intelligent judgments about the proper standards defining our civil liberties and an imaginative search for new avenues for implementing them. As a society, we must commit ourselves on the basis of an imperfect understanding of these problems before we do act, one way or the other. The question remains, though, whether we can trust the courts to choose wisely for us. Judges operate within an institutional framework which creates both advantages and disadvantages in this endeavour.

---

freedoms that the courts' decisions could be implemented. It is also interesting to note that the local judges who were supposed to apply the same legal framework did not hold the local governmental action invalid.

As I have reiterated throughout this book, the structure of an appellate court is oriented towards the task of adjudication. This creates a substantial risk of distortion in the court's perception of the civil liberties issues and the solutions it proposes. The question of principle is posed within the context of a concrete dispute which may colour our sense of the underlying conflict. These concrete disputes occur sporadically and are brought to the court pursuant to the accidents of litigation initiated by private interests. As a result, judges do not obtain a systematic overview of a problem area which can give them a feel for the on-going difficulties of the actors in the field (such as policemen). The adversary process assumes that there will be relative equality in presentation by both sides to give the court a fair picture of the competing interests, but this assumption is by no means always valid. Indeed, even when it is, the evidentiary process in litigation is not the best way to develop the policy or legislative facts which are relevant to the development of a new rule in an appellate court. Nor will the lawyers on the court, with their limited backgrounds and lack of specialization, be likely to have the ability to deal with the ambiguities of complex social situations. Aggravating all these risks in the immediate litigation is the inability of the court to make tentative proposals concerning its new policies and then receive feed-back from the primary actors about how sensible these standards are likely to be in operation.

These deficiencies cumulatively tend in one direction, one which we can see vividly in the recent work of the United States Supreme Court. Civil liberties cases carry a high symbolic load. They generate passions which are expressed in slogans: "police brutality" versus "law and order" is a prime example. Lawyers are prone to see in the concrete evil before them the operation of an abstract principle of justice. Too often they are ignorant of the social scientist's evidence of the real ambiguity in the factual patterns of the middle range. It is lawyers who control the administration of a Bill of Rights in the appellate courts. Once they write their general standards into the law, it becomes very difficult to retreat. In the rarefied atmosphere of the appeal process, it is easy to lose sight of the complexity of the real world. Once an individual interest achieves the label of a constitutional "right", no compromise or adjustment (on the grounds of mere expediency) can be justified. Concepts such as freedom of speech or the privilege against self-incrimination are "completely released from their moorings in the soil, either of historic or current reality. The slightest invasion of an interest is confounded with the worst. The most emotive sentiments are evoked by the most trivial occasion. The sense of proportion is forgotten."[45]

This is a risk inherent in the attempt to protect civil liberties through an adjudicative institution. Judicial excesses can trigger a popular re-

---

[45] Jaffe, *English and American Judges as Lawmakers* (1969), at 101.

action, almost of exasperation, which can endanger the court's role as protector of what is vital in a Bill of Rights. As a result, a wise court must always be careful in deciding when and how to intervene on this basis. This is what makes me so uneasy about the contrasting positions in *Drybones* and in *Wray* and *Osborn*. There are important reasons why the Court should have been much readier to undertake its supervisory role in the latter cases rather than in the former.

In the first place, *Wray* and *Osborn* could be decided by judicial elaboration of the common law. This is the real virtue of the Supreme Court's position as a final court of general jurisdiction. Most civil liberties claims can be handled through interpretation of statutes or revision of the common law, with the Bill of Rights in the background as a set of principles shaping the Court's reasoning. The virtue in this stance is that the legislature, with its greater resources, can still step in to revise the Court's solution, and substitute a more workable scheme of its own. The possibility of judicial collaboration with the legislature is greatly lessened when the Court must appeal directly to a Bill of Rights for a binding rule, as it did in *Drybones*, with the inevitable freeze this will place on legislative experimentation. I do not mean to suggest that the Court should never apply the Bill of Rights directly or that it must simply rubber-stamp legislative initiatives. However, it should be much readier to use the more discriminating weapons from its legal armoury.

There is a second reason for believing that *Drybones* would prove less amenable to judicial treatment, based on the kind of real life problems involved. *Osborn*, for example, presented the question of the scope of prosecutorial discretion in charging. The materials relevant to any legal standards regulating multiple charges are largely apparent on the surface of the immediate factual situation. The lawyers on the Supreme Court are probably as capable as anyone of appreciating their significance. In *Drybones*, by contrast, the reasonableness of special legislative treatment of intoxication of Indians can only be assessed in the light of complex scientific evidence which is not even hinted at by the circumstances of Drybones' offence. Judges are unlikely to have any special awareness of this background. The case by case method of incremental policy making seems to me to be the appropriate instrument for evolving standards to control the prosecutor from the radiations of the principle of double jeopardy. One must be very dubious about the likely success of a piecemeal judicial attack on the wisdom of the special legislative status of the Indian. The policy has a long history whose current effects cannot simply be wished away. Its many elements are interlocking in real life, though they may not so appear in isolated cases, and there is a real danger that the legal perspective could have disastrous results. In each of these respects, *Osborn* and *Drybones* are poles apart. The situation in *Wray* lines up somewhere in between,

216

though in my view much closer to *Osborn* in each of these respects. One's disquiet deepens, then, at the curious pattern in the Court's responses.

THE FRAGILITY OF JUDICIAL INFLUENCE

It may require fairly close attention to see these lessons which can be learned from the American experience about possibly unwise judicial innovation under a Bill of Rights. A casual observer, relying only on the news media, could not miss the tensions raised on the third dimension of institutional policy, the likely influence of judicial protection of civil liberties. How effective is a court likely to be in securing compliance with the restraints it may want to impose on legislative or official behaviour? Sometimes the court's symbolic authority as the oracle of "The Law" is sufficient. Many cases of intrusion on civil liberties are almost inadvertent and without much significance to the official. This does not mean that they are unimportant: if our neighbour accidentally puts his elbow in our face, we will want to let him know that he should stop. In that kind of case, when the court articulates a clear standard of behaviour to protect the libertarian interest and brings it to the attention of the official, this will be enough to secure voluntary compliance. The trouble case arises when the individual's claim conflicts with an important governmental objective whose proponents believe is more compelling. These are the situations which, in the United States, have produced 'massive resistance', 'backlash', and police disobedience of judge-made law on behalf of 'law and order'. We have not experienced these in Canada as yet, because the Supreme Court's civil liberties role is so new and as yet so tenuous. If our judges are prepared to establish new public policies in these critical areas, there will be entrenched participants in the government who will want to resist. The Court will need further weapons to implement its will, but it is sadly lacking in effective ones.

There is a famous expression used in the United States to describe the relative weakness of courts: "they wield neither purse nor sword". This characteristic again can best be understood as a natural implication of the structure of adjudication. The judicial process is designed to perform the central function of settling concrete disputes through authoritative and reasoned decisions, based on presentations made by the opposing parties. We capture the essence of this function when we say that courts are available, at the behest of the parties, to give a reading of the law applicable to a situation, and then to select the remedy legally appropriate for this reading be it a criminal penalty, monetary damages, or a mandatory order). The judges then retire to their chambers and leave it to the individual party concerned to enforce this specific relief. We want our judges to remain impartial and above the battle so they don't take any personal responsibility to see that their verdicts are implemented. There is of course a bureaucratic structure including sheriffs, police, and jailors to see that the court's orders are enforced. But the point is that this organization is not under the supervision of the judge, and these officials are not beholden to the courts for their wages, promotion, status, and other perquisites of the job.

Such a division of labour can be quite efficient in securing the specific remedy sought and obtained in the concrete dispute. Under a Bill of Rights, the judges have another critical objective. They want to define and protect fundamental freedoms through legal standards and to see that the general doctrines they announce are adhered to without the need for costly and time-consuming litigation in every case. Now let us hypothesize a case where the Court has formulated a new legal standard, controlling police behaviour for example. If the basic values expressed in the new standards are not accepted by the police (especially at the top of the police hierarchy), then there are serious deficiencies in this enforcement mechanism. Criminal law control of police (or other official) behaviour is notoriously weak, for obvious reasons. Private damage awards are too sporadic to be a good deterrent, dependent as they are on the accident of a private individual who will pursue and can prove a substantial, tangible harm. In this situation, effective judicial controls will usually require legislative help in setting up an enforcement mechanism (such as a police commission, civilian review board, ombudsman, etc.). The trouble is that legislative help requires the acquiescence of the majority whose wishes the Court may just have over-ridden in performing its task under the Bill of Rights.

There is one qualification to this scenario which has been played out in several areas in the United States in recent years. The judges do wield one direct sanction against the government within the structure of adjudication, that of "nullity". This is an immediate tactic which a court can use to enforce its views about the appropriate limits of state interference with individual rights. It can refuse legal validity to official actions which exceed these bounds, and thus deny the government the collaboration of the judiciary in imposing its contrary will. Each of our three cases is an example in point. In the case of the prosecutor in *Osborn*, the Supreme Court could have denied him the trial and conviction and thus frustrated the oppressive second charge. In *Wray*, the Court could have denied the use of the illegally obtained evidence at the trial. On the assumption that the primary incentive for the illegal police practice is the obtaining of evidence for a conviction, this presumably would lessen the incidence of the behaviour. In *Drybones*, the Court did deny the legislature the resources of the criminal courts for securing convictions against an individual on whom it had imposed unfair restrictions.

What are the implications of this kind of remedy? First, it is primarily designed for the achievement of a negative result, the prevention of certain kinds of official behaviour. It is not likely to secure positively beneficial actions from a government. Affirmative social policies need money raised through taxes, a fairly detailed programme for spending it, and a bureaucratic structure to oversee the details. In our constitutional framework these powers are held by the executive and legislature, the same institutions the court may be trying to control. There may be exceptional cases where a positive result is achieved when the judiciary propounds a new standard of conduct that is readily obeyed by its few and highly visible targets. Reapportionment of state legislatures in the United States is a clear example. However, the problem which is at the heart of *Drybones*, the provision of real equality to Indians within our legal and social structure, is not one of those tasks which is amenable to successful treatment in adjudication.

Secondly, the influence of the court varies in different contexts, depending on the officials' need for the collaboration of the court. Take the case of the prosecutor whose discretion was sought to be controlled in *Osborn*. He can only achieve his objectives if the courts will hear his charge. If the Supreme Court lays down standards for prosecution and promises to "stay" charges which do not respect these guidelines, it is reasonable to assume that the device will be effective. In theory the same logic should apply to police conduct in the investigation of crime, such as in *Wray*. If the Court decides that certain techniques will bring the administration of justice into disrepute, it can refuse to allow the "fruits" of these methods to be used as evidence at trial. Presumably this should lead police officers to adopt only those remaining methods which can be utilized to prepare a case for prosecution. This logic hinges on the assumption that the policeman is primarily interested in securing a conviction in court, and so can be influenced by changes in the law of evidence at trial. Empirical studies in the United States have cast doubt on that assumption. The police officer is directly attuned to his department's clearance rate, the prosecutor secures most of his convictions from guilty pleas without trial, and the system has available to it techniques of out-of-court harassment as an alternative to trial. In any event, the "illegally obtained evidence" rule has not been highly successful in changing police behaviour in jurisdictions where it has been tried.[46]

What about judicial conclusions that legislation is inoperative because it conflicts with a Bill of Rights? To the extent that the law ultimately relies on the courts for the application of its sanction, logically the denial of any validity to the law in court should prevent harm from these laws. There is such a variety of both governments and laws that it is difficult to make meaningful generalizations about real issues. I referred earlier

---

[46] Oaks, "Studying the Exclusionary Rule in Search and Seizure" (1970), 37 Univ. of Chicago Law Rev. 665. See also Amsterdam, "The Supreme Court and the Rights of Suspects in Criminal Cases" (1970), 45 New York Univ. Law Rev. 785.

to *Drybones* and its contrast to reapportionment decisions in the United States. Again the American experience in a variety of contexts (school prayer, obscenity, etc.) indicates that judicial innovations enjoy only mixed success in altering governmental policies. At this point, though, I must return to the comment I made earlier about the significance of such qualms in connection with judicial influence. Criticism of the effectiveness of exclusionary rules, judicial nullifications of statutes, etc. are valid counters to the belief that judicial review is a sufficient protector of our civil liberties. They are surely no proof against the usefulness of judicial efforts in tandem with political or administrative devices as, for example, the ombudsman.

Again we can see in the structure of adjudication a special advantage in the position of the judge. The distinctive feature of courts is that they entitle the individual to demand, as a matter of legal right, a public, reasoned pronouncement about the validity of a law or official decision. The private citizen cannot be fobbed off by arguments of political expediency or left to wander in a bureaucratic maze looking for someone with the responsibility of giving him an answer. I think that the most important contribution that courts make to the protection of civil liberties is that they give the ordinary person access to a body from whom he is entitled to have a decision one way or the other. As a result, many dubious official practices are brought out into the open where they may not be able to stand the light of day. In fact, I think this is the primary justification for the exclusionary rule, not its supposed deterrent impact on the police. One need only compare the level of debate and analysis of police practices in the United States and Canada to see the results of countless American cases reviewing police work in detail. Courts can only delay unjust legislation which a majority is determined to have, but more often it will initiate political and administrative actions to deal successfully with unfair situations the majority had not really appreciated before.

Indeed at this point, we can complete the circle in this dialogue about the place of active judicial protection of fundamental liberties. In the long run no court can successfully restrain a community from developing governmental policies which that community is thoroughly persuaded it must have. Ultimately the representative, political agencies of government hold the trump cards, because they can use the power of judicial appointment to change the views of the final court. However, the fact that a court cannot "save a society bent on self-destruction" is not an argument for judicial inaction. Instead, the existence of this final reservoir of political power is a partial answer to the qualms I raised earlier about the legitimacy and wisdom of judicial supervision of political decisions. Within this framework the courts can provide an essential forum to which under-represented minority groups can gain access and a sympathetic ear. The very fact of the Supreme Court's ultimate weakness is a source of the real influence it can have in enhancing the qualities of justice and freedom within our society.

THE UNCERTAIN
PATH AHEAD

The decision in *Drybones* can be of profound importance in the evolution of Canadian law and courts. I say this not only because of its obvious impact on the direction of civil liberties law in Canada but even more because of its potential for the substratum of legal reasoning in our courts. An ongoing legal system is always the expression of a theory of the nature of law, a theory which is shared at least by those dominant social groups which can influence the character of the system. At the heart of any such legal philosophy is a view of the proper criteria for justifying judicial decisions and defining the scope of adjudication. Ordinarily this tacit conception of the law in courts evolves over a long period of time. Judges gradually come to accept the relevance of particular factors in their decisions and adopt orders of priority between these different sources of law in cases where they conflict. Only rarely in the history of a legal system is such a fundamental issue graphically presented to a final court of appeal in one case, where it must choose between two different concepts of the legal structure. This rare event did occur in Canada in late 1969, and the Supreme Court seized the opportunity in *Drybones* to widen the perimeters of legal reasoning.

The question whether we should have judicial review of legislative action on behalf of civil liberties should always be approached in a tentative, even anxious, spirit. Sloganeering about whether one is for civil liberties, or against democracy, is never helpful. There are too many threads woven into the pattern to form any such strong contrasts as these. In my view, the activist judicial role adopted in *Drybones* can be justified in principle. The source of my unease is the fact that the opposite conclusion was reached in *Wray* and *Osborn*. The chief qualm I have in defending judicial review is the risk that decisions will be both unwise and irreversible.[47] Courts vary in their capacity to handle difficult and complex questions of public policy. The contrast in the results in these three cases suggests strongly that our Supreme Court is not ready

---

47 At least as a practical matter. Undoubtedly, some readers will have noticed that I have not dwelt on the fact that our Bill of Rights is not constitutionally entrenched. Parliament can legally reverse an unwise judicial interpretation by re-enacting the challenged statute with a *non obstante* provision. Of course, even if that interpretation arose under a constitutional Bill of Rights, it could legally be overridden by a constitutional amendment. In my estimate, the political feasibility of the first legal avenue in Canada is about the same as the second alternative in the United States —and small enough that it need not figure prominently in my analysis of the judicial role.

for the demanding task implicit in *Drybones*. And it is *this* Court which has the responsibility right now.

Thus, while I believe in the ideal of judicial review, I think that contemporary Canada would have been better served by the position advocated in the dissent. Despite Mr. Justice Ritchie's doubts, an attractive and important role for the courts can be founded on the combination of a Bill of Rights and the "clear statement" technique we saw in *Boucher*. The chief defect in the process of "interpretation" is the source of the standards the courts can use. A fundamental liberty such as freedom of expression may be implicit in our history, our institutions, or our community's values, but these are rather ephemeral materials for judicial reasoning. Such a standard is nowhere near so explicit in its authority or its demands as the principle of *mens rea* for example. Hence judges will always feel qualms about using it or appealing to it openly in opinions, thereby producing a coherent and consistent set of legal doctrines. The erratic pattern of results we receive instead is only to be expected.

The enactment of a Bill of Rights remedies exactly this defect. It is an authoritative legal expression of the community's basic values which it wants judges to protect in their use and elaboration of the whole range of legal doctrines. From this perspective we could conceive of the Bill of Rights as a set of legal principles which are to have great weight in legal reasoning, not legal rules which have overriding legal force. The reason is that they may admit of exceptions where the legislature clearly expresses this wish. No doubt this is not as perfect a restraint as the committed civil libertarian would prefer in an ideal world. However, I suggest that, for the moment at least, we might place greater trust in the virtue of our legislatures than in the infallibility of our courts.[48]

For the moment, the Supreme Court has taken the more radical route. It can do serious damage in this new role if it views the problem through the same legalistic blinkers it has donned in some of the areas we have looked at. Yet this style of reasoning is not inevitable. One may as well argue that when our judges come face to face with the Pandora's box they have unloosened in *Drybones*, they will open their eyes to a much broader conception of law. If this should happen, a new style of legal argument may have happy effects across the whole spectrum of the appellate court function.

---

[48] I would also add this point. If our judges treated the Bill of Rights as a source of principles of legal reasoning, this could conceivably enhance its present worth to civil liberties in Canada. The reason is that such an approach would be equally justified for legal doctrines within the legislative authority of the provinces where a large part of the dangers lie. Given the Supreme Court's holding that Parliament intended the Bill to be a set of rules limiting its own authority, the natural corollary is that it is totally irrelevant to the authority of the provinces.

The same crossroads can be viewed from another angle. Right now the Supreme Court of Canada is considered a non-partisan body, sitting above the social and political battle, and rendering impartial decisions in those few conflicts which take the shape of litigation. Its conclusions are treated with deference and followed as the dictates of an impersonal "Law". Even now it is apparent to any close observer that the picture has a large element of myth in it; the personal views and contributions of some judges are apparent at various points in the evolution of our legal system. However, if the Court must intervene in important and divisive civil libertarian controversies, the visibility of this factor will be greatly enhanced. The Court would eventually be drawn into the political maelstrom, the manning and jurisdiction of the Court at any one time would become partisan issues, and this could lead to an erosion in the popular acceptance of judge-made law. Again I point out that this infection would not likely be isolated from the whole range of the Court's appellate work.

These observations reflect a basic truth. The decision whether to allot an important new function, the protection of civil liberties, to the Canadian judiciary headed by our Supreme Court cannot be assessed simply by reference to its existing structure. The performance of this function will inevitably have a vital impact on the evolution of our judicial process. At the moment, the Supreme Court is much too heavily oriented to the purely adjudicative conception of the judicial role. I believe that the attempt to meet the intrinsic demands of this new task could eventually improve the Court's perspective and performance. Yet we must be aware of a possible dénouement much farther down this same path, a heavily politicized court, which is not a happy instrument for the more traditional judicial functions. Need I add that we can read alternative versions of this scenario in the American experience? Whichever choice we make, we gamble for the future. As Holmes once said, "certainty is an illusion, and repose is not the destiny of man."

Epilogue — The Lavell Case

Shortly before this book went into print, the Supreme Court rendered its decision in the case of *Attorney General of Canada v. Lavell & Bedard*.[49] As I noted earlier, the facts in that case would require the judges to confront the intractable problem of defining clearly such concepts as "equality before the law ... without discrimination by reason of race, national origin, colour, religion or sex." Unfortunately the Supreme Court seems to have marched up the hill to look at this problem and then turned around and marched right back down again!

Lavell was concerned with a provision in the Indian Act which deprived Indian women of their status when they married non-Indian

---

[49] (1973), 23 C.R.N.S. 197 (Can.).

men. The consequence of such loss of status was ineligibility for the several benefits of membership in the Indian band, including even residence on the reservation. The vice in that provision was that the same deprivations were not visited on Indian men who married non-Indian women. Hence, if the band council sought to turn the Indian woman out of her reservation home, could she be said to be discriminated against by reason of her sex and so denied equality before the law?

I would have thought it difficult to write an opinion which distinguished this case from *Drybones*; Mr. Justice Ritchie found this no more onerous a task than his earlier treatment of his effort in *Robertson & Rosetanni*. He said that *Drybones* involved "inequality of treatment in the enforcement and application of the laws of Canada before the law enforcement authorities and the ordinary courts of the land." That was totally different from this case which was concerned only with the "internal regulation of the lives of Indians on Reserves". But then we are not told how the band council can have the women ejected from their homes except by force of a judicial order secured from "the ordinary courts of the land". As the Toronto Globe and Mail put it:

> What the Supreme Court has done is throw us back to the sterile, jesuitical hair-splitting of a decade ago. What a pity.

Mr. Justice Laskin's opinion is better, but still not fully satisfactory. In essence he holds that any legal distinction based on "sex" amounts to "discrimination" and so denies "equality before the law". From that absolutist perch he can deny the relevance of the purpose of the legal classification, its history, or its presence in comparable legal systems such as the American. While we might agree with his conclusion in this particular case, surely the Canadian Bill of Rights does not make every legal provision expressed in sexual terms *per se* discriminatory and inoperative; if it does our whole Canadian law of sexual offences is in a shaky legal state. Only if the sexual classification is unreasonable or invidious can it be termed discriminatory and to make that value judgment a court must canvass the very materials which Mr. Justice Laskin too quickly ignored.

The same point can be tested in another way. Discrimination on account of race is equally offensive under the Bill of Rights as if based on sex; if that is so, how can the dissenting judges confine the benefits of membership in the Indian band to Indians alone? Mr. Justice Laskin would hold that Mrs. Lavell and Mrs. Bedard could not be denied homes on the reservation in situations when Indian men would not be. But how can Indian women legally enjoy that special benefit while non-Indians of either sex are excluded?

A Bill of Rights inevitably requires a Court to appraise the reasonability of value judgments made by a legislature. The truth of that proposition may be submerged for the moment in *Lavell* but not even the Supreme Court of Canada can play King Canute forever.

PART III

The Future Prospect

The Supreme Court in the Seventies and Beyond

CHAPTER 8

"The triumph of hope over experience" (Boswell)

The research on which this book was based covered the decisions of the Supreme Court of Canada from 1950 to 1970 or thereabouts. In that time the philosophical orientation of the Supreme Court changed direction sharply, sometime around the year 1960. This may or may not have had something to do with the departure of Justices Kellock, Locke and Rand from the Court. What is clearly apparent on the face of the reports is a sharp difference in reasoning style. In the sixties there are fewer opinions, they are shorter, they cite fewer legal authorities and draw them from a narrower range of sources, they deal with fewer legal issues and arguments and include much less analysis of the direction in which the law should grow. If we look at the broad sweep of decisions in the fifties, the Court was groping towards, and I think gradually achieving, what Karl Llewellyn has called the Grand Style of legal reasoning. The judges appreciated the complexity of the problems before them, canvassed a wider range of legal materials, adopted a critical view of the authority of any one of them and took their own personal but complementary paths to the underlying principle which pointed to the conclusion in the case. *Boucher* epitomizes that Court's style. In the sixties, the Court (composed of many of the same members) regressed to the heavily legalistic, Formal Style. The focus is on the facts of the immediate dispute, the law is assumed to be settled and clear and the truth of the Court's personal responsibility for the conclusion is disguised by a unanimous and mechanically argued opinion. *Carker* typifies that orientation.

It is too early to tell for sure, but I sense another fundamental change in direction in the seventies. The most visible, and perhaps the most important indicator, is *Drybones*, which carved out a new role for the Canadian judiciary. For reasons I need not repeat here, this decision will reverberate across the whole spectrum of the Supreme Court's work, though in ways which are as yet unpredictable.[1] At the same time we can

---

[1] The Supreme Court has not been reluctant to exercise this new authority. It has used the Bill of Rights in a fair proportion of the cases where it was relied upon in argument. I would single out *Brownridge v. R.*, [1972] S.C.R. 926, 18 C.R.N.S. 308, 7 C.C.C. (2d) 417, 28 D.L.R. (3d) 1, as the most noteworthy step forward

227

observe several recent examples of quiet but professional judicial crafts-manship in the revision of the common law. In *Horsley v. McLaren*,[2] the Supreme Court extended the duty to be a Good Samaritan and in *Highway Properties v. Kelly, Douglas & Co.*,[3] it revised the law of landlord and tenant. Both opinions, written by Mr. Justice Laskin, overruled the earlier doctrines embedded in Ontario law, but did so after careful examination of a wide range of legal materials and issues from which the basic legal principle was extracted and the legal anomaly overturned. In *Ares v. Venner*[4] the Court was confronted directly with the options of revising the law of hearsay itself (to take account of modern record keeping in an organization) or leaving this task up to the legislature. Mr. Justice Hall recognized that "this judge-made law needs to be restated to meet modern conditions" but, unlike the House of Lords (in *Myers v. D.P.P.*[5]) he refused to "leave it to Parliament and the ten legislatures to do the job". The Court saw its own responsibility for the quality of our law and was not afraid to exercise it.

We saw in the Supreme Court throughout the sixties an increasingly interventionist attitude towards the administrative process, epitomized in *Metropolitan Life* and the very generous doctrinal platform it erected for judicial review. Again I will not repeat the reasons I gave for believing this tendency to be misguided. There are hints in a recent decision, *Pringle v. Fraser*[6] that the Court may itself feel some qualms. In that case the full Court, in a unanimous decision, overruled the Ontario Court of Appeal and deferred to the statutory exclusion of *certiorari* supervision of immigration officers in the ordinary courts. I must hasten to add that this was a special case because the legislature had provided for an internal appeal to an Immigration Appeal Board with subsequent appeals on issues of law to the Supreme Court of Canada. Again we must await the future to tell whether the expressions of judicial restraint in the opinion will bear fruit in less obvious cases.

Finally, the Supreme Court's retreat in constitutional law is proceeding apace. *The Manitoba Egg Reference* will prove to be an accidental

---

and *R. v. Appleby*, [1972] S.C.R. 303, 16 C.R.N.S. 35, [1971] 4 W.W.R. 601, 3 C.C.C. (2d) 354, 21 D.L.R. (3d) 325, as the most dubious instance of judicial caution. Perhaps it is also worthy of remark that both of these cases dealt with challenges to laws designed to deal with impaired driving, as were several other important decisions on the Bill of Rights.

2 [1972] S.C.R. 441, 22 D.L.R. (3d) 545. I am referring here to the dissenting opinion of Mr. Justice Laskin with which Mr. Justice Ritchie's majority opinion agreed as to the law, but then took a different view of the facts.

3 [1971] S.C.R. 562, [1972] 2 W.W.R. 28, 17 D.L.R. (3d) 710.

4 [1970] S.C.R. 608 esp. at 623 ff, 12 C.R.N.S. 349, 73 W.W.R. 347, 14 D.L.R. (3d) 4.

5 [1965] A.C. 1001, [1964] 2 All E.R. 881 (H.L.).

6 [1972] S.C.R. 821, 26 D.L.R. (3d) 28. A Comment by Elliott in 7 U.B.C.L.R. 293 takes a very different view of the desirability of the approach in this decision.

and short-lived deviation from that trend. Much more indicative of the Court's prevailing stance is *Jorgensen v. A. G. Can.*[7] where it declined an invitation to subject Parliament's open-ended "declaratory" power under section 92(10)(*c*) of the B.N.A. Act to some judicial supervision.[8]

I don't mean to suggest that the situation is rosy, far from it. But there are more grounds for optimism than could be seen at the time I began my study of the Supreme Court in 1969. Several of the opinions which I believe, or at least hope, are harbingers of a happier future were written by Mr. Justice Laskin. I believe it is no accident that the picture brightened after his appointment in 1970.

No doubt, the judgments I have made about these several cases may appear rather cavalier and I do not intend to defend them here. I do believe they can be justified in the light of the position I have developed in this book. How might we summarize this conception of the judicial function whose detailed implications we have traced in the last five chapters?

The fundamental lesson is that we will not secure consistently good performance from a judiciary which does not share an adequate conception of the place of law in courts. The inevitable tensions between an appellate court's policy-making function and its adjudicative structure makes this a lot easier to propose than to achieve. But the truth must be faced that, at the present time, the Supreme Court's view is much too narrow. Its opinions focus on isolated legal rules and sources which it assumes will prescribe the answer, one way or the other. The judges appeal to legal materials which have much too brittle a texture to do the job that is demanded of them. The law is much more purposeful, evolutionary and systematic than any one legal rule would give us cause to suspect. An appellate court judge must always be asking how the rule developed, what objectives it now serves and how does it fit into the regulatory context of which it is a part? As he asks these questions, that judge will soon appreciate how much more pliable and elastic are the legal materials with which he works. Conscious of his creative role in the shaping of the legal system, he will always try to define the legal doctrines he finds into a more coherent and principled pattern, before using them to justify the result in the litigation before him.

---

[7] [1971] S.C.R. 725, [1971] 3 W.W.R. 149, 3 C.C.C. (2d) 49, 18 D.L.R. (3d) 297.

[8] I must mention the one area of those I have investigated in which no such happy tendency can be observed. The Supreme Court of Canada seems determined to dilute gradually the force of the principle of *mens rea*. In eight consecutive cases which have turned on this issue, the judges have accepted the Crown's position. The most recent expression of this attitude is *Lajoie v. R.* (1973), 20 C.R.N.S. 360, 10 C.C.C. (2d) 313, 33 D.L.R. (3d) 618 (Can.), where the Court significantly broadened the kind of "intention" which is sufficient for the crime of attempted murder (in an opinion which logically has very serious implications for the crime of attempt generally). As the Court's opinion recognized, the decision was a logical corollary of *Trinneer,* but then that is damning it with faint praise!

This is the critical message which the Supreme Court of Canada must hear from legal philosophy. To the Canadian public and Bar, my restatement of this message may seem novel, and perhaps disturbing. But I am perfectly aware that to Canadian legal scholars its conclusions will appear obvious, sometimes even trite. In the wider world of legal theory from which Canadian academics draw their intellectual sustenance, the assumption of judicial creativity is now the conventional wisdom. What is not always clear to that audience is that there are limits to this expansion of the concept of law. Of course, as far as the immediate redirection of Supreme Court performance is concerned, these boundaries are largely irrelevant to a body which is still so far from them. Still, it is important that the activist critic of Supreme Court timidity understand that there should be restraints on the creative role of the judiciary.

The institution of law in courts is a distinctive mode of governing and implementing public policies. The law is supposed to guide the behaviour of the citizens and officials whom it seeks to control, and the judicial position is designed for the adjudication of concrete disputes within that legal framework. The integrity of these institutional arrangements requires something more than the spongy character of pure judicial policy. Judges must have a sense of proportion in exercising their law-making powers, a sense which I think is illuminated by the theory I have sketched in this book. Within such a perspective we can understand why a court may be more creative in tort law than in labour law, in expanding criminal defences than developing criminal offences, and in controlling legislative behaviour to preserve civil liberties than in umpiring the federal system. Uncritical judicial activism is as unhelpful a refrain as is unthinking judicial passivity.

Those who are familiar with modern jurisprudence will realize that I have taken a rather conservative view of the proper ambit of the judicial function in Canada. I do not mean to prejudge the legitimacy of the wider mission for courts which is now the popular wisdom in the United States. Within the framework of analysis developed in this book, it is unlikely that significant generalizations about the judicial role can be applied across national borders (with their different governmental institutions, contrasting notions of legal policy, etc.). In any event, we need not worry right now about any risk that our courts will emulate American judicial activism in a fashion which is inappropriate for contemporary Canada. Our judges, led by the Supreme Court, are some distance removed from the boundaries of necessary judicial creativity in Canada. The problem, then, is how we can move the Court to fill this vacuum.

I think we should realize that the objective cannot be secured directly. A legislature may try to prescribe certain judicial attitudes to the interpretation of statutes, the use of common law precedents, or the administration of a Bill of Rights. The lesson of history is that wherever this has been tried, it has been singularly unsuccessful. The exercise of judicial creativity is a delicate art and craftsmanlike performance is a difficult achievement. External controls can prohibit harmful conduct and perhaps even require minimum forms of positive activity. They are crude and ineffective instruments for serving the kinds of human aspirations which we should have for our judiciary. Unless these are the operating ideals of the judges themselves in their work, we will not even approach them.

Yet there are some feasible reforms which could be indirectly conducive to this result. Any conception of the law in courts requires an institutional environment within which it can flourish. I shall briefly review some of the suggested structural reforms of the Supreme Court of Canada which might facilitate the reorientation in its vision which I have advocated.

Like most others who have written about the Court, I endorse the proposal to revise its jurisdiction. The composition of its workload must be radically altered. Appeals as of right should be abolished. Cases should come before our final court for resolution only because they present an issue of law which that body has certified as important. This will give the Supreme Court control over its expanding workload, rather than leaving it in the hands of private litigants. Even more critical, it will give visible, operative expression to the view that the function of the Supreme Court of Canada is to settle significant and ambiguous matters of legal policy. Once its members must select, day by day, those cases which meet the standard, it will be natural to adopt a very different stance in disposing of those cases.

At the moment I am not persuaded of the value of another current proposal—deletion of matters of provincial law from the jurisdiction of the Supreme Court of Canada. If the American experience with a federalized judicial system is any indication, it will produce real gains for lawyers but at substantial costs to litigants and the general public. Trying to sort out federal and provincial issues in every Supreme Court appeal and then using the multiplicity of common law decisions will only add to the undue complexity in our present law. Countervailing benefits would be largely symbolic (especially as long as provincial appellate judges are still appointed by the federal government). The notion that a desirable diversity in the common law would be produced by provincial judges sensitive to local conditions seems to fly in the face of the realities of judicial development of the common law, fed by sources from the whole English-speaking world. Given a Supreme Court which was truly composed of the cream of the Canadian legal world, I prefer a higher quality of law to greater diversity.[9]

---

9 I would enter two caveats to this judgment. A much better case could be made for giving provincial courts the final say in interpreting a provincial statute. Here the legislature has asserted that this is an area of provincial jurisdiction and has acted on the basis of local conditions and objectives. The balance of gains and

There has to be some major surgery on the appointment process. First of all, the retirement age should be reduced from 75 to 65, the normal point in just about every other walk of life. This does not mean we should go out looking for "young tigers" in their late 30's or early 40's (as a recent Minister of Justice has suggested). Perhaps my innate conservatism shows itself again, but I do think the ideal level of experience and maturity is attained around the age of 50 or so. Then I would like to see judges appointed for limited terms, preferably of 10 years but certainly no more than 15 years. In addition, the terms should be absolutely non-renewable in order to avoid any suggestion that the desire for reappointment could affect an incumbent's decision. The combination of these two proposals, reduction of the compulsory retirement age and a maximum length of service, is designed to produce a Court whose members retain the physical capacity to perform the arduous work needed for wise judicial policy-making, and who have not become stale and isolated in their judicial chambers in Ottawa. Though there are always exceptional cases, judges as a class are no more exempt than other officials from the inexorable operations of time. After a decent period in office, Supreme Court judges should move over to allow new and fresh faces their chance.

Changes must also be made in the actual procedure for appointment of Supreme Court judges, but here the greater danger is in the popularity of some wrong proposals. A standard suggestion promises lawyers a more prominent voice. I believe that committees of the Bar Association, with the natural composition they have, should not be given a vested say in the selection of a member of this Court which has such influence on the rest of us. I think that more Bar participation in the appointment of the lower court judges is a good thing. Not so in the case of the Supreme Court of Canada.

---

costs to a federal allocation of judicial power might be struck differently as a result. Secondly, there is the peculiar problem of the civil law in Quebec. Eminent French-Canadian scholars have suggested that the Supreme Court, applying common law techniques, has marred the purity and integrity of the civil law. This is the primary source of the proposed "federalism" reform of the Supreme Court's jurisdiction and could be assuaged by a "special status" for the Civil Code, giving finality to interpretation by the Quebec Court of Appeal. I will not express myself one way or the other on this issue, because I have not investigated the course of Civil Code decisions and, indeed, do not have the background to do so. (The best analysis is by Ledain, "Concerning the Proposed Constitutional and Civil Law Specialization at the Supreme Court Level" (1967), 2 La Revue Juridique Thémis 107.) I should say, though, that the controversy as it appears in the literature reflects an abstract and positivist conception of the nature of law, whether "civil" or "common". It would be peculiar indeed if these two bodies of law, as living in contemporary Canada and faced with the same technological, organizational, economic and other realities, should not have grown much closer together than was the case 150 years ago, no matter what the court in which they were ultimately administered.

I have qualms also about a second proposal, giving the provinces a say. This suggestion is fed primarily by concern about the Court's constitutional function. Since both levels of government are parties in interest, the federal government should not have unilateral selection of the umpire. My response is that the Supreme Court's federalism role is receding in importance and should be allowed peaceably to wither away. We should not try to reconstruct the Court so as to enhance its performance of that particular function. There is real danger that we would distort the capacity of the Supreme Court of Canada to perform its other critical functions—the craftsmanlike revision of less visible parts of our law and the independent protection of our civil liberties. These we need the Court for, but adjustments of the federal systems are better undertaken elsewhere.

The danger with institutionalizing a provincial voice is that it will deter certain kinds of appointments. The more people who have a say, the lower the common denominator which can satisfy all. The controversial figure, the person who has had experience with the issues and taken stands, will be shunned. The safe candidate will be the one with the right credentials but whom no one really knows too much about, because he has not been involved. Staffing our final court of appeal with that kind of appointee is the last thing we want!

I do think the appointment process has to be opened up somewhat. I would leave the selection of a nominee in the hands of the Prime Minister and the Minister of Justice but require them to refer the selection to an all-party committee of Parliament to examine the nominee's qualifications. A Prime Minister who enjoys the confidence of the House will have his nominee ratified, unlike recent American presidents. But this procedure will be a vehicle through which the Canadian public can start to think about the jobs it wants our Supreme Court to reform and the kinds of people it wants to use. I can think of no real harm in trying.

What about the working arrangements of the Supreme Court in reaching its decisions? The actual product—the Court's opinions—too often makes a meagre use of available materials and then presents a shallow analysis of the issues. Yet I can see little, if anything, in the way of procedural restrictions which accounts for these deficiencies. Extensive briefs, citation of a wide variety of sources, development of principled policy arguments, intervention by *amici curiae*, all these are now permissible. The judges have the aid of law clerks in appraising and supplementing these materials and adequate arrangements for internal conferences among themselves. What is needed is the will to use all these resources and thus to encourage counsel (who after all are trying to persuade the existing court in the immediate case) to provide even more in the future. This judicial will is directly dependent on the judges' conception of what are the proper elements in a legal argument, and the present arrangements do not block such an expanded vision of the law.

However, there are two procedural changes which might be conducive to this end. First of all, I think the full Supreme Court should sit to decide all the cases. Right now this would be a needless waste of effort, because so many current appeals turn on the facts of the immediate litigation. Given a new jurisdiction which filtered these cases out and presented only important and difficult legal issues to the Court, the full contribution of every judge to the proper solution should be secured. Not only would this be a symbolic expression of the Court's true role which should shape the members' attitude to their work; it would also eliminate the possibility of key decisions turning on the accidental composition of a panel and presenting real difficulties to the full Court in the future.

Secondly, I would like to see limitations placed on oral argument. Lawyers should be required to develop their full position extensively and coherently in their written briefs which can be studied by the Court beforehand. The oral argument, which will still be vital, should be devoted to an analysis of the crucial points in the respective positions which the judges have selected for discussion. I do not think we need a rigid rule of only one hour's oral argument as there now is in the U.S. Supreme Court. A better solution is to have time limits for each case set and communicated to counsel in advance. This could be done by the panel of the Court which has granted the application for leave to appeal. Nor need these time limits be immutable; as an argument develops, the Court may see the need for further time and grant an extension on the spot.

These suggestions comprise just about the sum total of changes in the structure of the Supreme Court of Canada of whose value I am persuaded at this time. I should make it very clear that I do not anticipate that these reforms would usher in any rejuvenation in Supreme Court performance. They would facilitate more polished judicial craftsmanship but cannot directly initiate it. That consequence is dependent on the attitudes of those persons who man the Court. What is their notion of what the Supreme Court should be doing and their understanding of how this should be done? The assumptions shared by the judges at this fundamental level will shape the product we receive from our final court of appeal.

Since I first began writing about the Supreme Court of Canada I have had many conversations in Toronto and in Vancouver with people who know something about its work, such as lower court judges, lawyers, law professors and law students. I have found a surprising consensus in their views. They find it difficult to see clear legal guidance in any one Supreme Court decision and the law becomes even murkier in a sequence of cases. There is concern about the lack of appreciation of the complexity of the issues in many important cases, the failure to canvass a wide range of legal materials, and the short, almost off-hand analysis with which the conclusion is produced. Reading the Supreme Court Reports, one becomes frustrated at the recitation of the facts and the procedural history of the case, the lengthy quotations from the transcript and lower court judgments, and the "scissors and paste" treatment accorded to legal authorities.

Underlying this litany of complaints is one basic theme: our Supreme Court is unduly oriented to the task of adjudicating the concrete dispute before it and, as a result, it exhibits much too narrow a conception of legal reasoning to do justice to the important legal policies it is settling for the Canadian polity. These are the fundamental attitudes which must be changed if we are to secure a better quality of judging from the Supreme Court of Canada.

I do not for a moment suggest that the Supreme Court is solely to blame for the deficiencies in our judge-made law. That Court is the tip of the iceberg of judicial law-making in Canada. Lawyers, legal scholars, lower court judges, administrative boards and others, provide much of the input on which the Supreme Court must ultimately rely. Without a satisfactory contribution from each of these groups, no final court could remedy the deficiencies on its own. Yet there are reasons for concentrating our attention on the Supreme Court which must provide the leadership in the Canadian judicial process. Without encouragement and receptivity at the top, it is hard to sustain interest and effort in the lower echelons of the process. Nor is it totally unfair to focus criticism on the opinion of the Supreme Court of Canada when the legal product is poor. If and when things get better, that body will receive the credit as well.

In fact, there is some ground for optimism about the near immediate future of the Supreme Court of Canada. A primary basis for this expectation is the increasing visibility of the Court. Following the growth in full-time law faculties and the increased interest in law among Canadian social scientists, extensive scholarly material is appearing, devoted to the Canadian judicial process and especially its highest court. At the same time we can see much more attention to the law in Canadian newspapers and magazines, which is fed to some extent by the academic work. Accordingly, the Supreme Court can no longer drift along, unconscious of the deficiencies in its present performance and unaware of alternative courses of action. Even better, the judges on the Court are coming out onto public forums and talking about how they view their own responsibilities for Canadian law.[10] In these lectures they clearly show that they are aware of what people are writing about them. In turn, their own

---

[10] Recent examples which have found their way into law reviews are Pigeon, "The Human Element in the Judicial Process" (1970), 7 A.L.R. 301; Hall, "Law Reform and the Judiciary's Role" (1972), 10 O.H.L.J. 399; Laskin, "The Institutional Character of the Judge" (1972), Israel Law Review 329.

contribution furnishes the materials for a much more realistic and informed analysis by outside observers of what we should expect from the Supreme Court of Canada. The dialogue which I believe is crucial for the improvement of Canadian judging has begun.

This book is my contribution to that exercise. Looking back I would single out one theme for final emphasis. Our judges must appreciate why they are given a particular legal role in order that they know how the task may be performed wisely. Why is the common law of criminal defences preserved by the Criminal Code? What is the purpose of a Bill of Rights? What do courts have to offer to the administrative process? Judges who understand the arguments addressed to fundamental questions such as these will be much better able to navigate successfully around the immediate problems presented to them for decision.

Moreover, these are the critical issues for modern jurisprudence. It is clear now that judges do make law and it is easy to point out the gaps and inadequacies in the reasoning of those judges who may not fully appreciate that fact. Since the advent of Legal Realism early in the 20th Century, there are innumerable examples in the literature of how this kind of analysis is performed by academic critics. It is much harder to be positive, to give constructive advice to judges about how they should exercise the room for judgment that a legal system necessarily leaves them. A court has to commit itself when it decides a case. A legal philosopher who dissents from the judicial product should do the same. Only in this way will our judges learn anything of real value to the performance of their difficult job. Nowhere has the need been better expressed than by Mr. Justice Cardozo:

> Implicit in every decision where the question is, so to speak, at large is a philosophy of the origin and aim of law, a philosophy which, however veiled, is in truth the final arbiter. It accepts one set of arguments, modifies another, rejects a third, standing ever in reserve as a court of ultimate appeal. Often the philosophy is ill co-ordinated and fragmentary. Its empire is not always suspected even by its subjects. Neither lawyer nor judge, pressing forward along one line or retreating along another, is conscious at all times that it is philosophy which is impelling him to the front or driving him to the rear. Nonetheless the goad is there. If we cannot escape the furies, we shall do well to understand them.[11]

---

[11] Cardozo, *The Growth of the Law* (1924), at 25.

Indexes

Index of Names and Cases

Subject Index

INDEX OF
NAMES AND CASES

The names of cases referred to in this book are set out below in italics. In many instances they are not the full names of the cases, but rather those by which they are popularly known. Although the report citations are not included in this index, full citations for each case will be found in a footnote on the first page on which a case reference appears.

241

SUBJECT INDEX